Christian Mythmakers

Christian Mythmakers

C. S. Lewis, Madeleine L'Engle,
J. R. R. Tolkien, George MacDonald,
G. K. Chesterton, Charles Williams,
Dante Alighieri, John Bunyan,
Walter Wangerin, Robert Siegel,
and Hannah Hurnard

Second Edition

ROLLAND HEIN

CORNERSTONE PRESS CHICAGO

CHICAGO, ILLINOIS

Second edition

Published by Cornerstone Press Chicago
939 W. Wilson Ave.
Chicago, IL 60640
www.cornerstonepress.com
cspress@jpusa.chi.il.us

Cover and book design by Pat Peterson/*wheatsdesign*
Cover illustration from *The Odes of Horace*, 1874, by William Morris;
Oxford, MS.Lat. class e.38, p.54:p.24. The publisher gratefully
acknowledges the Bodleian Library, Oxford, for use
of the photograph

Printed in the United States of America
Printed by United Graphics, Inc., Mattoon, Illinois
05 04 03 02 5 4 3 2 1

ISBN 0-940895-48-X

Library of Congress Cataloging-in-Publication Data

Hein, Rolland.
    Christian mythmakers : C.S. Lewis, Madeleine L'Engle, J.R. Tolkien, George
MacDonald, G.K. Chesterton, Charles Williams, John Bunyan, Walter Wangerin,
Robert Siegel, and Hannah Hurnard / Rolland Hein.
        p.   cm.
    Includes bibliographical references and index.
    ISBN 0-940895-48-X (trade paper : alk paper)
    1. Religion and literature. 2. Christianity and literature. 3. Literature, Modern—
History and criticism   I. Title.
    PN49 .H345   2002
    820.9'3823—dc21   2002005850
                                                            CIP

To my students

"I am a debtor to all, to all I am bounden"
—Edwin Muir

CONTENTS

Ⓦhat is Ⓜyth?

CLYDE S. KILBY

Myth needs to be seen in a certain context if it is not to appear negligible or silly. I want to try to describe that context.

The two most basic characteristics of man, beyond his mere physical needs, are to know and to worship. The great German psychologist, Carl Gustav Jung, thinks that the urge toward knowing is so persistent that it was this urge which brought about his birth and thus his consciousness. "Meaninglessness," he says, "inhibits fullness of life and is therefore equivalent to illness."

Our present age in particular is convinced that the main avenue to knowing is the making of statements. Yet all statements whatever, indeed all systems, in becoming statements and systems, become self-destructive. One is at sixes and sevens to translate a language of one hundred thousand words into a language of one thousand words. This is man's predicament. What man is, what he feels himself to be, makes a wasteland of language. Yet because of man's insatiable desire to know he requires some sort of verbal actualization. He is like the old woman who said, "How do I know what I think until I hear what I say?" Yet man's saying, i.e., his systematizing, is always inadequate. The more he defines, the more he abstracts, the farther a satisfying reality seems to fly. A young professor of philosophy said to me, "I feel I must write my own philosophy, yet by the end of the twenty years required to do the job, it will be so insufficient as to make the whole task rather foolish."

We intellectualize in order to know, but paradoxically, intellectualization tends to destroy its object. The harder we grasp at the thing, the more its reality moves away.

So what is to be done? Man finds in himself a third characteristic called imagination, by which he can transcend statements and systems. By some magic, imagination is able to disengage our habitual discursive and system-making and send us on a journey toward gestures, pictures, images, rhythms, metaphor, symbol, and at the peak of all, myth. Jung speaks of "the slender hints of the knowable" and the need to discover mythic means of bringing these hints together. Systematizing drives essentiality away, but successful creativity attracts it. While the basic requirement of systematizing is abstracting, myth is concerned not so much with parts as with wholes. Myth is necessary because reality is so much larger than rationality. Not that myth is irrational but that it easily accommodates the rational while rising above it.

Systematizing flattens, but myth rounds out. Systematizing drains away color and life, but myth restores. Myth is necessary because of what man is. The Roman poet Ovid in the first century said that man was formed in the image of the gods, and unlike animals, was given a "lofty countenance and ordered ... to contemplate the sky and to raise his erected face to the stars." The finest explanation of myth is a remark of long ago that man shall not live by bread alone. The truth is that man is less fact than he is myth. Owen Barfield thinks that man did not make myth but that myth made man. Shortly before his crucifixion, Jesus told His disciples that He was going away to prepare a place for them and added, "whither I go ye know, and the way ye know." But the rationalist Thomas promptly retorted, "Lord, we know not whither thou goest; and how can we know the way?" A great living whole is always the answer to essentiality. An advertisement for diamonds says that engagement is a time "when mind and heart and all the beauty of the world beat as one." Actually the wish for that condition is lifelong.

All statements, including the one I am now making, are unsatisfying because man is fundamentally mythic. His real health depends upon his knowing and living his metaphysical totality. In myth man discovers and affirms not his disparate nature but his mythic.

To define myth, as to define any other ultimate, is in part at least to destroy it. Myth is equally indefinable with man, life, reality. To search for definitions is less to define than to discover the paucity of words. It has been said that the only good definition of poetry is a poetic definition. So with myth. Myth is a way of going out into metaphysical space and saying, "Look back and see those mountains, those rivers, those great blocks of land that only now you can even see." A myth is a cosmic pattern which permeates man by some osmotic chemistry. Myth is one of the few means by which to understand and possess the blue flower, *Sehnsucht*, infinitude.

A blade of grass really seen, anything really seen, suggests the transcendental nature of myth. Myth is the name of a way of seeing, a way of knowing in depth, a way of experiencing—a way that in being disinterested contains the freedom of unending and vital interest. Mythic insight may tell us that plants and animals have "all the rights and privileges thereunto appertaining." It will cause an inevitable distinction between "thou" and "it." Lewis points out that enchanted trees give all ordinary trees a measure of enchantment. Myth is vision.

Jung makes much of consciousness. It has been pointed out that consciousness and conscience are from the same root and coincident in time. In man there is the exercise of consciousness toward knowing and the

exercise of conscience toward worship. Myth is, in
Mircea Eliade's phrase, "the nostalgia for eternity."
Man's concept of the absolute, he adds, "can never be
uprooted; it can only be debased." He points out that
sex was originally "a ritual with transcendent meaning
at every point." Those who indulge in promiscuous sex
perhaps know best the sordidness of its unritual and
animal uses. Our world is dispossessed of heirarchy.

Myth is like the green-belt of the world without
which, as the great British historian George Macaulay
Trevelyan says, man is brutish. Myth is a lane down
which we walk in order to repossess our soul, our
essentiality. Myth, said Charles Williams, consists of
"patterns of the Logos in the depth of the sun."
Coleridge said that symbol, myth's twin, is marked by
"the translucence of the eternal through and in the
temporal." Myth is ageless. Yet it may be experienced
in some everyday act or thought suddenly alive with
universal meaning. A friend asked William Blake,
"When the sun rises, do you not see a round disk of fire
something like a guinea?" to which he replied, "Oh no,
I see an immeasurable company of the heavenly host
crying 'Holy, Holy is the Lord God Almighty.' " Jean
Cocteau said that poetry is "a machine that manufactures love." Myth also manufactures love and truth and
essentiality, or rather reveals them.

A perfect good, as well as a perfect anything else, is
mythlike. The call toward perfect goodness is a mythic

call lying beyond the best possible set of rules and regulations. All systems are no more than statemental pointers and insufficient to the reality toward which they point. "Ah, how sick I am of 'therefore' and 'since,' and 'because!'" says a character in Gide's *Theseus*. "Sick of inference, sick of deduction. On their horizontal plane I have wandered all too often. The infinite calls me! It calls me! I cannot define what it is that summons me, but I know that my journey can have only one end: in God."

C. S. Lewis began a letter concerning *Till We Have Faces* by saying, "An author doesn't necessarily understand the meaning of his own story better than anyone else." That would be an almost insane remark except that his story is a myth, and in good myth an author puts not simply what he knows but what seems to have come to him from another world.

With this necessary framework, we can now come nearer earth and say that myth is a branch of literature. It is in fact embodied in words, though in true myth words are somehow enlivened with the aspects of the true Word, the Logos.

ACKNOWLEDGEMENTS

I am grateful to Wheaton College for granting me a sabbatical to begin this work and a reduced teaching load to complete it, and to the G. W. Aldeen family for establishing the fund from which financial support was drawn. Several friends have read the manuscript and offered helpful comments: John Estes, a graduate student; Christopher Mitchell, Director of the Wade Center; and Jill Pelaez Baumgaertner, Professor of English. Kathryn Lindskoog gave valuable input on the C. S. Lewis chapter, and David Davis commented on the Charles Williams chapter. I am grateful to Martha Kilby for giving me Clyde Kilby's statement on myth, and to the Wade Center, which now has Dr. Kilby's papers, for permission to publish it. And I acknowledge with pleasure the helpful suggestions from my editor, Jane Hertenstein.

Christian
Mythmakers

Introduction

"I wonder what sort of tale we've fallen into?" Sam muses to his master Frodo in J. R. R. Tolkien's *The Lord of the Rings*, as they near the completion of their courageous epic journey.[1] As they talk, they are aware that their actions are a part of a story being written on the high level of myth, and they wonder if their story will be an heroic one. So it is with people. In an inmost region of our beings we sense that our lives are part of a great story forming, with the quality of our actions determining the level upon which the finished story will exist. When the story is complete, we will be "home" in the eternally Real. "The real world is beyond time," Northrop Frye wrote, "but can be reached only by a process that goes on in time."[2] Such perceptions come to us through myth.

Myths are, first of all, stories: stories which confront us with something transcendent and eternal. Myth exists because life has a duality to it. All events and circumstances exist on a physical level, which we

1. J. R. R. Tolkien, *The Two Towers*, (New York: Ballantine, 1965), 407.
2. Northrop Frye, *The Great Code: The Bible and Literature* (New York and London: Harcourt Brace Jovanovich, 1981), 76.

3

apprehend sensuously, and on an anagogic level, apprehended with the intuitions of the spirit. Literary realism presents the former; literary myth attempts insights into the latter. The spiritual dimensions of any event are elusive, but it is only they that really matter. Literary mythmakers are successful when, working for the most part within the more congenial atmosphere of fantasy or fairy tales, their works stir the human spirit with visions of higher anagogic realities.

To experience myth truly is to have time stand still momentarily, to experience what has been called *kairos* time. Kairos time is transcendent time, as opposed to chronological—or clock time—with its regular rhythmic movement of hours, days, seasons, and years. Deity dwells in this other type of time, one in which, as the Bible states, "a thousand years is as a day, and a day is as a thousand years." We have momentary experiences of kairos time whenever we become so completely absorbed in something that we lose consciousness of ourself; it is as though the self is extinguished, and we become the other. Such moments, in which the spirit is illumined with a truth, are often called epiphanies. They help define what we truly are. And they can remain in a person's memory—sometimes for one's entire lifetime—repeatedly yielding pleasure whenever recalled. These epiphanies strengthen the sense that our true home and destiny is outside of chronos time. Wordsworth composed his great autobiographical poem "The Prelude" around such instances in his own life, affirming the conviction that:

> Our destiny, our being's heart and home,
> Is with infinitude, and only there;
> With hope it is, hope that can never die,
> Effort, and expectation, and desire,
> And something evermore about to be (6.604–8)

Kairos time defies the clock and the calendar; it seems as though it always *is*. The right sorts of stories will afford the sensitive reader such "spots of time." All who know them feel they have momentarily been touched by something transcendent, from outside of time itself.

All ancient peoples seem to have had their mythologies. In them they defined reality in terms of a transcendent world available only to the imagination. They participated in their stories through ritual in order to participate in higher reality. Many myths contain materials that to our sensibilities may seem absurd, base, even lewd and scandalous, as when for instance in the Daedalus myth the Queen of Crete cohabits with a bull and gives birth to the Minotaur. But even such aspects seem to command a certain power, and, while we quickly dismiss elements that are absurd, others grip us with a fascination and a force.

We are concerned in this study not with ancient mythologies as such, but with what is better identified as mythopoeia: stories that are composed in time, but which suggest (however dimly) something covert but eternally momentous. "A story must be told or there'll be no story, yet it is the untold stories that are most moving," Tolkien remarked. [3] Successfully done, mythopoeic writing intimates something that cannot be told, but when fully known will be eternally satisfying. It confronts us imaginatively, if only in flashes, with something that is beyond time, inexplicable but thrilling. Many people are oblivious to the possibility of such experiences. But if perchance their eyes are opened, the instances suddenly possess an incredible plausibility: "Yes, yes, this is what my life has really been about! Here is where my meaning and my destiny lie!"

THE DIVERSE USES OF THE TERM

One may muse that no term in the English language carries a range of meaning so seemingly antithetical as does myth. But its low meaning—as a discredited popular belief—is a complete degeneration of its high one, a means by which the eternal expresses itself in time. Between seem to lie as many gradations as there are scholars who use the term.

A brief overview quickly establishes the point. During the Enlightenment, the value and authority of myth was questioned by an increasing number of rationalist thinkers. In the nineteenth century Sir George Frazier set out to study mythology, especially as

3. Humphrey Carpenter, ed., *The Letters of J. R. R. Tolkien* (Boston: Houghton Mifflin, 1981), 110.

regards the widespread myth of the dying and rising god. He, together with scholars of similar mindset, exercised a scientific rationalist approach. They viewed myth as false explanations, pleasant lies no rightly reasoning individual would take seriously. In the twentieth century the famed anthropologist Mircea Eliade countered by arguing that myths do contain a record of genuine religious experiences emerging from sacred time. Freud and Jung exercised an immense influence by interpreting myth as imaginative and symbolic expressions of inner psychological states, first as regards the individual, and then as regards the collective subconscious of the race.

In our time, Joseph Campbell has done much to popularize a generally Jungian view of myth by suggesting that the source of myth is the human psyche itself. Impressed with such a reservoir of archetypal images within, he counsels us to submit to ourselves and find the solution to the perplexities and problems of life within the human mind. Such scholars tend not to dwell long upon such questions as *why* we respond as we do to the patterns of myth, *why* the human heart is so strangely moved and fascinated by them, and *where* they come from in the first place. Structuralists argue quite differently, affirming that myth is simply an inevitable expression of language coming to terms with social and economic conflicts. But, all the schools have this in common: they feel that understanding myth is an indispensable way of understanding ourselves.

Myth is, therefore, a term that means much more than a discredited popular belief.

Christian mythology is distinct in its claims. To the Christian, wisdom lies in submitting not to the self but to God; hence, the pattern of renunciation and rebirth, of continual renewal that so often occurs in the myths we are about to consider.

Many of the most significant literary writers in the twentieth century affirmed the role of myth to be requisite in imaginatively comprehending what it is to be human. Some, such as T. S. Eliot and James Joyce, drew upon both classical and Christian myths, whether seriously or ironically, in their depictions of the predicaments of the human condition. Others, such as W. B. Yeats and D. H. Lawrence, feeling Christian myths to be inadequate for their times, sought to devise their own mythological systems. All of these authors, together with many others, recognize that myth has an indispensable role in our lives, although they differ widely on precisely what that role is.

It is perhaps C. S. Lewis who defined this understanding of the concept with greatest clarity and force,[4] and it became one of the most basic elements in

4. Lewis discusses the concept in a number of places. See especially book 8, chapter 8 of *The Pilgrim's Regress* (Grand Rapids, Mich.: Wm. B. Eerdmans, 1989); chapter 15, footnote #1 of *Miracles* (New York: Macmillian, 1953); "On Myth," *An Experiment in Criticism* (Cambridge: University Press, 1965), 40–49; "Preface," *George MacDonald: An Anthology* (New York: Macmillian, 1948), 10–22; "Myth Became Fact," *God in the Dock: Essays on Theology and Ethics* (Grand Rapids, Mich.: William B. Eerdmans, 1970), 63–67; and "Tolkien's *The Lord of the Rings*," *Of This and Other Worlds*, ed. Walter Hooper (London: Collins, 1982), 112–121.

his thought. Lewis explained that the term designates a type of story that has—among other characteristics—a distinct extraliterary component whose presence is detected by an intuitive effect occurring in certain readers. Those who react with a pause and catch of breath, as though something "of great moment" has been conveyed, are encountering the dynamic of myth. They feel as though something numinous has confronted them. It is not so much that they receive a message, but rather that they seem to have a fleeting contact with some remote unbroken world, one in which, to borrow a stirring phrase from Flannery O'Connor, "the silence is broken only to shout the Truth." Much depends upon the sensibility of the individual reader, and, of course, skeptics will miss the experience altogether.

THE BIBLE AS SOURCE

J. R. R. Tolkien identified the gospel narrative of Christ's life, death, and resurrection as the ultimate fairy story.[5] He had no intention of denying the historical reality of the account, or in any sense diminishing its impact, but sought to place it in its proper literary genre. Both he and Lewis agree that myth is the indispensable aura of Truth. To us, in our finiteness, myth is the vehicle of Truth, so that it serves mankind in a manner rational analysis never can. In the Incarnation, myth becomes

5. J. R. R. Tolkien, "On Fairy Stories, *The Tolkien Reader* (New York: Ballantine, 1966) 33–99.

history. The distinguishing characteristic of the Christian faith is that actual historical time is invaded by ultimate Truth, and reality is defined.

Further, Tolkien and Lewis felt that what comes to us in biblical stories—accounts presenting pure and definitive sacred history—is foreshadowed, however vaguely or obliquely, in various mythologies. The pattern of the dying and rising god, ubiquitous in ancient mythologies, is one instance of this. "I believe that legends and myths are largely made of 'truth,' " Tolkien told a prospective publisher, "and indeed present aspects of it that can only be received in this mode; and long ago certain truths and modes of this kind were discovered and must always reappear." [6] Lewis saw ancient mythologies as a mixture of the diabolical and the divine, the latter elements being a *preparatio evangelica*, a divine hinting in poetic and ritual form at the same central truth which was later focused and (so to speak) historicised in the Incarnation. [7]

Scriptural narratives, therefore, stand in a class by themselves in that they present authoritative expressions of myth entering history as fact, of the ultimately Real invading time. The myths of other nations contain truth only to the extent that they adumbrate realities confirmed by the Bible. They are collections of—to use

---

6. Carpenter, *The Letters of J. R. R. Tolkien*, 147.
7. C. S. Lewis, "Religion without Dogma?," *God in the Dock*, 132.

Aristotle's terms—*mythoi*, whereas the Christian Scriptures are *logoi*. The writers we will consider in these pages see the Bible as the repository of ultimate Truth and salute its authority in all matters of faith and doctrine. Their literary myths are replete with its imagery and precepts.

The critic Northrop Frye built a notable career contending that, since the Bible is the ultimate source for the elemental images of Western literature, we can better understand the basic structure of the imaginary universe of literary art through the study of it. Frye freely acknowledged that he was inspired and guided in much of his thinking by the work of William Blake, who declared that "The Old and New Testaments are the Great Code of Art,"[8] and who in his complex mythology and compelling engravings detailed a spiritual vision reflecting his own understanding of the meaning of the Bible.

The sweeping pattern of images in the biblical text is that of creation, fall, redemption, and apocalypse; the dominant themes are those of struggle, calling, renunciation, and deliverance. Individual believers, Israel, the Church, and all of mankind are being called to spiritual journeys whose character and end are shaped by these essential ideas. One has only to consider the biblical narratives to see this to be true. The accounts of

8. Frye, *The Great Code: The Bible and Literature*, xvi. The phrase is from Blake's annotations surrounding his engraving of the Laocoon (*The Complete Poetry and Prose*, David V.Eerdman, ed., Rev.ed. (Berkeley: University of California, 1982), 274.

Abraham, of the Israelites moving through the wilderness from Egypt to the Promised Land, the peripatetic life of Christ, and the missionary endeavors of the apostles, all prominently contain journeys. Narratives of trial and struggle occur throughout Scripture, from Jacob's wrestling with God through the Book of Job to the trials of Christ and of Paul. God's extended indictment against Israel invests much of the biblical text with the air of continuous trial and the necessity for renunciation. Life itself, it would seem, is trial, but trial is necessary in the formation of character.

Whether or not people are aware of the fact, they cannot live without myth, nor can they reach full stature as people without true myths. Wrong myths destroy lives; those only partially true affect the human spirit like disease. A proper response to true myth is necessary to moral and spiritual health. Allowing its figurative language free play upon the imagination and yielding to its claims upon one's life is a means by which readers can come to well-being for time and eternity.

CHRISTIAN MYTHMAKERS

Literary fantasy provides the context most appropriate to mythic illuminations, and in this book we are mainly considering the mythic within the fantastic. But the possibility of such moments is by no means confined to literary fantasy. Many have experienced them in the essays of Frederick Buechner, Anne Dillard and

Madeleine L'Engle; the realist novels of Fyodor Dostoyevski, Walker Percy, and Flannery O'Connor; the poetry of William Wordsworth, Rainer Rilke, and Edwin Muir (as well as Muir's autobiography), and the works of many other writers.

The authors treated in this volume are diverse in many ways. All would lay claim to being Christian, though their theological convictions encompass about as wide a range as possible within the realm of Christian orthodoxy. But they hold in common an impressive command (consciously or unconsciously) of mythic imagery. Dante in *The Divine Comedy* presents an imagined world that has spoken to Western Man through the centuries as has no other single literary work. *The Pilgrim's Progress* is less ambitious but it commands a similar power, speaking more simply to common people. The mythopoeic tradition runs through the work of George MacDonald, G. K. Chesterton, Charles Williams, J. R. R. Tolkien, and C. S. Lewis, and finds engaging expression in the authors whose work we consider in the final chapter: Madeleine L'Engle, Robert Siegel, Walter Wangerin, and Hannah Hurnard. As one enters into their literary fantasies, one can experience the profound power and joy of myth.

But, a final caveat: to experience the power of myth, readers must respect story for its own sake and enter its precincts exclusively through the portals of the imagination. Give yourself to the story, for enjoyment's sake.

All pragmatic, utilitarian, or analytical attitudes must be abandoned. Such readers assume these writers have ingeniously contrived by means of symbols puzzles to be solved. Once the symbols are unlocked and their essential meanings extracted, the symbols themselves may be forgotten; only the abstract meanings matter. Actually, they could have saved us all time by stating their ideas directly in the first place. C. S. Lewis tries patiently to correct such thinking:

> Allegory gives you one thing in terms of another. All depends on respecting the rights of the vehicle . . . . We ought not be thinking 'This green valley, where the shepherd boy is singing, represents humility'; we ought to be discovering, as we read, that humility is like that green valley. That way, moving always into the book, not out of it, from the concept to the image, enriches the concept. And that is what allegory is for. [9]

It is in this willingness to move "into the book," to respect the images and through imaginative participation absorb their aptness and richness of implication, that readers experience the true genius of any story. If in mythopoeia revelations indeed seem to occur, they may be quite beyond the power of the mind to articulate. But they will give "a fleeting glimpse of Joy, Joy beyond the Walls of the world, poignant as grief." [10]

9. Roger Sharrock, ed., "The Vision of John Bunyan," *Bunyan: The Pilgrim's Progress. A Casebook* (London and Basingstoke: The Macmillan Press Ltd., 1976) 197, 198.
10. J. R. R. Tolkien, "On Fairy Stories," *The Tolkien Reader*, 86.

1

Dante Alighieri
The Beginning
(1265–1321)

The chief imagination of Christendom, Dante
Alighiere, so utterly found himself, that he has made
that hollow face of his more plain to the mind's eye
than any face but that of Christ.

—W. B. Yeats

canning the "Book Review" section of *The
New York Times* in 1999, I was fascinated to
see on the final page—a page generally
devoted to a human interest story—a full-color spread
of Dante's world as it is presented in *The Divine
Comedy*—hell, purgatory, and heaven—printed in bold
red with all the compartments fully labeled. It was
given without comment, save for a quotation from *Il
Purgatorio*, Canto 12: "O human race, born to fly
upward, wherefore at a little wind dost thou so fall?" I
will not speculate on the motivations of the editors for
printing it; I doubt they were intending to further
Christianity. The depiction, however, suggested two
things to me.

First, I daresay most readers were fascinated and amused. How far science has brought us from such a benighted myth! one hears them exclaim. That the myth of scientific rationalism with which the culture is presently enamored entirely ignores the soul does not concern them. Here is a fine illustration of the popular usage of that elusive term, myth. Dante's imagined world is a quaint and pleasant lie.

Second, the depiction also suggested the meaning of myth understood in its higher sense: a narrative embodiment of convictions concerning the transcendent held by a community of people. The latter meaning may at first seem antithetical to the former, but they are nevertheless related, in that both signify a view of the meaning and purpose of life and imply an answer to the question, "How should we then live?"

Is it not instructive that the picture in *The New York Times* needed no comment? Seven hundred years after Dante's composition, his images remain in the minds of knowledgeable people. They have a force and appeal that galvanizes the mind. The principles by which he shaped the images of *The Divine Comedy*, possessing great mythic power, continually answer to something deep within the human consciousness. It is the principles, not the images as such, that matter.

WHAT IT IS, AND ISN'T

Dante was as aware as is any novelist today that the bricks and mortar of narratives are images, images simply imagined. He was fully conscious that he knew no more about the actual realities faced by departed souls than does anyone else. But as a mature Christian he was completely convinced of the reality of hell, purgatory, and heaven, destinies shaped by the fundamental truths of Christianity. These convictions were the guiding principles with which his fertile imagination worked as it speculated upon the concrete forms these realities could well take. In giving narrative embodiment to these convictions, he expended as great effort in his project as does the most meticulous scientist today to achieve utter consistency, thoroughness, and comprehensiveness.

DANTE'S BEDROCK BELIEFS

Among the basic convictions that shape the story line of Dante's great poem are these:

People are responsible to God whether they know it or not.

The human race was created by a loving God whose purpose was for people to choose righteously through life, to become godlike, in order to see and be with God.

Because people possess free will, with their constant choices between good and evil shaping their experience of life for time and eternity, and because decisions are shaped by desires, people must learn to desire foremost God and his will.

Right understanding leads to right conduct, while wrong choices frustrate God's intentions and justly lead to negative consequences.

Unforgiven sin diminishes sinners, depriving them of their very humanity, whereas Christian virtues enable people to develop into the full stature God intended them to have.

These principles must not be confused with the sometimes peculiar and eccentric images Dante uses to convey them. Although the depictions may seem strange and eccentric, the principles are inexorable, the shaping forces of the myth.

God as Dante envisions him is no petty tyrant or vindictive divinity, as some cursory readers have concluded. Nor is Dante, writing as a political exile, a bitter curmudgeon gleefully assigning his friends to heaven and his enemies to hell. He is a great poet who has given the western world its most comprehensive narrative vision of Christian realities. These principles fully justify the eternal destinies he assigns to both contemporaries and historical figures. *The Divine Comedy* presents a stirring vision of the love of God evident in his government of the universe and in his grace fully expressed to humankind. The poem explores the central issues affecting the meaning and purpose of life and culminates in consuming praise for the wisdom of God's ways.

One should not assume, however, that it is a great theological treatise allegorically buried within a curiously medieval narrative, an intellectual puzzle to decipher. Dante is doing his utmost to engage our imaginations. *The Divine Comedy* is first of all an engaging story and should be read as one would read a novel, fully imagining the images and identifying with Dante the character as he gives testimony of how he was led on a complete tour of hell, purgatory, and heaven.

IN THE BEGINNING

In his famous opening lines, Dante introduces himself as a middle-aged man who was lost in a wilderness, having wandered from the right path:

> Ay me! How hard to speak of it—that rude
> And rough and stubborn forest! The mere breath
> Of memory stirs the old fear in the blood;
>
> It is so bitter, it goes nigh to death;
> Yet there I gained such good, that, to convey
> The tale, I'll write what else I found therewith.
> (*Hell*, I.4-9; Sayers trans.)

The reader readily understands the allegorical level: Dante has committed acts he knew to be wrong and is filled with distress and deep regrets. Whatever moral waywardness he had lapsed into, he gained from the experiences much good by coming to understand through them the nature of Reality. That understanding came from his learning of the seriousness of sin and its inevitable eternal consequences, the means by which he can be freed from being enamored of sin, and the glorious eternal destiny awaiting all who are liberated. He acquires this knowledge, and shares it with his readers, as we travel with him through the realms of the afterlife.

The reader identifies with the pilgrim Dante and receives with him the Christian truths appropriate to the episodes of the journey. Much of the instruction is imparted by Virgil, the image of the wisdom available to the natural man. Virgil has been sent by the heavenly Beatrice, who allegorically is first vehicle and later messenger of the love of God expressed to humankind. The wisdom these two impart brings ecstacy to Dante the pilgrim; Christian truth appeals to the highest aspects of the soul and transforms it, developing its full humanity.

Because Dante at the beginning of the poem is astray in a "rough and stubborn forest," his way up Mount Purgatory—which at the very beginning he sees in the distance—is blocked by a leopard, a lion, and a she-wolf. These signify respectively the sins of lust, pride, and fraud, acts that prevent people from attaining a practical righteousness.

Only after Virgil has led him through the nether

regions of hell, sternly impressing upon him the dehumanizing nature of all sins and their inevitable consequences to the self, can Dante understand the necessity of being freed from enslavement to them. The hell through which Dante travels is a region God intended for Satan and his followers, not for people. Sinners adamant in their sins, however, inevitably and justly experience its myriad horrors.

The figures Dante meets as he funnels downward from tier to tier to the very center of the earth are but the forms of their former selves, effigies bereft of any vestiges of humanness. They have, in Dante's famous phrase, "lost the good intellect" (*Hell*, III.18) and become the sins they embraced. The ultimate specimen is the great traitor Satan encased and immobile in Cocytus, the lake of ice at the center of the earth. The image of his immobility reinforces Dante's emphasis upon free will and human responsibility. The inhabitants of hell may not blame Satan for the course of life they chose.

STAIRWAY TO HEAVEN

Readers who may have doubts about the doctrine of purgatory can nevertheless greatly profit from reading the second portion of *The Divine Comedy* as instruction on nurturing the process of sanctification in this life. In addition of not submitting oneself to sin, completeness of being is impossible apart from a person's learning to desire God and his good above all else, then to see all things in relation to Him, and to act accordingly. This learning process is inseparable from being experientially freed from pride, envy, wrath, sloth, covetousness, gluttony, and lust. These natural tendencies must be replaced with the Christian virtues of humility, generosity, meekness, zeal, liberality, temperance, and chastity, all components of that holiness without which no one will see God. The qualities one has not acquired by the time of death must be gained in the next life. No careful reader of the *The Divine Comedy*, however, can conclude that Dante is suggesting a Christian can afford to neglect virutes now, nor that they are purely the product of human effort.

Triumphing over personal sins and mastering virtues here and now are tasks Christians dismiss to their own inevitable sorrow. Dante sympathizes with the largeness of the task and eagerly points his readers to the beauty and glory of the prize. The process of becoming holy is initiated by conversion: the three steps leading to the gate at the base of Mount Purgatory (Canto 9) signify confession, contrition, and blood satisfaction. The necessity of dying to the tyranny of sin is suggested by Cato, Virgil and Dante's guide up the mountain. Cato was a Roman statesman who, rather than submit to Ceasar, committed suicide. The rule of the mountain is that none can climb by night: God's enabling grace, symbolized by the sun, gives the essential light. At the top of Mount Purgatory he enters the Earthly Paradise—he has been restored to the condition of unfallen man. He has achieved wholeness of being in righteousness. Virgil bids him farewell with the benediction:

No word from me, no further sign expect;
Free, upright, whole, thy will henceforth lays down
Guidance that it were error to neglect,
Whence o'er thyself I mitre thee and crown.
(*Purgatori*, XXVII.139-142)

He now receives the heavenly Beatrice as his guide. The glories into which she then leads him stand quite beyond the reach of natural reason.

In real life, Dante had seen Beatrice only momentarily when both were children but even then he was attracted to her as the very incarnation of Love. Although both she and he married other spouses and she died as a young woman, her image remained in his mind throughout his life, bringing with it an inspiring and enabling inner power. Allegorically, she unites both *eros* and *agape*—love as desire and as self-giving. From heaven she commissions Virgil to help Dante regain the right road. In seeing natural reason and loving relationships as prime vehicles of the love of God, Dante is affirming all images as potential channels of grace. All of reality is sacramental; that is, any aspect of life can be a vehicle of the grace of God. *The Divine Comedy* is a prime expression of the Affirmative Way.

LAND OF THE FREE

In paradise Dante, guided by Beatrice, moves joyously
through a world where centers "every where and every
when" (*Paradise*, XXIX.12). Images of light, dance, and
music abound. Since thinking rightly is indispensable
to beatitude, Dante receives much theological instruction, the substance of which is generally shaped by the
thought of St. Aquinas. He converses with saints who,
no matter if they disagreed with one another on earth,
are now perfectly united in love, knowing complete
peace and joy. As Dante rises into the ultimate heights
of heaven, he is enraptured by a momentary vision of
the Triune God amidst an effulgence of light:

> And so my mind, bedazzled and amazed,
> Stood fixed in wonder, motionless, intent,
> And still my wonder kindled as I gazed.
>
> That light doth so transform a man's whole bent
> That never to another sight or thought
> Would he surrender, with his own consent;
>
> For everything the will has ever sought
> Is gathered there, and there is every quest
> Made perfect, which apart from it falls short.
> (*Paradise*, XXXIII.97-105)

Dante's engulfing rapture depicts the true end of
man, complete in righteousness, finding satisfaction,
contentment, and peace in fellowship with God. His
journey consummated, Dante closes his great poem by

affirming that his will and his desire are now "turned by love, / The love that moves the sun and the other stars."

JUST ANOTHER QUEST?

In shaping the great Christian myth, Dante inevitably turns many of the archetypal images of the mythological past—such as the hero, the quest, and the afterlife—on their heads. They are displaced by the Christian fulfillments they foreshadow, now invested with the moral imperatives that the divine revelation to the Judeao-Christian tradition brings to them. Historically, in the main, the transition from the pagan past to the Christian present is a shift in focus from external to internal reality. The image of the hero in pagan myths is that of the warrior who models on his quest such external traits as cunning, prowess, daring, resourcefulness, and pride. In *The Divine Comedy* Odysseus, Homer's hero, resides on the eighth level of hell. So much for daring, cunning, and pride in the Christian economy. Dante's Christian protagonist, on the other hand, stands as a model for the transformation of the inner man from his natural state to one of holiness. His quest, therefore, is the pursuit of virtues—such as self-sacrificing love, meekness, peacefulness, and moral purity—that are radically different from the *arete*, or manly excellence, modeled by the ancient Grecian warrior hero. Not being natural to fallen humankind, these Christian virtues must be acquired.

It is impossible to reconcile Christian virtues with the pagan ideal of the warrior-hero. Dante may be viewed, nevertheless, as attaining heroic status in a Christian sense, as he becomes the paradigm of being that God intends for humankind. Further, as a poet who has mastered and models Christian realities—completeness of the inner being—he is able to express with the highest command of language and literary form a comprehensive understanding of the divine purpose in creating and sustaining the universe and in redeeming humankind. The order and beauty of his great poem reflects his insights into the order and beauty of the Divine government of the universe. He epitomizes the Christian ideal for man.

The form and structure of *The Divine Comedy* symbolize unity and completeness. The numbers three (for the trinity), four (for man), and one (for final unity), making ten, are omnipresent. Consider the most obvious instances. The entire poem consists of three groupings of thirty-three cantoes which, with the addition of the introductory canto, make one hundred, the square of ten. Dante's *terza rima* stanzas consist of three lines each, with interlocking rhymes. Each canto ends with a one-line staza. Each of the three regions of the afterlife has ten compartments grouped into seven and three. Pythagoras is reputed to have said the world was created by number; Dante's world most certainly is.

The Divine Comedy offers compelling answers to all the questions about the meaning and purpose of life in light of the shaping principles of eternity. The mythopoeic writers that follow in Dante's wake each have their strengths, but none rise to the same level of comprehensiveness. Evidences of their debt to his achievement occur throughout their works, an obligation many of them overtly acknowledge. Theological systems within Christendom may differ from Dante's as to precisely how the ends he envisions are gained, but no Christian can disagree with the undergirding principles that shape his work, nor are images to be found which express these principles more graphically to the imagination. Were Dante with us today, he may ask to be forgiven his images, but he would affirm with joy the truths they convey.

2

John Bunyan
From Allegory to Myth
(1628–1688)

"I know of no book, the Bible excepted, as above all
comparison, which I, according to my judgment and
experience, could so safely recommend as teaching
and enforcing the whole saving truth according to
the mind that was in Christ Jesus, as in the Pilgrim's
Progress. It is, in my conviction, incomparably the
best *Summa Theologiae Evangelicae* ever produced by
a writer not miraculously inspired." [1]

 he Pilgrim's Progress has consistently fascinated not only people who are in general agreement with Bunyan's strong doctrinal views,
but also many who would surely have quarreled with
several of them, such as Winston Churchill, George
Bernard Shaw, and e. e. cummings. Even among fervent

1. Samuel Taylor Coleridge, *Coleridge on the Seventeenth Century*, Roberta Florence
Brinkley, ed. (Duke University Press, 1955), 475–76, as quoted in *Bunyan: The Pilgrim's
Progress: A Casebook*, edited by Roger Sharrock (London and Basingstoke: The
Macmillan Press Ltd., 1976), 53.

Christians today few would agree with all of Bunyan's theological convictions. How, then, may one account for the book's popularity?

The answer does not lie in its theology, but rather in the way the narrative ushers us into the the realm of myth and draws upon its stirring imaginative power. In accessing myth, Bunyan taps wellsprings of truth that appeal to all readers. His work is allegory, but—like the parables of Christ—it is the potency and authority of myth that makes the allegory speak profoundly to the soul. The essential point is that Bunyan handles dynamite in an imaginative way when he draws his images from the powder keg of Scripture, and his work has manifested this strength through the centuries.

Bunyan's *Pilgrim's Progress* has been regarded as "the most powerful literary expression of the essence of Puritanism." [2] Milton, his contemporary, is more learned and theoretical, but in his heterodoxies he may hardly be called the most typical Puritan. In spite of the many differences in ideas to be found among the innumerable Puritan sects, they adhered in the main to Covenant Theology, and Bunyan's vision is ultimately shaped by it. [3] Because he focuses our attention upon the inner life of Christian, he mutes theological

2. Kathleen M. Swaim, *Pilgrim's Progress, Puritan Progress* (Urbana and Chicago: University of Illinois Press, 1993), 47. See 6–13 for a helpful summary of the Puritan spirit.

3. Covenant theology teaches that God, in his dealings with Adam onward, bound himself by a series of agreements (covenants) that apply to his chosen people. To become Christian, the elect must be disabused of the Covenant of Works—which pertained to the Old Testament relationship between God and Israel—and come to

Barnes & Noble Bookseller
1701 E Empire
Bloomington, IL 61701
(309) 662-1506
03-09-03 S02590 R005

CUSTOMER RECEIPT COPY

Pilates Powerhouse: The   18.95
0738202282
Reclaim Your Spiritual. P   13.95
1561707082
Christian Mythmakers: C.   14.95
094089548X
Speedwriting Shorthand D   25.32
0026851512

SUB TOTAL   73.17
SALES TAX   5.49
TOTAL   78.66
AMOUNT TENDERED
MASTERCARD   78.66
CARD #:   ************9287
AMOUNT   78.66
AUTH CODE   009467

TOTAL PAYMENT   78.66
        Thank you for Shopping at
        Barnes & Noble Booksellers
#188063 03-09-03 05:31P J Byrd

Full refund issued for new and unread books and unopened music within 30 days with a receipt from any Barnes & Noble store.
Store Credit issued for new and unread books and unopened music after 30 days or without a sales receipt. Credit issued at <u>lowest sale price</u>.
We gladly accept returns of new and unread books and unopened music from bn.com with a bn.com receipt for store credit at the bn.com price.

Full refund issued for new and unread books and unopened music within 30 days with a receipt from any Barnes & Noble store.
Store Credit issued for new and unread books and unopened music after 30 days or without a sales receipt. Credit issued at <u>lowest sale price</u>.
We gladly accept returns of new and unread books and unopened music from bn.com with a bn.com receipt for store credit at the bn.com price.

Full refund issued for new and unread books and unopened music within 30 days with a receipt from any Barnes & Noble store.
Store Credit issued for new and unread books and unopened music after 30 days or without a sales receipt. Credit issued at <u>lowest sale price</u>.
We gladly accept returns of new and unread books and unopened music from bn.com with a bn.com receipt for store credit at the bn.com price.

Full refund issued for new and unread books and unopened music within 30 days with a receipt from any Barnes & Noble store.
Store Credit issued for new and unread books and unopened music after 30 days or without a sales receipt. Credit issued at <u>lowest sale price</u>.
We gladly accept returns of new and unread books and unopened music from bn.com with a bn.com receipt for store credit at the bn.com price.

allusions as such, so the text does not contain as many of his theological biases as are sometimes alleged.

The most basic values the text offers are those that arise from human experience viewed in the light of the primary mythical images that shape the biblical vision of life. The reader is seized with a compelling sense of life as a journey beset with perils and difficulties, trials demanding earnest effort to be overcome. To triumph over them brings the promise of a glorious afterlife. One must accept full responsibility for one's actions and face the consequences. But forgiveness for sins is available, triumph over trials is achievable, and a sublime destiny awaits those who overcome.

Bunyan has fired a burning in many hearts to follow in Christian's steps. In his vulnerability, humanness, and earnestness, Christian invites any reader's identification. His adventures impress one with the seriousness of human sinfulness, the need to accept its burden and find forgiveness in God, the necessity for making definite spiritual decisions and the difficulty in executing them, the motivating force of yearning after things of the spirit, the mandate for holiness in behavior, and the potential glory of the life triumphant. The narrative strengthens one's sense of

experience the Covenant of Grace. In it, salvation is in no sense a reward for performing good deeds; it is rather a free gift bestowed upon the believer by his being imputed the righteousness of Christ. The New Covenant, or Testament, therefore, is God's agreement to bestow his completely unmerited favor upon whom he chooses, granting them the indwelling presence of the Holy Spirit as a guarantee that in death he will grant them eternal life. Bunyan's own particular version of Reformed theology represents a Calvinism somewhat modified by a more Lutheran view of predestination.

the momentousness of the Christian struggle and the glory of its successful completion; it also inspires with the desire to be like Mr. Valiant-for-Truth, a champion for what is right.

Bunyan is often overtly didactic, but in presenting mythic images he taps a dynamic that is beyond his conscious control. Bunyan's frequent didacticism suggests—and his apology confirms—he was never free from the fear that the mythic level may exist beyond his mastery. Readers today may tend to overlook the didacticism to feed upon the myth.

The purity of mythic power is superbly appropriate to Truth and transcends Bunyan's sectarian attitudes. Critics tend to identify the latter alone as "Christian" while suggesting that all they see as valuable somehow belongs to a larger sphere. According to the critics, all didactic insistences are irrelevant to enjoying and profiting from the text. Kaufmann, for instance, devotes his attention to celebrating *The Pilgrim's Progress* as a work presenting action that deals in "the constants of the human condition." It "offers us the handsomely-articulated structure of literature's basic plot: the career of a human life." [4] True. Except such thinking allows him to conclude that *Pilgrim's Progress* deserves to be read as "something more than Christian pilgrimage." A truer view recognizes the integral relationship between

---

4. U. Milo Kaufmann, *The Pilgrim's Progress and Traditions in Puritan Meditation* (New Haven and London: Yale University Press, 1966), vi, vii, ix.

mythic images and the essential substance of Christian teaching, both of which are directly biblical. To Bunyan, and to all who are on the Christian Way, there is nothing "more" than Christian pilgrimage.

BUNYAN, THE PILGRIM

To understand the achievement of this earnest Puritan, one must see him in the context of his times and his place in society. Bunyan was born in 1628 in the humble village of Elstow, in Bedfordshire. To say he was a Puritan is not to identify him with a sect as such, but with a mentality that arose after King Henry VIII established the Church of England. Puritans wanted to "purify" Christian doctrine, which meant making it more Calvinist. This mindset existed both within the official church and in most of the proliferating non-conforming sects as well.

Charles I, that profoundly unenviable British king who could not control Puritan zealotry and in 1649 lost his head as a consequence, had ascended to the throne just prior to Bunyan's birth. During the 1640s, after the Puritans gained enough strength to control Parliament and wage war against the king's forces, Bunyan served for a time in the Puritan army. He returned to Elstow in 1647, married soon thereafter, and, following in the footsteps of his father, became a tinker—an itinerant tinsmith traveling from house to house mending pots and pans.

As a young man he became deeply agitated in mind and soul. An individual of keen conscience and tender sensibility, he experienced severe inner conflicts over a long period until he was at last converted, conflicts that are detailed in his classic *Grace Abounding to the Chief of Sinners*. Joining the Baptist assembly at Bedford and soon feeling a call into the ministry, he quickly developed his gift for preaching. In 1660 the Puritan Commonwealth failed and Charles II came to the throne. The Act of Uniformity was passed in an attempt to establish the authority of the Church of England, and penal laws were enacted against those conducting conventicles, or unrecognized religious assemblies.

Bunyan, who refused to cease his preaching, was arrested, tried, and imprisoned. Restless and with time on his hands, he strengthened his convictions by reflecting on the reality of his spiritual experience. *Grace Abounding to the Chief of Sinners* (1666), an elaborate spiritual autobiography, resulted. So taken with the realities of his conversion and spiritual experience, and utterly unwilling that his testimony should be stifled by his imprisonment, he turned his active imagination towards allegorizing his inner life, and *The Pilgrim's Progress* (1678) began to take shape, objectifying himself as "Christian." Bunyan wrote for his own spiritual enjoyment. "I did it mine own self to gratify," he explained in his preface. It was after the allegory was completed when he first considered its publication.

BUNYAN MIRRORS HIS OWN EXPERIENCE

In *The Pilgrim's Progress* Bunyan wrote to capture imaginatively the qualities of his own Christian life. He attributed to Christian his own compelling motivation: the consuming longing for salvation and heavenly glory. He had a keen fear of divine justice and a nightmarish vision of an eternal physical hell, but was possessed with a pervasive yearning after the eternal—what C. S. Lewis later referred to as *Sehnsucht*. This positive thrust contributed strongly to the appeal of the text.

The world of *The Pilgrim's Progress* is modeled after Bunyan's home district of Bedfordshire, where he journeyed daily over the hills and through the villages of the county, his pack of tools weighing heavily upon his shoulders. He must have passed the time of day with wayfarers met along the road, wary (like Christian) of the many dangers besetting travelers, and enjoying the rest and entertainment of inns in the evening. The blue hills, always on the horizon, may have suggested a distant destination, like the Delectable Mountains.

One can imagine the eagerness with which, after his conversion, he would talk with others concerning the Christian faith in both its practical and doctrinal aspects. His tone earnest and urgent, he considered and judged attitudes divergent from his own. Being a man deeply committed to his faith, he viewed the world and all its inhabitants entirely from this perspective.

Having become a preacher and pastor of the Bedford congregation, he was solicitous for the eternal welfare of all whom he met. Since he literally saw his fellow humans in terms of those attitudes that were obvious on their faces and in their gestures, allegorizing antagonistic attitudes was not difficult. In lifting to the level of myth the daily acts of ordinary people—as opposed to the concerns of the upper classes—Bunyan introduced into the tradition of Christian mythopoeia a new focus.

The strongest source of dramatic power in the text is in the tension between those who feel within themselves the urgency Christian feels and those who do not, the former becoming an anomaly and a spectacle to the latter. The dream world of the narrative enables Bunyan to establish the sense of antithesis between these two groups. Bunyan had a conviction that everything of worth in time and eternity is lost to those who refuse to sacrifice all to the spiritual values of life. That conviction fuels this tension.

The genius of the story lies in the landscape and the people who were formed and shaped by Christian's faith. He—together with those of like faith, such as Faithful and Hopeful—travels the narrow way. All phenomena are shaped by these travelers' views of reality. Christian has an entire range of difficult experiences only because he chooses to be Christian. He alone traverses the Valleys of Humiliation and the

Shadow of Death; he alone fights Apollyon. Talkative, Money-Love, and their ilk are spared such agonies and frustrations of spirit—to their eternal undoing. Pliable and By-ends, who see faith as a way of making life easy and palatable, purchase with their ease eternal loss.

BUNYAN'S USE OF THE BIBLE

No one would suggest that Bunyan did not know Scripture. If one discerns a problem, it most often lies in what he excludes from Scripture, and in his extreme literalism. While the text conveys Bunyan's awareness of communicating to an audience, it focuses our attention on personal experience contemplated in the light of biblical statements. It possesses a strong air of reality because of the author's masterful use of detail (sparse though it be) together with the fact that he entertained no doubts concerning the validity of his thinking. This is experienced truth imaginatively viewed, not simply detailed theological opinion. Molding it all in a simple but compelling narrative mutes any feeling that he is preaching to us directly.

The Bible is at the core of the text. *The Pilgrim's Progress* is, in effect, Scripture reorganized; biblical statements and imagery constantly echo through it, reflecting Bunyan's profound knowledge of the Bible. His thoughts seem more completely possessed of Scripture than those of any other author, in part because he evidently read so little else, but also because he gave the Bible supreme authority. To the Puritans, Scripture was the Word of God, the official voice in all spiritual matters. They saw it as primarily propositional and doctrinal, with all its narratives and images serving doctrinal ends. Their personal experiences had validity and authority only insofar as they conformed strictly to biblical statement; hence, Bunyan's elaborate scriptural glosses. He interpreted the Bible literally, the Old Testament as well as the New.

But the Scriptures that Bunyan relied upon throughout his writings are those that confirm the tenets of Calvinism; those that seem to contradict his system he ignored or dismissed. For instance, in one of his written sermons he speciously explains Paul's statement in Romans 11:32, "For God has consigned all men to disobedience, that he may have mercy upon all:"

> Here again [John 12:32 is the first instance] you have all and all, two alls; but yet a greater disparity between the all made mention of in the first place, and that all made mention of the second. Those intended in this text are the Jews, even all of them, by the first all that you find in the words. The second all doeth also intend the same people; but yet only so many of them as God will have mercy upon. . . . The all also in the text, is likewise to be limited and restrained to the saved, and to them only." [5]

5. From the sermon "Come and Welcome to Jesus Christ," as quoted in G. B. Harrison, *John Bunyan: A Study in Personality* (Garden City, N.Y.: Doubleday, Doran & Company, 1928), 179.

Beyond its questionable nature, his thinking seems callous and harsh. But in such passages Bunyan's mind is opposing his heart; he was in fact—in contrast to the stereotypical Puritan—a remarkably sensitive and generous person.

Writing in *Grace Abounding* concerning his conversion, he recounted how, after an extended period of inner turmoil and agony, he was sitting by the fire one evening, when the words suddenly came to him: "I must go to Jesus." When his wife could not tell him the location of the scripture, he heard an inner voice adding: "And to an innumerable company of Angels." Recalling the passage was in Hebrews 12:22–24, he turned eagerly to it, and a marvelous change swept over him. He recorded that afterwards, "I could scarce lie in my bed for joy, and peace, and triumph, through Christ. . . ." The passage was thereafter a favorite of his. We learn much about his spiritual struggles that followed and their consequent resolutions by reading *The Pilgrim's Progress.*

LIFE AS SACRED JOURNEY

"This book will make a Traveller of thee," Bunyan affirmed in his opening poem, "The Author's Apology for his Book." The metaphor central to the entire Bible, that of life as a journey, is perhaps most succinctly expressed in Hebrews 11:13–16. Bunyan would have used the King James Version:

These all died in faith, not having received the
promises, but having seen them afar off, and were
persuaded of them, and embraced them, and con-
fessed that they were strangers and pilgrims on the
earth. For they that say such things declare plainly
that they seek a country. And truly, if they had been
mindful of that country from whence they came out,
they might have had opportunity to have returned.
But now they desire a better country, that is, an heavenly: wherefore God is not ashamed to be called their
God: for he hath prepared for them a city.

The passage is archetypal and richly mythical. The
journey image is directly associated with eternity. As
such, it arouses the longing for immortality and the
hope for a more blissful and glorious afterlife, emotions
deep within the human heart.

Further, Bunyan established an air of authority by
reminding his readers of the prevalence of metaphors in
the Bible, such as those present in the teachings of
Christ. They were to him not as sugarcoated capsules of
doctrinal truth, but more as lamps that send mysterious
illumining rays into the human spirit. They "make truth
to spangle, and its rays to shine," he insisted.

Bunyan had a strong conviction that life is an
extended contest and enduring struggle until its consummation in eternity, with future glory depending
upon our continually overcoming and finally triumphing. By incorporating this vision into the journey

image, Bunyan intensified the mythic power of his text. He would have agreed with Dostoyevski's Dmitri Karamazov that life is a perpetual spiritual struggle between God and Satan, the battlefield being the human heart. To Bunyan's Christian, divine triumph brings joy and peace, so that he concludes many of his trials with a song, even a trial so dire as the execution of Faithful, his close companion, in the city of Vanity Fair. Bunyan's vision is one of complete fusion between the physical and the spiritual, not so much in a sacramental sense as in the perception that all human experience involves eternal consequences. All of life is sacred.

Bunyan melded the two levels of the narrative into a unified vision with his allegory. Normally, one thinks of allegory as narrative with two levels of meaning, that of surface images and that of abstract meaning, with the second level so overshadowing the first that the latter is hardly noticed. Christ's parable of the sower, for instance, is not often discussed as a story of an irresponsible farmer. Bunyan would probably have been familiar with some of the mechanical attempts by prior Puritans to allegorize the Christian life, efforts that tend to be no more than laborious sermons. But *The Pilgrim's Progress* is more than a Puritan sermon.

We take the first level seriously because it is that of ordinary life realistically presented. A man, distressed and anxious, leaves his home and family in one city and makes a long journey to another, meeting many travelers along the way. The second level is that of spiritual significance, in which every meeting issues in either eternal success or failure. The completeness with which Bunyan unites these two levels establishes within the minds of his readers the conviction that all of life, rightly viewed, has infinite consequences. Everyday life is a sacred journey. The ubiquity of a spiritual dynamic invests all of life with the aura of myth.

THE JOURNEY BEGINS

The Pilgrim's Progress contains two parts, the first giving the story of Christian's journey from the City of Destruction to the Celestial City, and the second recounting how his wife and family followed in his footsteps, their journey being somewhat different from Christian's initial one. The narrative begins with a familiar device—the dream. In it Graceless (who soon becomes Christian), possessed of Bunyan's own feelings as described in *Grace Abounding*, is a burdened and bedraggled sinner with the Bible in his hand. Evangelist urges him to "Fly from the wrath to come." The course he chooses is simply preposterous to the worldlings around him. But, consumed with desire and conviction, he "put his fingers in his Ears, and ran on crying, Life, Life, Eternal Life: so he looked not behind him. . . ." He has but dimly seen the light from afar, but he sacrifices all to find the Gate. We feel his urgency. The depiction seems at once both absurd and filled with the force of the simplest logic.

In the beginning of the narrative Christian begins to experience what the Puritans called the Work of Grace. Its first manifestation is conviction of sin (as Faithful later explains to Talkative). Christian has on his back an immense burden. Among Bunyan's tinker's items contained in the Bunyan Museum in Bedford is his sixty pound anvil—a toadstool shaped affair rounded on top to receive upturned pots and pans. The anvil and necessary tools would have indeed been a burden to carry, readily suggesting to him the burden that besets Christian at the beginning of his journey.

As Christian is convicted of personal sin, he must gain a sense of relief found in personal salvation. Many of those with whom he first converses represent false approaches to salvation, such as Worldly Wiseman (whose path runs perpendicular to Christian's). Lacking Christian's sensitivity to sin, they subsequently have no appreciation for the peace he feels when the burden is finally lifted. Bunyan is keenly convinced of Solomon's observation that there is a way which seems right to man but its end result is death; his fecund imagination overflows with erring ways.

The most dangerous of these erroneous ways is that of trying to find relief from the burden of sin by means of the Covenant of Law; Christian's early trials rehearse the perils. Mr. Worldly Wiseman, from the town of Carnal-Policy, represents the error. Christian is at first deceived. But no one can perfectly keep the law: he stands quaking before the sight of the hill on the way to Mr. Legality's house. Then, Evangelist meets him and directs him to the Gate. Christian's fears and frustrations not only exhibit the impossibility of achieving salvation through good works, but they make us the more appreciative of the Evangelist's message. The function of the law is to bring one to grace.

AT THE CROSS

The cross represents the Covenant of Grace, or the New Covenant, in which the sinner repents of his sins and receives forgiveness. Christian finds, however, that the wicket gate opens to the narrow way, but not yet to the cross. Proper teaching is vital to the success of Christian's journey. He first must approach the House of the Interpreter, knock, and be shown "excellent things" that will make the experience of the cross efficacious for him. The man at the gate is Good-will, or grace, by which, in the words of Ephesians 2:8, people are saved. Christian, however, does not immediately know deliverance from his burden, and nothing he can do can bring it about: "be content to bear it, until thou comest to the place of Deliverance; for there it will fall from thy back itself," Good-will instructs him.

The scene of Christian identifying himself and his sense of purpose to the Interpreter at the door is memorable and important. Christian must have a clear sense of his identity as a pilgrim whose foremost purpose in life is to reject the world and travel to Zion. It is after he makes such a commitment and clearly expresses a desire to be helped on his journey that the candle is lit—an inner illumination of mind is granted him—and he is shown a series of pictures.

These pictures are instances of the emblem, a vital tradition in Renaissance literature. [6] Emblems are word pictures contrived to convey moral or religious truths. They are to religious literature not unlike what stained glass windows are to cathedrals: a means of focusing the observer's mind upon edifying images. Bunyan is especially adept in creating emblems that provoke contemplation of fundamental Christian realities.

Some expositors of *The Pilgrim's Progress* see the Interpreter as the Holy Spirit and his house as the Bible. [7] But the various emblems Christian is shown do not represent specific biblical statements so much as a general Puritan understanding of scriptural teaching. The first picture—that of "a very grave Person" whose eyes are lifted to Heaven, "the best of Books in its hand, the Law of Truth was written upon its lips, the World was behind its back; it stood as if it pleaded with Men, and a Crown of Gold did hang over its head"—

6. E. Beatrice Batson, *John Bunyan: Allegory and Imagination* (Totowa, NJ: Barnes & Noble, 1984), 87–101. See also Lynn Veach Sadler, *John Bunyan* (Boston: Twayne Publishers, 1979). Bunyan published in 1686 *A Book for Boys and Girls, Or, Country Rhymes for Children* composed of seventy-four emblems.

7. Kaufmann, *The Pilgrim's Progress and Traditions in Puritan Meditation*, 61–79.

presents the ideal person in the Puritan imagination. [8]
As a paradigm it contains mythic energies, but its
prototype is not Christ, but the Puritan preacher. He is
the Puritan Evangelist, the possessor and proclaimer of
divine truth whose work is to "know, and unfold dark
things to sinners," effecting by his labors the eternal
destiny of multitudes. He, Christian is told, is "the only
Man, whom the Lord of the Place whither thou art
going, hath Authorized, to be thy Guide." Christian
may on his journey meet others who pretend to lead
him rightly, but they will in fact lead him to death.
Christian's safe arrival in Zion is dependent upon his
following the voice of Puritanism.

This emblem of the ideal man was of mythic proportions to Puritan minds. It occupied a position not
unlike the Grecian or Roman heroes Odysseus or
Aeneas occupied in the mind of classical man. From a
biblical standpoint it is incomplete—one doubts that
Paul, Peter, or John would recognize it as the most
direct or complete depiction of the characteristics they
attribute to the Christian life. When Bunyan's fellow
Puritan, Milton, attempted in *Paradise Lost* to describe
the Christian ideal by having the Archangel Michael
list the necessary qualities to Adam, the emphasis falls
upon gentler virtues. Milton stops short, however, of
imaginatively incarnating them in a character. The

8. Swaim, *Pilgrim's Progress, Puritan Progress.* Swaim identifies the figure as Christ
(87), but it is so only in the sense that for the Christian the ideal is reposited in
Christ. Kaufmann more correctly sees him as Evangelist (67).

poem ends with Adam and Eve making their way out into the world.

The issue of what constitutes Christian heroism in the real world is a large one, one upon which many Christians would disagree. Clearly, classical paradigms will not do. Christian himself presents a provocative pattern. The ultimate paradigm to the Christian imagination is Christ, but, although he was fully human, he was sinless and divine; the Christian hero must begin in sinfulness and, in the realm of time, can go only so far in approximating the Christlike ideal. Given his Puritan understanding of Scripture, Bunyan is committed to the essence of heroism being the individual's triumphing over sin and achieving holiness. One thinks of Dante's narrator in the *Divine Comedy* and Spenser's Red Cross Knight as important antecedent attempts at portraying Christian heroism. It is doubtful that Bunyan knew anything of either, or that he would have allowed himself to be much impressed if he had. His emphasis is upon the struggle to overcome, with all its inherent perils.

Through a series of emblems given in the House of the Interpreter, Christian receives the extensive knowledge which Bunyan feels essential to an accurate understanding of the Christian life. One, a Christian pilgrim must understand the ineffectuality of the law and the genius of the gospel in relieving the weight of sinfulness; two, the need to wait patiently until the next life for the rewards of virtue; three, the paradox that the work of grace in the heart is nurtured by its conflict with evil; four, the need for courage and decisive action in entering into Christian experience; five, the danger of falling into apostasy; and six, the certainty of final judgment.

At the cross, in exchange for his burden, Christian receives from three angels assurance of forgiveness, a new coat, a mark upon his forehead, and a sealed roll. The coat—in accordance with Covenant theology—signifies that God will see him from this moment on as a righteous person; the mark, his assurance of predestined salvation; and the roll, the statements from Scripture that encourage him to persevere and receive salvation upon his death. Christian believers today may be surprised that the Person of Christ is absent from this scene. To Bunyan, Christ seems preeminently a Judge—the "Man that sat on the Cloud" in the prior emblem, casting the reprobate into the burning lake—not the gracious Savior who risks all to reclaim the lost person. [9] Bunyan's understanding of Christian conversion stands in interesting contrast to that of American evangelicalism. To Bunyan, the *work* of Christ is more essential than a sense of union with his Person.

The point that a correct knowledge of Christian doctrine is vital is reinforced at the end of part 1. Ignorance, even though he affirms he believes in Christ for his justification, is cast down to hell from the very

9. See the parable of the lost sheep and similar ones in Luke chapter 15.

gates of heaven because he lacks a precise understanding of the doctrine of imputed righteousness.
According to today's thinking this may seem intolerant
and cruel. But Bunyan, who has read Scripture with
Calvinist glasses firmly in place, sees no alternative to
doctrinal precision. Ignorance is like the unprofitable
servant in Christ's parable of the pounds who in judgment is cast into outer darkness. Christian's accurate
knowledge is the result of Interpreter's having taken
him by the hand, an image that suggests his being
taught truths he could not have attained on his own,
and willingly receiving them.

The righteousness of Christ in which Christian is
robed is a necessary element in his journey, distinguishing him from all other impostures. Formalist and
Hypocrite, whom he soon meets, profess to be as able
as Christian to abide by laws and ordinances; besides,
they follow the customs the Church has practiced for
over a thousand years. Christian, however, has his coat,
together with the roll and mark; that is, he is confident
in a righteousness not his own. Thus armed, he stands
supreme in his individualism against everything external to himself.

THE PALACE BEAUTIFUL

As a good Baptist Bunyan saw the importance of the
Church, and the Church is an important institution to
Christian. It is a spiritual entity, the Palace Beautiful.

Christian does not come upon it until he has recovered his roll which he had lost on the Hill Difficulty. During this period several trials cause him to doubt momentarily, losing the assurance of his salvation. When he recovers his roll, the promises of Scripture found in it refresh his spirit. He is now able to give a testimony of his personal experience that satisfies the daughters of the palace. In having Christian recount his experiences to the local church, Bunyan is reinforcing the essential steps to conversion, but he is also presenting the process whereby anyone would become a member of a Baptist conventicle. The purpose of the Church is to strengthen and secure the individual in the Christian life through fellowship and inspiration received from the teaching of biblical narrative and doctrine. Nothing is said of worship, and certainly not of honoring and perpetuating ecclesiastical traditions. The model to which the Puritans looked was that of the early church as presented in the book of Acts. When Christian goes on his way, Discretion, Piety, Charity, and Prudence accompany him, and he descends into the Valley of Humiliation.

PASSING THROUGH THE VALLEYS

There Apollyon awaits him. The confrontation and battle that follows may be seen as the dramatic center of the entire narrative. Apollyon is Satan, whom Paul teaches is the god of this world, the prince and power of the air, the spirit present in all people who are not actively obedient to the word and will of God. Apollyon is, therefore, the spirit behind all Christian's confrontations. Bunyan wisely refrains from allegorizing this confrontation with Satan in terms of any specific temptation. Apollyon views Christian as a rebellious subject and tries to entice him back with an "all is forgiven." If he persists in traveling on the King's Highway, Apollyon threatens to kill him. Christian's two-edged Sword, the Bible, gives him the victory. The entire passage is filled with imagery from Ephesians 6.

The scenes describing Christian's inner struggles tend to suggest periods of depression, discouragement, and confusion; whereas those that Faithful is soon to recount suggest more carnal struggles. The Valley of the Shadow through which Christian must journey—a biblical image occurring in Job, Jeremiah, and the Psalms—suggests gloom and apprehension, with the ditch on one hand probably suggesting doctrinal error and the quag on the other an engulfing sense of guilt and confusion. Christian, groping through darkness for the path, desperately avoiding the mouth of hell, may symbolize Bunyan's struggling for theologically correct answers to the difficult questions of his experience, questions which his keen mind and hypersensitive conscience kept asking. His fear of having unconsciously blasphemed the Spirit of God, detailed in *Grace Abounding*, is a case in point. The figures of Pope and Pagan likewise suggest the besetting dangers of opposing systems of thought. Correct conclusions are vitally necessary, the text insists, or else one falls into eternal perdition.

Christian's experience in the Valley of the Shadow arouses within him a longing for company, a desire soon satisfied when he meets Faithful. Their conversation affords Bunyan yet another opportunity to review the steps by which the Christian journey is begun, with variations appropriate to Faithful's more extroverted nature. Faithful is attracted to the more physical temptations of life. Like Christian, he had his encounter with the law, mistaking Moses for Christ; but unlike him, Faithful is at first deceived into thinking Talkative a fine fellow.

Christian has better discernment concerning Talkative than does his companion: "all he hath lieth in his tongue, and his religion to make a noise therewith." Vital as correct thinking is, in itself it is insufficient if unaccompanied by deeds. True Christianity is a matter of the heart as well as the head. The heart yields an active and glad obedience to the will of God. Faithful's artful exposing of Talkative's error is one of the more amusing passages in *The Pilgrim's Progress*.

VANITY FAIR

The difficulty of obedience is intensified by the temptations of the secular world, as the famous episode of Vanity Fair illustrates. The pilgrims' way takes them inevitably through the town of Vanity where a fair is in progress. Fairs were common among the towns and smaller cities of England, and Bunyan on his travels would often have encountered them. The fair the pilgrims visit was no doubt suggested to him by the huge one given annually in the village of Sturbridge, near Cambridge. Covering an area of half a square mile, it attracted merchants not only from around England and Scotland, but also from other European countries and the American colonies. All manner of entertainments were there. [10]

A fair to Bunyan, therefore, was a vivid image of the world in microcosm. The entire order that characterizes secular society is permeated with a spirit alien to that of Christianity. Bunyan has the attitude of the apostle John in mind: "For all that is in the world, the lust of the flesh, and the lust of the eyes, and the pride of life, is not of the Father, but is of the world" (1 John 2:16, KJV), and he glosses the text with the assessment of Ecclesiastes: "Then I looked on all the works that my hands had wrought, and on the labour that I had laboured to do: and, behold, all was vanity and vexation of spirit, and there was no profit under the sun. . . . for all is vanity and vexation of spirit" (2:11, 17, KJV).

Vanity Fair is run entirely by Apollyon and his ilk. It encompasses all the relationships of life in a civilized society: Bunyan's listing is breath-taking. His point is not that the necessary activities and relationships of life cannot be conducted in a way that honors God, but rather that before God all human activity is permeated with evil, and humans even at their best are ever and always in the wrong.

Bunyan's pilgrims are at such cross purposes with the inhabitants of Vanity that they are indicted and must stand trial. The tone and intensity of the narrative is derived from Bunyan's own experiences of arrest and imprisonment. His numerous confrontations over a score of years with the authorities of his day is evident in his indignation at their injustice. The scene illustrates vividly how attitudes of the community at large can turn Christian conduct into a spectacle. Bunyan felt with the apostle Paul that "all that will live godly in Christ Jesus shall suffer persecution" (2 Tim. 3:12, KJV). The brunt of the persecution falls upon Faithful, resulting in his death, while Christian escapes. Since Faithful's temptations pertained more to the physical aspects of life while Christian's were more intellectual, his clash with the lusts of Vanity Fair was more intense.

Faithful dies, but is assured the crown of life. Christian goes on his way accompanied by a new companion, Hopeful. The allegorical transition from faith to hope suggests a certain progress or spiritual growth on Christian's part. Hope, inasmuch as it gains its energies from a vision of the world to come, implies a more thorough rejection of this world. Christian's struggles, though they shift somewhat in character, do not lessen in intensity.

CONTINUING CONFLICTS

After the conflicts in Vanity Fair, Bunyan fixes his reader's attention less on the process of salvation and more on the types of temptations that beset the Christian. Browning remarks at the beginning of "Easter Day" how hard it is to be a Christian; Bunyan explicitly defines the difficulties. The central symbol of these episodes is that of Lot's wife who, although she escapes one judgment—the destruction of Sodom— falls by another—the sin of covetousness (as Bunyan reads the event). So Christians, having been delivered from damnation through the death of Christ, may still fall to the judgment of fruitlessness. One is tempted to observe that Bunyan's diagnosis is prophetic of the Puritan movement at large. During the nineteenth century the Puritan spirit was weakened by many turning their attention to prospering in the world economically, becoming convinced that riches were the appropriate rewards for righteous living.

The pillar of salt that was Lot's wife stands beside the highway just beyond the Plain of Ease and the hill Lucre (riches), where both By-ends and Demas meet their untimely ends. Covetousness precipitates their falls: it undermines one's proper values and drains one's energies away from spiritually productive labor. Christian keenly understands and avoids the peril. The extended episode is redolent with Bunyan's shrewd awareness that the Christian life is most quickly diffused whenever principle is sacrificed for personal gain. Life is beset with such opportunities—By-ends has many relatives indeed.

Christian, however, remains appealingly human. On the one hand, he is "progressing" in inner strength and fortitude, as well as in a deft ability to choose appropriate biblical narratives and apply them to life-situations. For instance, he soundly destroys Mr. Hold-the-World's question concerning whether it is lawful to become a Christian in order to advance one's material position in the world. He wisely admonishes: "If it is unlawful to follow Christ for loaves. . . , how much more abominable is it to make of him and religion a stalking horse to get and enjoy the world," and then proceeds to marshal an elaborate and precisely organized listing of scriptural passages. Christian's conversation with Hopeful that follows also shows his growth in such virtues as trust, humility, and thoughtfulness.

On the other hand, Christian is vulnerable to doubt, despair, and flattery. Doubting Castle, with its proprietor Giant Despair, lies not far from the pleasant River of the Water of Life, even as the hill Lucre lies by the Plain of Ease. Apparently, experiences that give the spirit refreshment or relaxation contain the danger of relaxing one's guard against temptation. Christian has a ready antidote: he has but to recall the biblical promises.

In contrast to the backward looking aspects of the earlier narrative, such as when Christian, through various images and devices, recounts the steps in the process of his salvation, his attention is now increasingly focused on the life to come. The Shepherds of the Delectable Mountains—suggesting teachers of sound doctrine within the church—both warn the pilgrims of various errors and, through their "perspective glass," grant them a glimpse of the Celestial City. Through Hopeful's recounting of his spiritual odyssey, and a dismissal of the errors of Ignorance and Temporary, the pilgrims come at last to the culmination of their journey, the Country of Beulah.

At this point in his narrative Bunyan generates dramatic tension between the dazzling beauty of the Celestial City and the pilgrims' dismay at the River of Death they must cross to attain it. Beulah means "married"; in death divine faithfulness marries human frailty. The fusion has a vivid existential dynamic:

> Then they asked the men if the Waters were all of a depth. They said no; yet they could not help them in that Case; for said they, You shall find it deeper or shallower, as you believe in the King of the place.

Faith is the essential virtue of Christian's character from the inception of his journey to its conclusion. His painful struggles and misgivings make him the more human and appealing as a real person, while his victorious arrival enhances his preeminent mythical qualities. The sense of ascension and joy effect a fitting climax to the tale.

PART 2: CHRISTIAN'S WIFE
BEGINS A JOURNEY

Part 2 complements part 1, adding a richness to the allegory. As Kathleen Swaim observes, part 1 invites us as readers to contemplate a reader reading his book; part 2 presents the fictional reader himself as a text to be read. [11] In making Christian a text to which his wife Christiana refers, Bunyan reinforces the mythic nature of the Christian life, affirming both its particular and its universal aspects. Hers is the same journey, yet experienced quite differently. He also softens somewhat the former rigidity of his prescribed steps to salvation. "I pray for all them that believe on me, by what means soever they come unto me," Christ, the keeper of the gate, tells Mercy. That different personalities have approaches afforded them appropriate to their needs was not told to Christian. Perhaps Bunyan's directing the text of part 2 to the needs of women prompted his new-found latitude. All the distinctions in gender that

11. Swaim, *Pilgrim's Progress, Puritan Progress*, 16, 17.

characterized Puritan thought are present, and these account for many of the differences in the narratives between the two parts. [12] Temptations to sexual sins are all but absent from part 1; they occur almost immediately in part 2. For Christiana and Mercy to consent to the two ill-favored men intent on sexual favors would have imperiled their salvation.

Beyond the weaknesses Bunyan intimates are endemic to women in general, he envisioned a procession of weaker individuals: Ready-to-halt, Feeblemind, Despondency, and Much-afraid. God mercifully accommodates his grace to all sincere seekers, compensating for their weaknesses. In the years between writing part 1 and part 2, Bunyan, a keenly observant pastor, noted many more struggles and potential pitfalls besetting the pilgrim's way; he is now more concerned with the weak and struggling than with the stubborn and opinionated.

Mercy is Christiana's companion. In replacing the figures of Faithful and Hopeful with Mercy, Bunyan emphasizes not only that such is God's dealings with mankind, but also that the pilgrim should show a merciful concern for others, a sentiment immediately expressed by both Christiana and Mercy. In general, the dynamics of salvation are more horizontal, although perhaps not less vertical, than in part 1. The reader is made to be more aware of the function of the

12. Swaim discusses gender differences, *Pilgrim's Progress, Puritan Progress*, 160–97.

community of Christians in their mutual salvation. And Mercy does not receive a direct invitation from the King as does Christiana. This seems to suggest that a conscious conviction of one's election is not requisite to receive salvation.

In part 2, Bunyan identifies the keeper of the gate as Christ, with whom Christiana and Mercy have an extended conversation. Part 1 is somewhat obscure in presenting the role of the person of Christ as regards the pilgrim. In retelling Christian's pilgrimage, Bunyan allows no possible misunderstanding that salvation begins with a direct confrontation of the soul with Christ. Nor is there any possible confusion concerning the nature of the narrow way: it is "the way of his Steps." At the conclusion, Mr. Stand-fast in death affirms: "I have loved to hear my Lord spoken of, and wherever I have seen the print of his Shoe in the Earth, there I have coveted to set my Foot too."

In general, Christiana and Mercy seem to lack Christian's tender sensitivity of conscience and the intensity of his driving desire for salvation. One reason for this might be that they have not a burden upon their backs as he did, and they seem quite content to rest in inns (now more liberally occurring) along the way. They not only do not fall into the Slough of Despond, but Mr. Great-heart and Honest slay Giant-Despair and even demolish Doubting Castle. Clearly, Bunyan is not acknowledging that despair may be pathological. By annihilating doubt, he may be indicating how far he has progressed in his own odyssey from his early days, but he weakens the text by discounting completely the quantity of uncertainty which inevitably characterizes the human condition.

The journey of part 2 is considerably safer and more secure, in spite of the allegorical encounters. The party is not called upon for heroic action with the urgency and sense of eminent danger that beset Christian, and the dramatic dynamic of the text is less intense. The need of the women pilgrims is more one of understanding than overcoming, to be strengthened within rather than to confront and resist temptations. Greatheart is a more constant companion and active protector than Evangelist was to Christian; he is more of a mentor and less of a sign-post.

Dramatic intensity increases as part 2 draws to its close, and the narrative achieves an effective climax. Bunyan's view of election did not preclude the sense of the pilgrims' constant peril to the very conclusion of the journey. Being seized by the paralysis of the Enchanted Ground or yielding to the enticements offered by Mrs. Bubble—temptations occurring immediately prior to the pilgrims' entrance into the Land of Beulah—represent real threats, dangers that could have negated all their preceding efforts and triumphs. "What Danger is the Pilgrim in, / How many are his foes, / How many ways there are to Sin, / No living

Mortal knows" summarizes the essence of Bunyan's vision.

Bunyan's genius in narrative is perhaps nowhere more evident than in the climax of part 2, as the Messenger brings from the King personal tidings to each of the pilgrims that they are expected in His Presence. To Christiana "the Token was, An Arrow with a Point sharpened with Love, let easily into her Heart, which by degrees wrought so effectually with her, that at the time appointed she must be gone." The imagery is remarkably successful in presenting the reality of a person's final pain and demise. Mr. Despondency is bidden to "be ready with thy King, by the next Lords Day, to shout for Joy for thy Deliverance from all thy Doubtings." The sense of triumph and joy which should surround dying in faith could hardly be more movingly expressed.

Bunyan's allegory is significant in that he focuses on the spiritual experience of common people, adopting an intimate tone of urgency. In this he is distinct from earlier writers such as Edmund Spenser and John Milton, to whom in his religious interests he may be compared. Their mythological heroes are removed from ordinary life. In fashioning lowly characters, Bunyan demonstrated how common and widespread are the foundational aspects of spiritual experience. In presenting with simplicity and purity image patterns drawn directly from the Bible, he showed how deeply rooted in myth are the issues of the human spirit. He penetratingly discerned and delineated the mythic substructure of life, demonstrating that myth is the indispensable language of Truth.

The popularity of *The Pilgrim's Progress* takes the measure of its success as an outstanding example of mythopoeia. It has passed through more editions and been translated into more foreign languages than any other book written in English.[13] Since it was written, it may be the most widely read book next to the Bible. Bunyan is not the pioneer mythmaker, but he is a pioneer in making imaginative literature available to common people: he did more than any other writer to make myth accessible to a wide range of readers. He is a permanent point of reference to all subsequent writers of mythopoeia, a genre that has grown from his time to our own.

In their imaginative contemplation of the ordinary individuals who would live the Christian life, myth-makers penetrate deeply into the nature of Christian experience. The result is an essential companion and supplement to the bulk of rational and discursive analyses of Christian realities. Because Bunyan's work reaches steadily forward to the world of today, we will have several occasions in this study to recall him.

13. Robert G. Collmer, ed., *Bunyan in Our Time* (Kent, Ohio: Kent State University Press, 1989), 1.

3

George MacDonald
Myth and Symbol
(1824–1905)

Most myths were made in prehistoric times, and I
suppose, not consciously made by individuals at all.
But every now and then there occurs in the modern
world a genius—a Kafka or a Novalis—who can make
such a story. MacDonald is the greatest genius of this
kind whom I know. But I do not know how to classi-
fy such genius. To call it literary genius seems unsat-
isfactory since it can co-exist with great inferiority in
the art of words—nay, since its connection with words
at all turns out to be merely external, and, in a sense,
accidental. Nor can it be fitted into any of the other
arts. It begins to look as if there were an art, or a gift,
which criticism has largely ignored. It may even be
one of the greatest arts; for it produces works which
give us (at the first meeting) as much delight and (on
prolonged acquaintance) as much wisdom and
strength as the works of the greatest poets. [1]

---

1. C. S. Lewis, *George MacDonald: An Anthology* (New York: Macmillan, 1948), 16.

enuine mythmakers are indeed rare. It was some two hundred years after John Bunyan when George MacDonald was born. In England the Enlightenment had given way to the Romantic Movement and scientific rationalism had engendered the Industrial Revolution. Wesley's Great Revival had revitalized British nonconformist Christianity and, in part due to Wesley's movement, it had become evangelical in tone. But British Evangelicalism tended to be a stern and rigid affair. For all that may be said in its behalf, much of it was unduly narrow and austere in tone and attitude. Reformation rationalism had come to lack the joyous celebration of mystery. In such a time, George MacDonald undertook to rediscover it through myth.

Though raised in Scottish Calvinism, as a youth MacDonald loved the Gaelic lore and Celtic fairy tales that came to him through his stern but life-loving father. While attending King's College in Aberdeen, he discovered the rich, mythic fantasies of German authors E. T. A. Hoffmann and Novalis. George MacDonald's achievement lies in his accomplishing a consistent and coherent system of thought derived from the best of these traditions of Calvinism and romanticism. His muscular intellectualism is evident in his published sermons. His mythopoeia demonstrates an imaginative reach towards Truth, achieving a splendid literary consummation.

MACDONALD'S CAREER

As a theologian, MacDonald's strength lies in his humanizing the stern Calvinist image of God. He insisted that God could not be less righteous than an upright, kindly father. His own father's spiritual stature was his inspiration, who, upon the loss of his wife in 1832, raised his family of boys as a model parent, being to them both mother and father. George MacDonald gave his life to communicating the idea that if people knew who God really was, they would believe in Him. Seeing his age in spiritual bondage to an attenuated image of God, he kept insisting: "But hear me this once more: the God, the Jesus, in whom I believe, are not the God, the Jesus, in whom you fancy I believe: you know them not; your idea of them is not mine. If you knew them you would believe in them, for to know them is to believe in them." [2]

After graduating from King's College, Aberdeen, he went down to London in the late 1840s, joined an evangelical church, and became a tutor to the children of an evangelical merchant. There he clearly saw Victorian attitudes where Christian commitment seemed only an intellectual assent to precisely stated doctrines, with little concern for obedience. Once assent was given, people felt free to pursue material and pragmatic ends in life—what the British termed "getting

2. MacDonald, *Paul Faber, Surgeon* (1879; reprint Whitehorn,Calif.: Johannesen, 1992), chapter 54.

on"—unhampered by any serious consideration of the ethical precepts of Christ. A copy of *The Pilgrim's Progress* could readily be found in most homes across the land, with people abiding by its stern doctrinal insistences and moral imperatives. Christian morality was a legalist affair, to be gauged in external terms, having more to do with maintaining Sunday blue laws than with a loving relationship to one's neighbors.

MacDonald soon felt called to become a prophet to his society. His strongest literary gift was to perceive and communicate the realities of Christ through myth. He opposed the prevailing religious climate by infusing it with imaginative works that vibrate with mythic energies. It is this mythic component that makes his stories and tales continue to live today.

Although his mature ministry involved preaching and lecturing, he gained his widest influence through writing. After two volumes of poetry he published *Phantastes* (1858), a fairy tale for adults. When public reception to it was unenthusiastic, he turned to the novel, publishing over two dozen during his lifetime. His novels—theological romances in which he contemplated human life and behavior from a carefully conceived Christian point of view—are distinguished by the degree to which they integrate a mythic vision, such as in *Sir Gibbie*. The books sold widely in England and especially in America, rendering MacDonald one of the most widely read writers of his period. His fantasies continue to delight both children and adults today. In this chapter we will examine *Phantastes, At the Back of the North Wind, The Princess and the Goblin, The Princess and Curdie, The Golden Key*, and *Lilith*.

ROMANTIC THOUGHT WITHIN
CHRISTIANITY

In contrast to Bunyan's Enlightenment rationalism, MacDonald's sensibility was romantic. In twentieth-century literary criticism, the term romantic is often seen in opposition to Christianity. The definition of the romantic spirit, expressed in many of the nineteenth-century authors (e.g., William Wordsworth) manifested the following characteristics: (1) a strong sense of the ideal; (2) a conviction that the only reality is spiritual, the physical world existing as a manifestation of it; (3) a primary interest in inner reality; (4) an insistence upon the importance of perception, with the imagination being defined as the faculty by which the mind perceives the world (which is quite different from popular usage today as creative fantasizing); [3] and (5) an intense

---

3. Samuel Taylor Coleridge gives the classic definition of the imagination: "The primary imagination I hold to be the living Power and prime Agent of all human Perception, and as a repetition in the finite mind of the eternal act of creation in the infinite I AM. The secondary Imagination I consider as an echo of the former, co-existing with the primary in the *kind* of its agency, and differing only in *degree*, and in the *mode* of its operation. It dissolves, diffuses, dissipates, in order to recreate; or where this process is rendered impossible, yet still at all events it struggles to idealize and to unify. It is essentially *vital*, even as all objects (*as* objects) are essentially fixed and dead." *Biographia Literaria*, chapter 13.

interest in nature as a manifestation of the immanent presence of God. When these tenets are combined with firm Christian convictions, as they are in MacDonald, the result is a vibrant and challenging Christianity.

Viewed in this light, much of traditional Christian thought is romantic: The sense of the ideal in the Sermon on the Mount; the life of faith epitomized by Abraham and defined by the apostle Paul; the insistence on the primacy of the unseen as opposed to the seen; the command that Christians develop eyes to see and ears to hear spiritual realities; the love of nature because in some undefinable sense it manifests aspects of the divine; and the awareness that all worship centrally involves the imagination. All these make up the romantic spirit, and all are emphasized in MacDonald's thought. Some of these traits are anticipated in Bunyan; all of them generally characterize the authors considered in this study.

George MacDonald's strong celebration of the imagination attracted him to Bunyan's mythic paradigms. For years his family—he and Louisa raised eleven of their own sons and daughters, together with several foster children—formed an acting troupe and gave renditions of *The Pilgrim's Progress*, part 2, in public halls throughout England and Scotland. Their unusual ministry cohered around their oldest daughter Lilia's portrayal of Christiana, Louisa's of Mistress Much-afraid, and MacDonald's of Great-heart.

In contrast to Bunyan's cautious view of the imagination given at the beginning of *The Pilgrim's Progress*, MacDonald saw its exercise as indispensable to our humanity. The imagination is the faculty of all perception. [4] His thinking is essentially an extension of the teachings of Samuel Taylor Coleridge, a romantic poet of the previous generation. MacDonald believed that the human imagination is on the finite level as God's creating power is on the infinite level. Everyone receives images through the senses and interprets them—in effect, creating one's own world. The story writer creates with words a reality that is both more ideal and more unified than that of daily life. Because human creation is confined to using images derived from experience, a person who interprets the world rightly is thinking God's thoughts after him. "Our imagination is made to mirror truth . . . and when we are true it will mirror nothing but truth." [5]

The artist unifies and idealizes images taken from his perceptions, offering in his art a fresh interpretation of them. He "ought to learn of nature, but not in his work *imitate* nature," MacDonald states. "His work is, through the forms that Nature gives him, to express the

4. See MacDonald's essays "The Imagination: Its Functions and Its Culture," *Orts* (London: Sampson Low, Marston, Searle & Rivington, 1882) and "The Fantastic Imagination," *The Light Princess and Other Fairy Tales* (New York: G. P. Putnam's Sons, 1893). A Cutting of the first and the entirety of the second may be found in Rolland Hein's, *The Heart of George MacDonald* (Wheaton, Ill.: Harold Shaw Publishers, 1994), 416–28.

5. MacDonald, *Unspoken Sermons: Second Series* (1886; reprint Whitehorn, Calif.: Johannesen, 1997), 113.

idea or feeling that is in him." [6] The artist who is pure in heart has valid feelings and expresses truths he perceives God has placed at the heart of things.

SACRAMENTAL SYMBOLISM

MacDonald's fantasies spring from deep within the emotions of his own soul; his images, which are filtered through his highly romantic sensibility, are spiritual responses to his own experiences. At times they may seem to veer near to allegory, but they are seldom allegorical in the sense that much of Bunyan's work is. "He must be an artist indeed who can, in any mode, produce a strict allegory that is not a weariness to the spirit," he mused. [7] His images often function as symbols: that is, the abstract values they designate are less definite and more suggestive than in allegory.

Symbols have the capacity to reach very high—towards something ineffable—and arouse wonder; to attempt to define their significance precisely is to diminish them. To interpret, for instance, the rose fire in MacDonald's Curdie stories as an image suggesting personal trials is perhaps true, but it is also shockingly reductive. The image is redolent with suggested meanings that lie beyond one's ability to articulate, meanings that concern the need for proper preparation for service, for purgation, and for the ultimate union of

6. MacDonald, *Donal Grant* (1883; reprint Eureka, Calif.: Sun Rise Books, 1990), chapter 11.

7. "The Fantastic Imagination," *The Heart of George MacDonald*, 426.

purity and beauty in the economy of God. The effect is one of awe and desire. Responding to an allegorical image, such as Bunyan's Mr. By-ends, for instance, is more simply an intellectual exercise. To define the spiritual type he depicts is simply to enrich our intellectual understanding.

To MacDonald, symbols portray spiritual truths. He conceived of the world as sacramental, with all the images in one's experience having the potential to convey grace to the beholder. Grace is conveyed according to one's spiritual need. He wrote:

> "All about us, in earth and air, wherever the eye or ear can reach, there is a power ever breathing itself forth in signs, now in daisy, now in a wind-waft, a cloud, a sunset; a power that holds constant and sweetest relation with the dark and silent world within us. The same God who is in us, and upon whose tree we are the buds, if not yet the flowers, also is all about us— inside, the Spirit; outside, the Word. And the two are ever trying to meet in us; and when they meet, then the sign without, and the longing within, become one in light, and the man no more walketh in darkness, but knoweth whither he goeth." [8]

Shades of Coleridge's thinking are present in this excerpt. Images function as symbols when they convey divine meaning and grace to the sensitive reader. The moment in which the image from without and the

8. MacDonald, *Thomas Wingfold, Curate* (1876; reprint Whitehorn, Calif.: Johannesen, 1996), chapter 82.

spirit within meet and "become one in light" is an illumined moment, similar to what some authors term an
epiphany—thus, myth.

These anagogic moments concentrate the mythic
impulse. Images that induce them seem to penetrate
beyond time itself, bringing to us glimmers of light
from the borders of those "high countries" that faith
envisions. One has the sensation of truth encountered,
though one can articulate precisely what truth only to
a meager point. The experience defies intellectualization. MacDonald would himself explain the fact
that different readers recognize different significances
in any given symbol by observing that each reader's
spiritual state at a given moment is different; he
believed that the Spirit of God keeps offering to each
person what is most needed for one's spiritual growth
at that time. Therefore, "the best thing you can do for
your fellow, next to rousing his conscience, is—not to
give him things to think about, but to wake things up
that are in him." [9] What is awakened is a sense of the
ideal. MacDonald's steadfast focus upon this inner
sense of the perfect—what people may become—
motivates his portrayal of characters, investing them
with mythic dimensions. Commenting on the characters in his novel *Paul Faber: Surgeon*, he explained in a
letter to his friend William Cowper-Temple that his
purpose was "to make them true to the real and not the

9. "The Fantastic Imagination," *The Heart of George MacDonald*, 427.

spoilt humanity. Why should I spend my labour on
what one can have too much of without any labour! I
will try to show what we might be, may be, must be,
shall be—and something of the struggle to gain it." [10]
Something of this is what Lewis had in mind when he
hailed MacDonald as the greatest master of mythic
writing he knew. [11]

THE SPIRITUAL NATURE OF FAIRY LAND

C. S. Lewis relates how as a young agnostic his imagination was "baptized" by his reading *Phantastes*. [12] In
Phantastes and the fairy tales MacDonald took his
readers into Fairy Land, an image he used as a symbol
for the realm of spiritual realities. His primary undertaking in his fantasies—as in all his writings—was to
arouse within his readers an interest and a desire after
higher truths. He imaginatively created fictional
worlds in which moral and spiritual realities were
accentuated, worlds whose atmosphere and values
allude to the divine. Human life is presented as he
imagined God saw it. The fictional world in George
MacDonald's works is pure, fresh, and childlike.

These fictional regions generally contain imaginative depictions of the protagonist's inner reality. "The

10. MacDonald to William Cowper-Temple, 13 January 1879. Held by the Trustees of
the National Library of Scotland.

11. Lewis, *George MacDonald: An Anthology*, 14.

12. Lewis regarded MacDonald as his master, saying he never wrote a book but what
he did not quote from him. See especially his tributes in his preface to *George
MacDonald: An Anthology* (New York: The Macmillan Company, 1948) and *The Great
Divorce* (New York, The Macmillan Company, 1946), chapter 9.

world which we see is our own minds turned inside out," MacDonald was fond of saying. [13] The characters and terrain the protagonist encounters depict the spiritual quality of his mind, and the adventures he has are peculiarly adapted for his spiritual growth. The forms they take are most appropriate to his needs. "That which is within a man, not that which lies beyond his vision, is the main factor in what is about to befall him," [14] Vane, the protagonist in *Lilith*, concludes.

The image of the journey in the fantasies tends to depict movement to a further spiritual experience or a higher spiritual state. In the two adult fantasies, *Phantastes* and *Lilith*, the protagonists go through a series of life stages—moving away from their bondage to a life lived in ignorance of the truth, to the triumph of a new life transformed into a high degree of spiritual maturity. They participate in "a story without a beginning," [15] which "will never have an end," but which ultimately ascends. Each adventure is a further trial, which is an opportunity to grow.

MacDonald's beliefs as to the nature of the Christian life contrast with Bunyan's. His journeys do not begin with the protagonist having a certain understanding of doctrine, but rather with a yearning or a curiosity. MacDonald's journeys are also dangerous,

13. "The Imagination," *The Heart of George MacDonald*, 418.
14. George MacDonald, *Lilith* (1895; reprint Whitehorn, Calif.: Johannesen, 1994), chapter 16.
15. George MacDonald, *Phantastes* (1858; reprint Whitehorn, Calif.: Johannesen, 1998), chapter 4.

but if protagonists fail, their destiny does not seem jeopardized. They experience necessary consequences for their mistakes and are afforded another adventure appropriate to their state. In contrast to Christian's constant peril on Bunyan's narrow way, MacDonald's characters are more secure on their journeys.

PHANTASTES

Phantastes is a rich, complex, and highly subjective fantasy, certainly not to be approached as though it were allegory—nor, for that matter, as a second *Pilgrim's Progress*. Incidents and events are symbolic. Many of the scenes are autobiographical, reflecting something of the author's own experiences and struggles to find his orientation to life as an aspiring artist. He composed it during the final two months of 1857, intending to write for his English audience a fairy tale for adults in the tradition of the German märchen, such as Novalis's *Heinrich Von Ofterdingen* or E. T. A. Hoffmann's *The Golden Pot*, both of which he greatly admired. The fantasy has generated mythic moments for many of its readers, such as the young C. S. Lewis.

At the time of writing, MacDonald and his wife had undergone several trials and the future seemed uncertain. In the eyes of the world he had failed as a minister, having lost his church. Severe illness had almost taken his life. He wanted to be a man of letters, but getting published had proved to be immensely difficult. Living off of the dole of parents and in-laws was a continuous necessity. He counseled Louisa in a letter, "We must be saved from ourselves by very unpleasant things, and have no choice whether it shall be by toothache or living on other people's means." [16] *Phantastes* is shaped by this central principle of the spiritual life, that "we must be saved from ourselves." The theme of renunciation has more to do with vices within the self, rather than, as in Bunyan, worldly attitudes. One must abandon self-centeredness and live altruistically. Biblically, he was exploring the process whereby one comes to experience Christ's message that those who lose their lives will save them. The kernel of wheat must die to bear fruit. (John 12:24, 25.)

The process of spiritual rebirth in a sacramental world is the chief thematic concern of *Phantastes*. Anodos's journey follows the archetypal pattern of trial and deliverance. His focal experience occurs in chapter 18 when he determines to die by plunging into an ocean. The trials he has undergone to this point have driven him to utter despair. In jumping to his death, he experiences not oblivion but sudden transformation into joy. Deliverance comes not through his valiant effort, but through Something mysteriously meeting and transforming him after he has exhausted all the resources of self.

16. See Rolland Hein, *George MacDonald: Victorian Mythmaker* (Nashville: Star Song, 1993), 134. The original undated letter is in the Beinecke Rare Book and Manuscript Library, New Haven, Conn.

Prior to this pivotal occurrence, Anodos's adventures have resulted in disappointment and failure, sometimes horror. In chapter 1, he finds his way into Faerie through his being awakened by a "tiny woman form" to an intense desire or yearning after Fairy Land. C. S. Lewis will later identify this emotion as *Sehnsucht* and build much of his apologetic for Christianity around it.

Once in the country of Faerie, Anodos's desire focuses upon a marble lady, a symbol of that for which he longs deep within his soul, an embodiment of the ultimate ideal combining truth, beauty, and goodness. But his pursuit of her degenerates quickly into a self-centered sensuality that issues in images of horror, death, and corruption. Not yet spiritually reborn, he is unable to relate rightly to her. The authoritative warning of the trees that he received shortly after his admittance to Fairy Land proves true: he has mistaken the Maid of the Alder-tree for his Marble Lady, and as a consequence he narrowly escapes death at her hands.

By not having learned the importance of self-denial, he was certain to fail. The refrain occurring later gives memorable expression to the theme:

Alas, how easily things go wrong!
A sigh too much, or a kiss too long,
And there follows a mist and a weeping rain,
And life is never the same again.

The "Ballad of Sir Aglovaile," in which the refrain occurs, celebrates the necessity for spiritual dying and rebirth, the only antidote for spiritual failure.

Anodos's spiritual health also momentarily suffers when he succumbs to cynical attitudes. His encounters with his shadow underline one of MacDonald's central themes, one that will come to culmination in *Lilith*: individuals have multiple selves and must learn to deny all inferior ones. The shadow is Anodos's alter ego, which is at first his skeptical self, characterized by rationalist attitudes that prevent any perception of the spiritual import of things. Later in the story, this becomes his own prideful self-image that imprisons him, momentarily removing him from effectual endeavors.

His skeptical self is quiet during his visit in the Fairy Palace, a symbol of the realm of such imaginative activity as that of art. In MacDonald's romantic view, artistic composition is imaginative and inspirational, as opposed to rationalist and ironic. As an aspiring young Christian artist, he explored in this complex center section the spiritual temptations he had himself experienced in his artistic pursuits. Many have to do with wrong attitudes toward love and sexuality; it would seem that the artistic desire to capture the ideal may quickly degenerate into a self-centered sensuality.

The tale told in chapter 12 is set in another world and describes people who are deprived of the communion of love because they are sexless. It underscores the preciousness of human sexuality and uncorrupted passion. Although the "souls" of the passions are pure, possessing "glory and wonderment" (as we are told—explicitly—later), they may still become corrupted. The Cosmo story near the center of *Phantastes* explores how in the love relationship a person can imprison and tyrannize one's beloved, destroying the relationship, unless, like Cosmo, the person learns to abandon possessiveness and sets the beloved free. This is a recurring subject for the Christian mythmakers associated with this study. The story presents another version of the theme of dying into life, as does "The Ballad of Sir Aglovaile."

Following the pivotal experience of spiritually dying and being reborn in chapter 18, Anodos enters the foursquare cottage of the Wise Woman. The episodes are autobiographical, with MacDonald contemplating through Anodos's adventures his own past and future. As a young author aspiring to the very difficult task of addressing the larger religious community of his day and attempting to alter their attitudes, MacDonald was uncertain as to how to begin to change them. In the story, the Wise Woman instills Anodos with confidence that a great good is coming to him and sends him out to "do something worth doing." The spiritual quality of one's life is defined in terms of what one does, not in terms of introspection and contemplation.

Such episodes as his joining in the war against the giants, his working with the knight to help the little girl find butterfly wings, and his dethroning the great wooden image that receives the homage of so many, are all symbolic depictions of the types of tasks MacDonald himself will undertake over the next forty-some years as he wrote about the shortcomings of Victorian Christendom. Through indefatigable writing and lecturing, he never quit in his attempts to defeat the giants of secularism and the false religious idols of his day.

Phantastes suggests the characteristics any Christian ministry must have in order to be effective and endure: it must be motivated by self-abandoning love; be free from self-centeredness, cynicism, and pride; and be in harmony with the divine energies that sacramentally pervade the universe. Great good is constantly coming to such servants. The adversities of life—"what we call evil"—are the only forms out of which some types of good can come. As Anodos's experiences suggest, only when self-contemplation is replaced with a consistently humble pursuit of one's work will one's ideal become one's life. "I learned that he that will be a hero will barely be a man; that he that will be nothing but a doer of his work, is sure of his manhood," he concludes. [17]

Anodos's journey, therefore, brings him to see life in its spiritual dimensions. Through myth the reader

17. MacDonald, *Phantastes*, chapter 22.

imaginatively perceives the divine realities that ultimately measure the worth of life. Perception begins
with his ability to see the fairies—the realities of the
spiritual world—and proceeds through adventures in
Fairy Land that continually illumine his spirit. A certain sensitivity and discernment is essential to progress
on the journey successfully.

THE CURDIE STORIES

Among the many themes that MacDonald develops in
the fantasies that follow, the nature of belief with its
accompanying perceptions is perhaps most basic. A
person is unable to see a better world than one's nature
allows one to see, nor is one able to perceive a higher
God than one's belief allows. That individuals respond
to God as each understands him to be is a shaping
principle of these fantasies. The image of the great-
great-grandmother in the sequels *The Princess and the
Goblin* and *The Princess and Curdie* symbolizes visita-
tions of the divine presence that occur within a person;
she governs the nature and quality of one's spiritual
journey.

The Princess Irene, in *The Princess and the Goblin*,
discovers her great-great-grandmother living in the
attic of the castle, while hordes of goblins live deep
within the caverns under the mountain upon which the
castle stands. The grandmother suggests the manner in
which the divine presence accommodates itself to dif-

ferent people. It appears in various forms according to the ability of a given individual to perceive the divine nature. In chapter 7 of *The Princess and Curdie*, Curdie is confused by the manner in which the grandmother not only appears to different people in different forms, but by the way she appears to him in various guises as well. He inquires about this and receives a revealing reply:

> "Then would you mind telling me now, ma'am, for I feel very confused about it—are you the Lady of the Silver Moon? . . . . now I see you dark, and clothed in green, and the mother of all the light that dwells in the stones of the earth! And up there they call you Old Mother Wotherwop! . . ."
>
> "I could give you twenty names more to call me, Curdie, and not one of them would be a false one . . . . It would want thousands more to speak the truth, Curdie—and then they could not. But there is a point I must not let you mistake about. It is one thing the shape I choose to put on, and quite another the shape that foolish talk and nursery tale may please to put upon me. Also, it is one thing what you or your father may think about me, and quite another what a foolish or bad man may see in me. For instance, if a thief were to come in here just now, he would think he saw the demon of the mine, all in green flames, come to protect her treasure, and would run like a hunted wild goat. I should be all the same, but his evil eyes would see me as I was not."

MacDonald is expressing a principle established by the psalmist David: "With the loyal thou dost show thyself loyal; with the blameless man thou dost show thyself blameless; with the pure thou dost show thyself pure; and with the crooked thou dost show thyself perverse" (Ps. 18:25, 6, RSV). MacDonald gives this divine principle many artistic expressions throughout his writings.

The nature of Christian faith and obedience, closely allied to perception, is probed throughout the Curdie stories. In *The Princess and the Goblin*, Irene's nurse Lootie is unable to believe, but she is not to be blamed for not believing. "People must believe what they can, and those who believe more must not be hard upon those who believe less," the grandmother tells Irene. When Irene takes Curdie to introduce him to her grandmother, he is able to see nothing but "a tub, and a heap of musty straw, and a withered apple, and a ray of sunlight. . . ." He is not yet ready to perceive her.

Later, in delirium, Curdie receives a visit from the grandmother, and in the beginning of the sequel he receives her visit and obeys her commission to him. When individuals reach a certain juncture in their spiritual odysseys, the divine presence appears to them, but at her bidding, not theirs. The visit signals their inception into the kingdom of God and invitation to work within it to accomplish the divine will in the world.

Curdie's task is to foil the goblins' plan to conquer the castle. When he is imprisoned by the goblins, Irene's task is to rescue him. Her unwavering obedience to the grandmother's instructions, exemplified by her following the string from the ball the grandmother has given her, indicates that explicit and unquestioning obedience is necessary to serving God.

The goblins are creatures of low and distorted spiritual natures, prideful, contriving, contentious and ambitious. Some scholars see in the heirarchy of great-great-grandmother, Irene, and the goblins foreshadowings of the Freudian model of the human psyche, with these images vaguely corresponding to the superego, ego, and id respectively. [18] MacDonald did develop a theory of the unconscious in his writings, but his thinking is distinctly Christian; the apostle Paul is appreciably more present in his work than Freud. To see the goblins as expressions of the id seems wide of the mark: they hardly suggest libidinous energy, nor are they much concerned with pleasure. They are more aptly understood as depicting the base and vulgar aspects of human nature. They dwell deep within the mountain. Insofar as the structure of the tale symbolizes the inner reality of the mind, with the great-great-grandmother suggesting the perception of the divine presence, and Irene the perceiving self, the goblins do

18. Richard Reis, *George MacDonald* (New York: Twayne Publishers, Inc., 1972; Eureka, Calif.: Sunrise Books, 1989), 41, 81.

suggest the Pauline "old man" or one's baser tendencies. Their presence in the mountain is a threat to the spiritual health and stability of the castle; for them to seize control would be disastrous, just as capitulating to one's baser instincts is spiritually perilous.

Curdie's next encounter with the great-great-grandmother and the subsequent way in which it affects his spiritual journey becomes the subject of *The Princess and Curdie*, published some ten years after the first story. When he had completed it, MacDonald told his wife Louisa he felt it to be the best he could do in this genre, a judgment with which many would concur. Among its strengths are its various depictions of the theme of "spiritual becoming." The tale concerns Curdie's killing a pigeon belonging to the great-great-grandmother, and then repenting. He is then commissioned by her to rid the kingdom of Gwyntystorm of a gang of conspirators against the king and help the king restore order. He and Irene marry and reign. The kingdom in time reverts to its former ways and falls to destruction. The fate of the city serves as final illustration of a spiritual principle Curdie learned early on from the grandmother: "When people don't care to be better, they must be doing everything wrong." Failure to consistently pursue righteousness will eventually result in a fatal destiny.

MacDonald insisted that both individuals and nations are on spiritual journeys of either becoming better or worse. He gave the concept as memorable imaginative depiction in this fantasy as anywhere in his writings. "All men, if they do not take care, go down the hill to the animals' country. . . . many men are actually, all their lives, going to be beasts," the grand-mother instructs Curdie. But in the animals' country they may eventually come to the end of their degener-ating course and begin on the long slow journey of learning righteousness. Lina, the monstrous but servile animal who aids Curdie in his mission, illustrates the paradigm of ascent from moral depths. The details of her downward journey are never divulged; we only see her as beginning to serve the grandmother by being Curdie's helper, and in the end, like Dante's pilgrims through Purgatory, eagerly enters the refining fire. Those who, like Curdie, awake to their moral plight, repent, and begin working at becoming virtuous in this life are far ahead of Lina in their spiritual journey .

The refining fire is essential to the growth of both. The grandmother's fire of roses (perhaps T. S. Eliot's inspiration for the imagery of fire and roses in *The Four Quartets* [19]) is one of MacDonald's most memorable images. It is a graphic portrayal of divine love, a creative love terrible in its insistence on genuine goodness:

> For love loves unto purity. Love has ever in view the
> absolute loveliness of that which it beholds. Where
> loveliness is incomplete, and love cannot love its fill

19. Kathryn Walls, "George MacDonald's *Lilith* and the Later Poetry of T. S. Eliot," *English Language Notes* 16 (1978): 47–51.

of loving, it spends itself to make more lovely, that it may love more; it strives for perfection, even that itself may be perfected—not in itself, but in the object. . . . Therefore all that is not beautiful in the beloved, all that comes between and is not of love's kind, must be destroyed.

And our God is a consuming fire. [20]

MacDonald's earnest conviction concerning the role of adversity and trial in the improving of one's spiritual character is rooted in his own experience. Beset throughout life with poverty, illness, and the deaths of those he loved, he nevertheless saw each adversity as contributing to his own spiritual growth. "So sure am I that many things which illness has led me to see are true, that I would endlessly rather never be well than lose sight of them," he avowed. [21]

Curdie holds his hands in the fire, convinced the pain will kill him if he lets go: one must receive adversity with patience and endurance, else one is overcome and loses the final reward. The grandmother seems to Curdie to have been weeping as he suffered. The perception echoes that of Blake in his poem "On Another's Sorrow":

> Till our grief is fled and gone
> He doth sit by us and moan.

In all our afflictions God is afflicted.

20. MacDonald, "The Consuming Fire," *Unspoken Sermons* (London, 1867; reprint Whitehorn, Calif.: Johannesen,1997), 27, 28.

21. MacDonald, *Paul Faber, Surgeon*, chapter 36.

THE GOLDEN KEY

MacDonald's conviction that life is a sacred journey shapes much of the imagery of *The Golden Key* and *Lilith*.

The Golden Key has as its compelling charm Mossy and Tangle, children who enter the Kingdom of Heaven in childhood, marry, grow old as loving man and wife, and pass into eternity, each experiencing deepening perceptions of the divine presence. Mossy takes with him the golden key which he discovers at the foot of a glorious rainbow just within Fairyland. The scene, vivid and enchanting, suggests that of the fortunate child receiving imaginative faith in the context of the true Church. In the middle of the magnificent colors of the rainbow are men and women steadily rising amidst its columns of color; all are in the process of being redeemed. Mossy is fortunate in having a grandmother who instills within him a love for the right type of literature, reading which nourishes his imagination and his faith.

Tangle, on the other hand, is disadvantaged by having been neglected as a child in a wretched home. She, being frightened into Fairyland, is led by strange air-fish, heaven-sent messengers who providentially serve her greater good. A fish takes Tangle to her first encounter with the divine presence, whom she perceives as a beautiful grandmother. She lovingly cleanses her and ministers to her needs. Mossy also arrives, and the grandmother sends them forth as life-long companions, hand in hand.

They grow old together. As a couple steadily deepened in their love for one another and in their spiritual perceptions of life, they are charmed by how all the images of life are like a sea of shadows, shadows that arouse their deep yearning for "the country from which the shadows come." But at the same time, the shadows increasingly disappoint. The fascination for and yet gradual disillusionment with this life on the part of those who are experiencing healthy spiritual growth, together with their growing desire for eternity, are perhaps nowhere else in literature so graphically depicted.

At their deaths, Mossy and Tangle proceed on separate ways through the nether world until they are again united at the foot of the rainbow, where Mossy's golden key helps them ascend. The tale concludes dynamically as they climb within the rainbow, together with "beautiful beings of all ages," towards the desired country, the ultimately Real. The atmosphere is of joy and anticipation; their prior difficulties have prepared them for their triumph. Unlike Dante, MacDonald refrains from any suggestion of their achieving a condition of stasis; growth into full divine sonship continues beyond the furtherest reaches of the imagination.

Crucial to their journeys are the successive theophanies, the Old Man of the Sea, of the Earth, and of

the Fire. Tangle's encounters with these figures symbolically portray essential phases in spiritual growth:
the cleansing administered by the Old Man of the Sea,
the life of faith demanded by the Old Man of the
Earth as he counsels her to throw herself in to a great
hole with no stairs, and the purifying of her nature in
the refining that precedes her meeting with the Old
Man of the Fire. Her growing spiritual awareness after
her bath is shown by her eyes themselves emitting a
light to see by, her hearing the Old Man of the Earth
"though not with her ears," and finally her acquiring
the illumining perception of the significance of all that
has happened to her in her past: "she understood it all,
and saw that everything meant the same thing, though
she could not have put it into words again."

The Old Man of the Fire is but a child, arranging
balls in various harmonious designs, patterns that contain "infinite meaning"—though Tangle cannot fully
comprehend them. But the "ravishing smile" too deep
to appear on the child's face suggests that the ultimate
secret of the universe is too glorious for the imagination to image forth. The increasing youth of these three
figures suggests one of MacDonald's fondest ideas,
derived early in his life from the writings of Emanuel
Swedenborg, that in heaven the angels keep growing
younger. Spiritual bodies, that inhabit the "high countries" to which the travelers go, keep becoming younger
in physical vitality and more childlike in spirit.

AT THE BACK OF THE NORTH WIND

One of MacDonald's favorite texts was the saying of Christ, that unless one becomes as a little child, one will not enter into the kingdom of heaven. [22] In *At the Back of the North Wind* he envisions the childlikeness that makes for spiritual health. It involves a spirit of wonder, a willing trust, a readiness to begin a new venture, and a faith that God is so ordering life that good may come out of evil. In this myth Diamond, the child protagonist, learns that a still greater good awaits him in the next world, a good quite beyond the ability of the human imagination to depict.

Diamond, the small son of a poverty-stricken London coachman, has his bedroom located in a loft above the stall of his father's horse—also named Diamond. When he falls ill, The North Wind, which on occasion blows strongly through the cracks in the wall, speaks to him, revealing herself to be a kind and gracious lady. She portrays the divinely appointed presence of adversity in life, the "evil" that issues in good for those who receive her in the right spirit. Making a cradle for him on her back, in her long and flowing hair, she takes him with her on various errands of tumult and destruction. She shows herself obediently and pur-

22. See Matt. 18:3. In "The Child in the Midst," the initial sermon in *Unspoken Sermons: Series One*, MacDonald enlarges upon the concept, suggesting that the nature of God himself is childlike, as the Old Man of the Fire in *The Golden Key* intimates. The sermon was published in 1867, the year before *At the Back of the North Wind* began to appear serially in the children's magazine, *Good Words for the Young*.

posefully obeying a Higher Power whose government she knows to be wise and good, although even she does not understand it. When Diamond perceives her as beautiful and good, she cautions him: "Ah, but . . . what if I should look ugly without being bad—look ugly myself because I am making ugly things beautiful?" and stresses that however she may seem momentarily to appear to him, he must not let go of her hand. [23]

She takes him on a journey to the far reaches of the north and bids him pass through her person into the land "at the back of the north wind." It is a sort of vestibule of heaven, where departed souls, while they await the greater bliss of the resurrection, may look back and see what their loved ones are doing back on earth. Diamond's adventures with her so transform him that when she returns him to his home he lives an ideal life of Christian servanthood, helping to bring goodness and cheer into situations of reversal and misery. At the conclusion he becomes ill again and is taken finally to the land at the back of the North Wind.

LILITH

MacDonald never tired of conceiving in his fiction the region to which the soul may travel beyond death. The vision in *Lilith* is shaped by theological convictions held throughout his life, but this myth is not to be approached as a story sermon. As in Bunyan, one does

23. MacDonald, *At the Back of the North Wind* (1871; reprint Whitehorn, Calif.: Johannesen, 1997), chapter 1.

not have to agree with all the theological nuances one may detect in order to be moved by the myth. Whatever stature the work has must be measured in terms of its success as myth. It is a vision which seems first to have come to him as an inspiration, which he then proceeded painstakingly to rework over the period from 1890 to 1895. [24]

When towards the end of his career he undertook to write his masterpiece, he chose to rewrite the Jewish myth of Lilith, investing it with a final exploration of this and related major themes. MacDonald's version of the myth, derived from the Cabbala—a system of Jewish mysticism—is found in chapter 29. Lilith is Adam's first wife, an angelic being that, after rebelling against Adam and her task of childbearing, fled to "the army of the aliens" and ensnared the "great Shadow," who makes her queen of Hell. Henceforth, she seeks to kill her child, but by her very nature she can neither create nor destroy, only live "by the blood and lives and souls of men." She epitomizes selfishness. "The one principle of hell," MacDonald wrote, "is 'I am my own,' " [25] a thought repeated by C.S. Lewis in *The Great Divorce*.

Although at times MacDonald's symbols in *Lilith*

24. Eight manuscript revisions are held by the British Museum. The first, a shorter one, has hardly any revisions; the next four are elaborately revised. These have been published by Johannesen Printing and Publishing of Whitethorn, CA., as *Lilith: First and Last* (1994) and *Lilith: A Variorum Edition* (1997). For a fuller account of its composition, see Rolland Hein, "Beyond Ideas: the Intrigue of the *Lilith* Manuscripts," *Seven: An Anglo-American Literary Review* (1997) 14:45–52.

25. MacDonald, "Kingship," *Unspoken Sermons: Third Series* (London, 1891; reprint Whitethorn, Calif.: Johannesen, 1997), 102.

may seem to veer uncomfortably close to allegory, their strength lies in their suggestive character. The narrative keeps our attention firmly upon the anagogic level of life through symbolic representations. Vane, whose name at once suggests pride, futility, and a direction of travel, falls in love with Lilith, as well as with her daughter, Lona. Lona is the spirit of redemptive love, paradoxically born of Lilith, just as the love that redeems is necessitated by the spirit of selfishness within humanity. As representative man, Vane is both attracted to selfishness and longs for purity of being. MacDonald's insistence that at the heart of truth is paradox is demonstrated by the seemingly contradictory prophecies pertaining to Lilith: she will be saved in childbearing, and her child will be the death of her. Both are true, inasmuch as Lona is largely instrumental in her finally dying into life.

During that part of the tale in which Vane is attracted to Lilith and almost seduced by her, he is himself sinking on the scale of becoming. But he delivers her finally to Eve's charnel house where, after an appropriate struggle, she accepts sleep. After having delivered her, Vane is himself ready to sleep.

As is true in the prior fantasies, so here: Vane's perilous journey is an inner one, a journey of the spirit that suggests the spiritual destiny of everyman. Instead of Fairy Land, we now have the protagonist stumbling into "The region of the seven dimensions." Perhaps

MacDonald thought that his end-of-the-century readers, whom apparently he envisioned to be more sophisticated, man-of-the-world, rationalist types (like
Vane), would not take another trek through Fairy Land
seriously enough. In any case, the way into this world
is through the human heart. The adventures encountered there are determined by the spiritual state of the
traveler. MacDonald succinctly stated:

> [W]e make our fate in unmaking ourselves . . . men,
> in defacing the image of God in themselves, construct
> for themselves a world of horror and dismay; . . of *the
> outer darkness* our own deeds and character are the
> informing or inwardly creating cause . . . if a man will
> not have God, he never can be rid of his weary and
> hateful self. [26]

Life has a dual nature, with people shaping their
immortal spiritual destinies by their acts today; the
eternal is coincident with the present. Good people can
through their conduct invest that world with delightful
realities. For example, prayers become lovely flowers
and birds there.

In his first meeting with his Raven mentor in this
realm, Vane is startled into realizing that he cannot
identify himself: "What is at the heart of my brain?
What is behind my *think*? Am *I* there at all?—Who,

26. George MacDonald in his preface to *Letters from Hell*, anonymous, 1884 edition.
When an unnamed Dutch author first published this work in 1866, it immediately
went through numerous editions. Impressed when he read it, MacDonald offered to
write a preface, which appeared in the 1884 edition. The work also impressed C. S.
Lewis, giving him the kernal idea for *Screwtape Letters*.

what am I." [27] Much of the imagery of the tale concerns one's sense of identity and self-knowledge, emphasizing how a Christian handling of these issues differs from that of the humanist. The latter may be quickly summarized in the Socratic command, "Know thyself." But MacDonald vividly shows that an accurate knowledge of the self is impossible. Persons are possessed by various inferior selves; one's self-image is at best an illusion, as Mara tells Lilith later in the tale. Only God knows the true self; we gain in perception as we grow in knowledge of Him.

No individual is trapped in the unreal who chooses otherwise. God's true idea of one's self is an ideal which He is working to bring into being in each person. He alone knows a person's true name and will bestow it when that person has reached that spiritual maturity which is essential to one's final being. One's self-identity must finally be left with God; it is enough that He knows who the individual is. Similar to *Phantastes*, dying into life, which here takes place in Eve's house, is crucial to the development of the soul's true self. Eve is the mother of all living in a spiritual, as well as a physical, sense. Until Vane is willing to sleep, he is spiritually dead, as are all in their natural state.

Before he can sleep, Vane must repent. Mara (a biblical image meaning "bitter") symbolizes the sorrow of

27. MacDonald, *Lilith*, chapter 3.

repentance. She is a good example of an image that veers near to allegory but emits intriguing symbolic suggestions. Not unlike the North Wind in the prior fantasy, she controls all events that may generate sorrow. MacDonald was convinced that the spiritual milestones in one's life are most apt to occur during incidents of adversity or trial. These are effected by the missions of Astarte, the white leopard that emanates from Mara; her opposite, the spotted leopard that emanates from Lilith, epitomizes all the sorrows that issue from selfishness and that bring only pain, but no redemption.[28] For Vane to name Mara negatively—for instance, to call her "bad luck"—would signal a low spiritual state; for him to receive her more positively would suggest his willingness to obey the Pauline mandate to "rejoice in our sufferings" Romans 5:3 (RSV). To persevere is to become more spiritually mature.

The images Vane encounters in the realm of seven dimensions depict various spiritual states: the skeletons, the people of Bulika with their babies, the Little Ones, and the Giants. The skeleton lord and lady "without faces" suggest the spiritually perverse among the higher social classes. Their disintegration is checked and they begin to acquire substance the moment they start exercising altruistic attitudes towards each other. C. S. Lewis takes the title of his

28. Cf. 2 Cor. 7:10: For godly grief produces a repentance that leads to salvation and brings no regret, but worldly grief produces death (RSV).

masterpiece, *Till We Have Faces*, from this scene. Bulika is MacDonald's Babylon, its inhabitants are possessed of secular attitudes. Their offspring are fought over by the two leopardesses; those rescued by Mara's leopardess are taken into the woods—suggesting spiritual confusion (as in Dante)—to be found by Lona, or redemptive love, and nursed into becoming Little Ones. They are, in other words, people evangelized.

The childlike attitudes of the Little Ones are commendable; their childishness is not. They have yet to sleep in Eve's house. Here MacDonald is lamenting the reluctance of Christians to become spiritually mature. They neglect the Waters of Life which richly flow underground, waiting to be accessed. Instead, some from among them become lazy, greedy, and stupid, growing into deformed Giants. They are like people in the institutional church who forsake essential Christian attitudes and, as MacDonald suggests, tend to become its leaders, lording it over others to the detriment of the Little Ones.

The value of *Lilith* lies in MacDonald's poignant reading of spiritual laws, those which shape the anagogical level of experience. Many of these are brought to a climax in the scene in Mara's house between her and Lilith. It establishes the paradigm of spiritual awakening for recalcitrant souls. Lilith, having experienced the consequences of her self-centeredness and for the second time reduced to strengthlessness, must repent before she can know the sleep of death that leads to life. She is captured by Vane and the Little Ones and taken to Mara's house. Repentance is more than sorrow: she must forsake her many delusions, the central one being her misconception of freedom, and experience a completely different set of her will.

The images of worm and fire that figure prominently in the scene are derived from Christ's description of hell, where the worm never dies and the fire is never quenched. The fire suggests the divine glory from which mankind has been created (as the Raven has previously told Vane), and the worm the essential human. (See Mark 9:48; Heb. 12:29; Ps. 22:6.) When Lilith is on Mara's couch, the worm crawls from her into the fire, is purged, and, reentering Lilith, affords her a vision of her two selves: the moral horror she has made herself to be and the moral splendor God intended her to become. Faced with the alternatives of, on the one hand, dying into life and the long slow process of making right her wrongs, and, on the other, annihilation, she chooses the former and submits to sleep. Adam severs her clenched hand, the symbol of inveterate acquisitiveness.

Mara tells Lilith that death is the atonemaker. While sleeping in Eve's house, the sleeper passes into various dream states where all wrongs must be righted. MacDonald is not denying the role of Christ's death in salvation; Christ is mankind's atonement with God. All the concepts portrayed in Lilith rest upon God's revealing His divine love and intentions for humankind in the life, death, and resurrection of Christ. But the necessity for everyone to be completely "at one" with all others remains, and must be achieved experientially. When Vane himself sleeps, he makes "atonement with each person" he had "injured, hurt, or offended." [29]

Two themes that are especially characteristic of MacDonald predominate in the closing of Lilith. The one affirms the necessity for explicit obedience, the other the inevitability of doubt. Before Vane can sleep, he must bury Lilith's hand. The temptations he resists in doing so demonstrate his newly acquired ability to obey. Burying the hand releases the glorious River of the Waters of Life: once the final vestige of self-centeredness is obliterated, they can begin to flow.

In addressing doubt, MacDonald confronted an issue that had long concerned him. Like Vane when he is sleeping and dreaming, MacDonald vacillated between moods of euphoria, when he entertained glorious imaginative visions for the future of mankind, and feelings of misgiving and doubt, together with loneliness. These became more pronounced in his old age. In Lilith, Vane expresses MacDonald's own problem when he asks Adam whether one can trust one's dreams. Adam responds that, until a person is himself perfectly true, a quantity of doubt is inevitable: "That

29. See MacDonald's sermon "The Last Farthing," Unspoken Sermons: Series Two, 98–114. MacDonald has Matt. 5:23–26 in mind.

which thou seest not, and never didst see save in a glass darkly—that which, indeed, never can be known save by its innate splendour shining straight into pure eyes—that thou canst not but doubt, and art blameless in doubting until thou seest it face to face, when thou wilt no longer be able to doubt it." Full truth will finally be experienced by the one who, through consistently obeying the truth, comes to know complete purity.

The myth ends on an air of dynamic expectation. Vane, awaking on "the glorious resurrection morning," finds himself wondrously changed. He feels harmoniously related to all things in nature and is now able to read their spiritual importance: "every growing thing showed me, by its shape and colour, its indwelling idea." He proceeds with his party towards the Father of Love and Life, who at the same time is proceeding towards them, and in the distance they glimpse the glorious City of God. Amidst this crescendo of anticipation, he is returned to his earthly life in the library.

The reader may be perplexed by the ending, wondering why Vane does not try to return to the glories of the realm of seven dimensions. Vane waits, like the biblical Job, until he is bid reenter. For him to seek to go back would not only be to second guess God, who will summon him when his present life is properly over, but it would also be a rather base attempt to enjoy this ethereal realm sensually, from mere curiosity. Early in the tale when Vane sought entrance to Eve's house simply out of curiosity and desire for adventure, he was refused. All things have their proper time in the divine economy.

MACDONALD AND MYTH

MacDonald felt a freedom Bunyan did not feel to honor the imagination and consciously follow its leading into myth. He sought to avoid allegory and invested his images with the more open-ended symbolic suggestions upon which myth thrives. His distinct interpretation of Scripture together with his sensitive apprehension of its spirit allowed him to penetrate a considerable distance into mythical reality. Like Bunyan, he discerned there the pervasive dominance of the great images of journey, trial, renunciation, and deliverance. His romantic sensibilities prompted him to develop the themes of the need to love and be loved, and of the necessity for one's being to grow into full goodness.

The doctrinal differences between these two mythmakers are obvious, but they did have much in common. Both authors saw life as a journey that has God as its author and full communion with Him as its destination. God provides redemption through spiritual transformation and growth. The trials and perils of life are overcome by one's renouncing negative and self-aggrandizing attitudes and cooperating with the divine grace readily available. MacDonald's sacramental model of reality stands in appreciable contrast to Bunyan's, but both yearned for communion with the same God and saw the virtuous life as indispensable to that end. Both Bunyan and MacDonald went far in accomplishing their ends by wielding the power of myth.

4

G. K. Chesterton
Myth in Everyday Life
(1874–1936)

The aim of life is appreciation; there is no sense in
not appreciating things; and there is no sense in
having more of them if you have less appreciation of
them. . . . In short, as it seems to me, it matters very
little whether a man is discontented in the name of
pessimism or progress, if his discontent does in fact
paralyse his power of appreciating what he has got.
The real difficulty of man is . . . to enjoy enjoyment.
To keep the capacity of really liking what he likes;
that is the practical problem which the philosopher
has to solve. And it seemed to me at the beginning,
as it seems to me now in the end, that the pessimists
and optimists of the modern world have alike missed
and muddled this matter; through leaving out the
ancient conception of humility and the thanks of the
unworthy. . . . I, at least, leaned more and more to the
old philosophy which said that their real rights came
from where the dandelion came from; and that they
will never value either without recognizing its source.

And in that ultimate sense uncreated man, man merely in the position of the babe unborn, has no right even to see a dandelion; for he could not himself have invented either the dandelion or the eyesight. . . . For the first thing the casual critic will say is "What nonsense all this is; do you mean that a poet cannot be thankful for grass and wild flowers without connecting it with theology; let alone your theology?" To which I answer, "Yes, I mean he cannot do it without connecting it with theology, unless he can do it without connecting it with thought. . . ." [1]

 o G. K. Chesterton, life was a mystery with a rightness at its heart. To see it accurately is to worship. He had a singular appreciation for the common things in life. The result of this attitude was the mythic vision, one that saw existence as a type of "pleasant surprise." A favorite riddle of his was "What did the first frog say?" to which the proper answer is, "Lord, how you made me jump!" [2]

Chesterton is no mere optimist. His gift was to state concisely and forcefully "what's wrong with the world." [3] He penetrated to the heart of issues with an attractive combination of shrewd common sense and unfailing good humor. In his many books, he created

1. G. K. Chesterton, *The Autobiography of G. K. Chesterton* (New York: Sheed & Ward, 1936), 347–48.

2. *Orthodoxy* (1908; reprint Wheaton, Ill.: Harold Shaw Publishers, 1994), 55.

3. See *What's Wrong with the World* and *Heretics* in various reprints, or in *G. K. Chesterton: Collected Works* with introduction and notes by David Dooley (San Francisco: Ignatius, 1986.)

within his readers a sense of humility and awe as he caught glimpses of the real beyond the everyday things of this world. In *Orthodoxy*, certainly a classic in the genre of spiritual autobiographies, he commented on the practical effect of seeing all of life freshly and appreciatively from the perspective of myth:

> My first and last philosophy, that which I believe in with unbroken certainty, I learnt in the nursery. . . . The things I believed most then, the things I believe most now, are the things called fairy tales. They seem to me to be the entirely reasonable things. They are not fantasies: compared with them other things are fantastic. Compared with them religion and rationalism are both abnormal, though religion is abnormally right and rationalism abnormally wrong. Fairyland is nothing but the sunny country of common sense. It is not earth that judges heaven, but heaven that judges earth; so for me at least it was not earth that criticized elfland, but elfland that criticized earth. [4]

Much of the secret of Chesterton's success lies in his ability to capture inside of his writings the air of the fairy tale—the mythic mode of thought. The identification of fairyland with the realm of the spirit, which is the locus of pure common sense, suggests the direct influence of MacDonald.

G. K. Chesterton paid deep tribute to MacDonald in an introduction to Greville MacDonald's biography

4. Chesterton, *Orthodoxy*, 49.

of his father, especially noting the effect upon him as a child of *The Princess and the Goblin*. He said it was a book that "made a difference to my whole existence, which helped me to see things in a certain way from the start." He went on to say that the fairy tale is the "inside" and not the "outside" in all of MacDonald's stories, those classified as novels as well as the fantasies. "In other words, MacDonald had made for himself a sort of spiritual environment, a space and transparency of mystical light, which was quite exceptional in his national and denominational environment." [5] Chesterton's writings are similarly imbued. Such "light" is what C. S. Lewis appreciated and identified with the term myth.

A VOICE FOR HIS TIME

A Londoner who earned his living by his pen over the first four decades of the twentieth century, Chesterton produced an immense amount of material. He was chiefly a journalist, but he also wrote poetry, literary criticism, biography, and Christian apologetics, so that he became one of the most prolific writers in all of English literature. As a controversialist and avid debater, his primary interests were political and social. His writing deftly responded to the welter of opposing views and positions that occurred during the span of his career. Keenly aware of the great political disturbances

5. *George MacDonald and his Wife* (London: George Allen & Unwin, 1924), 9, 12.

taking place—the various Marxist and fascist upheavals
and the cries of the anarchists—he responded steadily
with his clarion voice of common sense.

Opposed to both capitalism and communism (both
systems concentrate the control of wealth in the hands
of a few people), he argued for a more equitable
distribution of wealth and work. Chesterton would
have been quite familiar with the work of William
Morris, a leader of the Arts and Crafts movement and
author of socialist fantasies. He believed that through
the arts and crafts humanity could recapture the joy of
creation and avoid the ugliness of industry and the repetition of manufacturing—a view close to Chesterton's
ideals. Seeing the common man as rightful owner of
property and practitioner of a craft, Chesterton
thought the impersonal and massive aspects of industrialism injurious to the spiritual health of a nation.
The family was, to him, the essential social unit and the
center of a healthy society. And he believed each person should maintain a direct relation to nature;[6] all
these themes are present in his writings.

As a young Englishman of independent mind, he
came to Christian faith by first deciding his own views
on the core issues of life and then discovering his conclusions coincided with those of historic Christianity.

6. Known as Distributism and sanctioned by the Roman Catholic Church, these
views were a viable political movement a century ago. Chesterton was a leading pro-
ponent as was his associate Hilaire Belloc. The American counterpart was known as
Agrarianism, and was advocated by writers such as John Crowe Ransom and Robert
Penn Warren.

He observed concerning his convictions: "I have discovered, not that they were not truths, but simply that they were not mine. When I fancied that I stood alone I was really in the ridiculous position of being backed up by all Christendom. It may be, Heaven forgive me, that I did try to be original; but I only succeeded in inventing all by myself an inferior copy of the existing traditions of civilized religion."[7] His thinking led him to join the Roman Catholic Church in 1922.

Chesterton's imaginative writings tend to be more like those often classified as fantasies, such as Swift's *Gulliver's Travels* or Oscar Wilde's *The Picture of Dorian Gray*, rather than works known as romances, like the works of Cooper, Dickens, and Melville. It is not with undue modesty that he remarked concerning them: "In short, I could not be a novelist; because I really like to see ideas or notions wrestling naked, as it were, and not dressed up in a masquerade as men and women."[8] His interest in "dressing up" ideas, preferring the discursive over the imaginative, together with his determination to address social and political issues, tends somewhat to dilute or render uneven the mythic tone. Perhaps his fantasies could have been more purely crafted, but they certainly convey a rich zest for life and experience. For our purposes we will consider two works: *Manalive*, and *The Man Who Was Thursday*.

7. Chesterton, *Orthodoxy*, 6.
8. Chesterton, *The Autobiography of G. K. Chesterton*, 298.

MANALIVE

Chesterton began *Manalive* very early in his career, some fifteen years before it was published. [9] The main idea is quite thoroughly captured in the title: man rightly oriented to reality is man renewed. The farcical tone of which Chesterton is master gives this story a forceful impact.

The story is set in Beacon House, a London boarding establishment inhabited by an assortment of listless men and women possessed by characteristic modern attitudes. They are bored, cynical, flippant. "You can't help your temperament," one explains. "Humanity . . . really consists of quite different tribes of animals all disguised as men." [10] Suddenly blown into their garden on a delightfully windy day is Innocent Smith, a gigantic man dressed all in "gay green holiday clothes." (Chesterton was himself gargantuan). His seemingly irrational affirmations and fantastic antics—he climbs trees, makes up games with the wind, and sponsors a picnic on a rooftop—give all the boarders a change of mood. They find a new zest for activity and creativity and begin to enter into new relationships.

Their activities are characterized, not by random impulses, but by order and pattern. Chesterton remarks:

9. Alzina Stone Dale, *The Outline of Sanity: A Life of G. K. Chesterton* (Grand Rapids, Mich.: Wm B. Eerdmans, 1982), 39. *Manalive* was published in 1912.
10. Chesterton, *Manalive* (London: Thomas Nelson and Sons, 1912), 58.

The truth is that when people are in exceptionally high spirits, really wild with freedom and invention, they always must, and they always do, create institutions. When men are weary they fall into anarchy; but while they are gay and vigorous they invariably make rules. This, which is true of all the churches and republics of history, is also true of the most trivial parlour game or the most unsophisticated meadow romp. We are never free until some institution frees us, and liberty cannot exist till it is declared by authority. [11]

Such remarks represent Chesterton at his best, opposing popular assumptions with affirmations that insist upon a rightness existing at the heart of things in spite of human depravity.

In their high spirits, the people at Beacon House jokingly make a pact to hold their own court and sit in judgment upon each other's supposed misdeeds. Innocent Smith insists, however, that the idea should be treated seriously: the group should assume authority over themselves and their conduct. "Let us begin the League of Free Families!" he announces. "Away with Local Government! A fig for Local Patriotism! Let every house be a sovereign state as this is, and judge its own children by its own law...." [12] Chesterton is championing on the comic level one of his favorite insistences, that the family is the most important unit to the health of society.

11. Chesterton, *Manalive*, 63–64.
12. Chesterton, *Manalive*, 74–75.

Ironically, Smith is the first to be tried in this court. The distinguished Dr. Warner, a young physician visiting at Beacon House, concludes that Smith is insane, and he enlists the help of a famous American criminologist, Dr. Cyrus Pym, to apprehend him and bring him to justice. Possessed of the attitudes and "authority" of the modern scientific community, these prosecutors approach their task by expounding in contemporary jargon the latest behavioral theories. They claim to have found conclusive evidence for Smith's having committed a long list of crimes.

Warner and Pym press their indictments. They allege Smith's attention has been especially fixed upon one of the women boarders, Mary Gray, a rather silent and modest woman slightly older than the others. After a seemingly short acquaintance and whirlwind courtship, he proposes to her and she accepts. The incredulous members of Beacon House try to prevent what appears to them the height of impulsive folly. Warner and Pym accuse him of desertion and bigamy, for it is alleged he has in the past suddenly left his family to court and marry other young women; of attempted murder, for he has a habit of threatening people with a pistol; and of burglary, for he is a socialist, taking back wealth stolen by capitalists.

Chesterton devotes the larger half of the fantasy to the trial, taking opportunity to expose with great ridicule the attitudes of modern "scientific" thinking that—in its supposedly superior methods of analyzing reality—ignores what a common sense understanding of the individual and human experience reveals. The trial proceeds by the learned prosecutors arguing deductively from psychological and sociological theories of the day, together with written statements of eyewitnesses to the alleged crimes. Their rationalist mentality acts as a blinder to keep them from seeing life in its truer character.

Innocent Smith has been living his life in correspondence to mythic realities. Michael Moon, a journalist boarding at Beacon House who is convinced of Smith's innocence, defends him. Each accusation is disproved by actual facts coming to light. As regards the charge of attempted murder, Smith is revealed to be "manalive" who has been trying to get people to recognize the true nature and value of life. In his threatening to murder pessimists, he was attempting to bring "a wholesome scare to those whom he regarded as blasphemers." His efforts brought them to affirm life over death and rejoice in existence itself. "I am going to hold a pistol to the head of Modern Man. But I shall not use it to kill him—only to bring him to life," he insists. [13]

The other charges against Smith are similarly handled with amusing dramatic irony. As regards the charge of burglary, Smith actually broke into his own

13. Chesterton, *Manalive*, 226.

home in order to instill within himself a greater appreciation for his own property; he is "a man who tries to covet his own goods instead of his neighbor's."[14] As regards the charge of desertion, he left his wife and family periodically in order to return to them with renewed appreciation. Smith explains:

> I do believe in breaking out; I am a revolutionist. But don't you see that all these real leaps and destructions and escapes are only attempts to get back to Eden— to something we have had, to something at least we have heard of? Don't you see one only breaks the fence or shoots the moon in order to get home?[15]

One recalls MacDonald's achieving similar mythic effect by using the image of longing for "home" to identify the sense of being displaced from eternity.[16] Chesterton is suggesting that wisdom consists in recognizing and appreciating the vestiges of Eden present in the here and now. People need eyes to see.

Smith returns to his home and family with a renewed love for them and a (very English) conviction that, whatever heaven is like, it will not be unlike the hearth and native land God has given individuals to love. The sentiment anticipates lines from T. S. Eliot's *Four Quartets*: "We shall not cease from exploration / And the end of all our exploring / Will be to arrive

14. Chesterton, *Manalive*, 286.
15. Chesterton, *Manalive*, 314.
16. See, e.g., *Lilith*, chapter 3.

where we started / And know the place for the first time." Eliot may well have gotten the idea from Chesterton, whom he admired.

The climactic charge, that of bigamy, appears to be irrefutable until it is revealed that all the women that Smith has been seen to woo and win have been the same one, his wife, who has cooperated with her husband's efforts to keep their marriage fresh and alive by assuming a variety of roles in assorted situations. "He seriously sought by a perpetual recapture of his bride to keep alive the sense of her perpetual value, and the perils that should be run for her sake." [17] Michael Moon summarizes:

> If Innocent is happy, it is because he *is* innocent. If he can defy the conventions, it is just because he can keep the commandments. It is just because he does not want to kill but to excite to life that a pistol is still as exciting to him as it is to a schoolboy. It is just because he does not want to steal, because he does not covet his neighbour's goods, that he has captured the trick (oh, how we all long for it!), the trick of coveting his own goods. It is just because he does not want to commit adultery that he achieves the romance of sex; it is just because he loves one wife that he has a hundred honeymoons. If he had really murdered a man, if he had really deserted a woman, he would not be able to feel that a pistol or a love-letter was like a song—at least, not a comic song. [18]

17. Chesterton, *Manalive*, 368–69.
18. Chesterton, *Manalive*, 372–73.

Such depiction carries the impulse of myth. It arouses a desire that good people feel towards a level of living that is more satisfying simply because it is both morally pure and, in that purity, more adventurous and exciting. Chesterton's vision contrasts vividly with that of the stereotypical Puritan's narrow rigidity and sterility, something he seldom overlooked an opportunity to disdain. In tone he stands in stark contrast to Bunyan, yet their respective ends, that of recommending the pure and virtuous life, are much the same.

The journey image is tellingly evoked at the end of *Manalive*, as Innocent's wife recommends their novel way of living to a boarder of Beacon House: "You go down the king's highway; for God's truth, it is God's" [19] To perceive life truly and guilelessly is to apprehend the divine presence that helps to make it a stimulating and fulfilling journey. The fantasy begins— and ends—with the imaginatively provocative image of a wind tearing across England from the west, "like a wave of unreasonable happiness." It suggests the sacramental energy Chesterton sees at the heart of things, a force that would deliver people from enslavement to stale human conventions and patterns. The attitude of taking life for granted makes people oblivious to the presence of grace in things as they are, a grace which, when discovered, issues in praise.

19. Chesterton, *Manalive*, 380.

THE MAN WHO WAS THURSDAY

Chesterton's most provocative and artistic depiction of this presence occurs in *The Man Who Was Thursday*, a fantasy that remains his most popular and, perhaps, his most artistically impressive. Subtitled *A Nightmare*, it sustains a surrealistic tone. The narrative revolves around another gargantuan figure, Sunday, who mysteriously appears and disappears throughout the story, confronting, commanding, fleeing from, and being pursued by other characters. As they come under Sunday's aegis, each is given the name of a different day of the week. Sunday is similar to the great-great grandmother in George MacDonald's *The Princess and the Goblin*, in that he is the divine presence as it is perceived in human experience. Like all perceptions, it corresponds to the state and capacity of the perceiver, and alters as the perceiver matures.

In this book Chesterton combines a farcical tone with intense dramatic irony and paradox. One may be delighted but also puzzled: What on earth is he saying?. Like MacDonald, his best images are symbolic and bathed in myth. As with all literary symbols, one must be careful to discern the precise ideas that they may suggest and reject incongruous ones. True interpretations must harmonize with the gist of the whole piece.

The story begins by exposing how wrong the contemporary attitudes of the aesthetes were towards art.

Two poets are in conversation: Gregory, who depicts
the decadent and fin de siècle posture with which the
young Chesterton, as a student in an art school during
the 1890s, was revoltingly familiar; and Syme, whose
view of the poetic office presents Chesterton's own
position. Gregory boasts of being an anarchist, a member of a great "Anarchic Council" of which the head is
the massive Sunday, and all members have the name of
a day of the week. He is about to be appointed to the
post of Thursday. He boasts that the anarchists have
abolished right and wrong and wish to abolish God.

Syme believes that order, regularity, and precision
should characterize poetry simply because these are the
characteristics of the universe itself. To him, nature has
at its center order and design; to Gregory, it epitomizes
chaos and meaninglessness. As a representative of
modern relativism and nihilism, Gregory, for instance,
disdains a lamp post, seeing it as dull and sterile, and
celebrates a tree, admiring its profusion of seeming
irregularity. "You only see the tree by the light of the
lamp," Syme replies. "I wonder when you would ever
see the lamp by the light of the tree." [20] The tree is to
Syme sacramental, a type of all of nature, quite capable
of being as a light enabling one to see all of experience
rightly. To prove his seriousness, Gregory takes Syme
to a meeting of the Anarchic Council. There, Syme

20. G. K. Chesterton, *The Man Who Was Thursday* (1908; reprint London: Penguin, 1986), 17.

cleverly makes himself to appear a better candidate for anarchist than the real one, Gregory, and gets himself appointed as Thursday.

The two levels of appearance and reality are intensified when the reader learns in chapter 4 that Syme had formerly been commissioned as a "police detective." Prior to his meeting Gregory, he had met a "philosophical policeman" who insisted there was abroad "a purely intellectual conspiracy" of both artists and scientists who are "bound in a crusade against the Family and the State." The policeman's analysis expresses the alarm that Chesterton himself felt concerning his contemporary England. The moral and ethical attitudes of the intelligentsia (positivism and relativism were two main thrusts) offered the most perilous threat to society at large. Impressed by what he had heard, Syme asked to join the New Detective Corps. He was taken to a dark room, where a man of massive stature, his back towards him, accepted his enlistment and, curiously, sentenced him to death. Syme, then, as "detective" has become a spy at the Central Anarchist Organization. We later learn that the massive man in the dark room was Sunday, the same one who is the head of the Anarchist Council.

The metaphors of detective and spy suggest that Syme was closely examining the workings of the anarchic group, and one can conclude that he represents—at least in part—the young Chesterton, who was at the time warily considering various philosophies of existence himself. But if Sunday in some sense represents God, how is it that he is both the commissioner of police detectives and the head of a group of anarchists?

The adage that what one treasures the most is one's god applies here. Add to that the principle that pervades many of MacDonald's fantasies, that each person serves the god he perceives to be, and that one's perceptions are governed by one's nature. The anarchist serves an anarchist, the policeman a police commissioner. Further, the true God existing beyond human perceptions of Him is, after all, in charge of His world, securing even from the wrath of men His own purpose and ultimate praise. He is in control of even the anarchist, but in a manner that honors his free will and holds him responsible for his decisions. That Sunday operates in such a dual capacity is the central dramatic irony of the tale.

Dramatic ironies abound as the tale progresses. When the Anarchic Council meets, with Sunday at its head, Syme sits among them feeling exceedingly uncomfortable. To his amazement, however, he discovers afterwards in a series of encounters with the various members that all are, like him, disguised policemen. Each has been appointed by Sunday, whom each has met briefly and mysteriously in a dark room. Symbolically, the image suggests that all people are really on a quest to figure life out. They will come (it is hoped) to reject the world's false philosophies and arrive at a true one. It is God who commissions the quest. People tend to see their own quests as unique, but a closer view reveals that everyone is similarly engaged. The heart of the quest is dying into life.

The "detectives," who now consciously feel they are rebelling against Sunday, are in truth serving him. Since they fear him, they make a pact to dethrone him, and since none are really anarchists, they set out to foil a supposed plan assumed to have been instigated by the Anarchic Council to set off a bomb in Paris. Chesterton is suggesting that the rebellion against God in which many spiritual journeys begin may be a God-ordained phase of the voyage towards Him. When the group of detectives arrive in France, they suddenly perceive that a mob of people sent by Sunday are in pursuit of them. When a person attempts to dethrone God, one is fleeing not only from God and His Church, but also from the divinely established control of humankind in general.

The mythic aspects of the narrative come further into focus in the final three chapters. Suddenly, in the fashion of a nightmare abruptly becoming benign, the threat of all the pursuing crowd vanishes, and the detectives return to London. They resolve to confront Sunday, determined to discover precisely what he means, or, as Syme remarks, "I think it is six men going to ask one man what they mean." [21] They find him and, in one accord, demand to know. Rising slowly to incredible proportions, Sunday roars:

> "I? What am I?. . . . Bull, you are a man of science. Grub in the roots of the those trees and find out the truth about them. Syme, you are a poet. Stare at those morning clouds. But I tell you this, that you will have found out the truth of the last tree and the topmost cloud before the truth about me. You will understand the sea, and I shall be still a riddle; you shall know what the stars are, and not know what I am. Since the beginning of the world all men have hunted me like a wolf—kings and sages, and poets and lawgivers, all the churches, and all the philosophies. But I have never been caught yet, and the skies will fall in the time I turn to bay." [22]

The persistent resolve of the rational mind is impossible to satisfy, inasmuch as the finite may never comprehend the infinite. The ultimate question, What is God? can never be finally answered.

While much about God may be learned from a right view of the universe itself, God Himself will never be fully comprehended. In one of the more intriguing portions of the fantasy, Sunday suddenly flees, eluding all his pursuers. He escapes first in a cab, then in a fire engine, an elephant, and finally a balloon, all the while teasing them with messages that make no sense. None

21. Chesterton, *The Man Who Was Thursday*, 153.
22. Chesterton, *The Man Who Was Thursday*, 154–55.

of the pursuits of God can yield rational certainty. Exhausted, the detectives recount their impressions of Sunday and find that they each describe him in terms of some aspect of the universe. They agree he appears ugly to a person viewing only his back, but unspeakably beautiful to the person afforded a glimpse of his face. So with the universe: the back of the world seems brutal, but "everything is stooping and hiding a face." [23] One may recall Vane's similar description of Mara in *Lilith:* the presence of God in human experiences can appear terrible until one catches a closer view.

While God can at best be imperfectly known, each person stands in a unique relation to him. The penultimate chapter ends with a metaphoric simulation of death, in that the pilgrims are finally summoned by a messenger to appear before Sunday. (The scene faintly echoes the close of *Pilgrim's Progress*.) Sunday sends his servant with chariots to escort each. Of all their adventures, "not one had carried them so utterly off their feet as this last adventure of comfort." At their destination each enters "a splendid suite of apartments that seemed to be designed specially for him," and is given appropriate apparel, garments that do "not disguise, but reveal." [24]

The climax comes as the detectives appear in Sunday's "very large old English garden," each dressed

23. Chesterton, *The Man Who Was Thursday*, 170.
24. Chesterton, *The Man Who Was Thursday*, 175.

in splendid garments, the color and design suggested by the creative energies of the day whose name each bears—Monday the austerely thinking person, Tuesday the transparently simple, and so forth—yet each "seemed to be for the first time himself and no one else."[25] Again, as in MacDonald, the text emphasizes the preciousness of individuality. Sunday appears in quiet majesty, bidding each be seated on his appropriate throne on the terrace, while around them occurs the eternal dance of all living things. Sunday addresses them "dreamily":

> 'We will eat and drink later. Let us remain together a little, we who have loved each other so sadly, and have fought so long. I seem to remember only centuries of heroic war, in which you were always heroes—epic on epic, iliad on iliad, and you always brothers in arms. Whether it was but recently (for time is nothing), or at the beginning of the world, I sent you out to war. I sat in the darkness, where there is not any created thing, and to you I was only a voice commanding valour and an unnatural virtue. You heard the voice in the dark, and you never heard it again. The sun in heaven denied it, the earth and sky denied it, all human wisdom denied it. And when I met you in the daylight I denied it myself.'[26]

A vision of the spiritual history of humanity has seldom if ever had so condensed and yet comprehensive

25. Chesterton, *The Man Who Was Thursday*, 176
26. Chesterton, *The Man Who Was Thursday*, 179.

expression. The above excerpt captures the existential aspects of faith, with its strange combination of certainty and uncertainty, together with its persistent quality of otherness.

With dramatic intensity, the various detectives vent outrage and voice strong objections, unable to accept this vision and "forgive" Sunday. Sunday quietly hears their complaints and then accepts yet another, that of the anarchic poet Gregory who expresses his repudiation of the entire divine scheme. The reader may be reminded of Mephistopheles' cynical rejection of all creation in Goethe's *Faust*. The crux of Gregory's objection is that he alone has suffered; the detectives have all enjoyed the protection of divine providence. They have been safe, the power of the universe on their side, while he alone has agonized in opposition.

The lightning conclusion strikes with extraordinary effect, offering a rationale for suffering. Syme expresses the crowning insight:

> 'I see everything. . . . Why does each small thing in the world have to fight against the world itself? . . . For the same reason that I had to be alone in the dreadful Council of the Days. . . . So that the real lie of Satan may be flung back in the face of this blasphemer, so that by tears and torture we may earn the right to say to this man, "You lie!" No agonies can be too great to buy the right to say to this accuser, "We also have suffered. [27]

27. Chesterton, *The Man Who Was Thursday*, 182–83.

When Gregory, with burning enmity, asks Sunday, "Have you ever suffered?" the latter's face abruptly enlarges to fill all of space, and he asks, "Can ye drink of the cup that I drink of?" The mystery and magnitude of divine suffering suddenly confronts one afresh, and the biblical assertion that Christians share in the sufferings of Christ acquires fuller meaning. (See Phil. 3:10; 1 Pet. 4:13; 5:8–10.)

Much of the force of the final scene comes from the pattern of dramatic irony that has been working throughout, in which all that has been sinister and threatening is now seen to be innocuous and benign. But Chesterton does not dismiss the essence of evil. Much that one assumes to be evil may be good in disguise, but its dark and terrible reality cannot be dismissed.

The final page of the fantasy returns the reader to the conversation between Gregory and Syme with which the narrative began; all else has been a vision. But precisely when did the vision begin? Perhaps it was during Syme's early conversation with Gregory's sister. Because the initial transition Chesterton accomplishes from the real to the fantasy world is smooth, our return at the end seems incongruous. This weakness, nevertheless, does not detract from the impact of the myth.

THE ETERNAL IN THE TEMPORAL

To the extent the narrative recounts Syme's spiritual odyssey it also presents much of Chesterton's own thought. One feels in the text the strength of personal experience and conviction. The issues and struggles of everyday life are seen, as Chesterton felt they must be seen, against the backdrop of eternity and the far reaches of one's actions. The result is the strongly mythic force of the narrative. Franz Kafka, whose existential myths were being written at approximately the same time, is quoted as having said of Chesterton: "He is so gay, one might almost believe he had found God." [28]

Chesterton's contribution, then, to the tradition of literary mythmaking lies in his assertion that everyday life is permeated with mythic qualities. One must have the eyes to see and the ears to hear. He caught the mythic vision from George MacDonald, and many of his themes can be traced back to MacDonald's penetrating spiritual insights. Chesterton adds to his mythic vision an inimitable wit and command of irony, suggesting that all the struggles of life—the social, the political, and the personal—should be seen in the light of myth. One's spiritual quest is vitally related to the everyday aspects of life. Chesterton's vision of the eternal in the temporal is a message for

28. As quoted in Dale, *The Outline of Sanity: A Life of G. K. Chesterton*, 113.

the modern world. He anticipated fellow Catholic authors Flannery O'Connor and Walker Percy, whose realist stories also present people as desperately needing to see the true nature of reality.

5

Charles Williams
Myth and Power
(1886–1945)

I have always believed that he would have been equally
at ease in every kind of supernatural company; that he
would never have been surprised or disconcerted by
the intrusion of any visitor from another world,
whether kindly or malevolent; and that he would have
shown exactly the same natural ease and courtesy, with
an exact awareness of how one should behave, to an
angel, a demon, a human ghost, or an elemental. For
him there was no frontier between the material and
the spiritual world. [1]

f the writers mentioned in this study, Charles
Williams is the most unconventional. In his
seven fantasy novels he created an original
vision of both the fatal character of evil and the true
beauty of mature Christian conduct. Like Chesterton,
he saw clearly the supernatural in the everyday; his

1. T. S. Eliot, Introduction, *All Hallows' Eve* by Charles Williams (Grand Rapids,
Mich.: Wm. B. Eerdmans, 1963), xiii–xiv.

realistic portrayals of its presence are more persuasive and his vision of evil more pernicious. He lacks Chesterton's wit and engaging style, but he makes his fictional world more convincing. A person cannot think of the state of the newly dead in the same way after reading the opening chapter of *All Hallow's Eve*, nor of the complexity of interpersonal relationships after reading *Descent into Hell*.

OXFORD AND THE INKLINGS

Charles Williams joined Oxford University Press, in London, in June of 1908. For thirty-seven years he worked at the Press, finding time in the midst of his editing responsibilities to publish seven mythopoeic novels, works of poetry, drama, history, theology, and literary criticism, and a constant flow of articles and reviews. Academically, his most distinguished work was *The Figure of Beatrice*, a profound study of Dante's *Divine Comedy*.

Near the beginning of World War II, when London was threatened by bombing, the Press moved much of its operation to its Oxford offices; Williams moved with it. There he joined the Inklings, an informal group of writers and their friends who met regularly in C. S. Lewis's rooms in Magdalen College to discuss their works. [2] Having already established himself as a

2. Humphrey Carpenter, *The Inklings: C. S. Lewis, J. R. R. Tolkien, Charles Williams, and their friends* (Boston: Houghton Mifflin, 1979), 115. Carpenter's work is a ready source of information on this interesting group.

literary scholar and critic (although Williams attended University College, London, he never took a degree), he lectured on poetry at Oxford University, and in 1943 was granted the degree of Honorary Master of Arts.

Preoccupied with the patterns of the ideal world which he saw within the real one—within the city of London was the City of God, and within every loving relationship was God as Love—he was so intensely interested in the supernatural he sought to know more of it not only through the Church of England but through fringe groups as well. As a young man he studied Rosicrucianism, and joined the Fellowship of the Rosy Cross in 1917. While neither movement saw itself as opposing Christianity, both used secret rituals and Christian symbols in a gnostic pursuit of spiritual power.

His novels show an intricate knowledge of occult attitudes and practices; they also show how thoroughly he saw them as self-centered quests for personal power, the essence of evil. In the novels, such portraits as that of Gregory Persimmons in *War in Heaven* or Father Simon in *All Hallow's Eve* clinch the point.

Williams, like the poet William Blake, discerned the spiritual in all things physical: in human love, in the way all images may convey grace, and in the complex and vital interdependencies that pervade social relationships. In *The Figure of Beatrice* he expounds the first. [3] In short, knowing the beloved is a means of knowing God as Love; the effect is humility and a desire to be virtuous. Upon falling in love with his future wife Florence Conway, Williams immediately wrote her a sequence of eighty-four love poems, although it was not until nine years later, when he was past thirty and she nearly so, that they married. When she tried to see the lighter side of their relationship, he nicknamed her Michal, after David's wife who laughed at him when he danced before the Lord.

Anyone who has genuinely fallen in love can vouch for the moral and spiritual aspirations that attend the experience. The effect is not primarily sexual. A danger for someone of Williams's intense spiritual sensitivities was that of seeing the beloved as a means to an end and cherishing the emotion more than the person. Another danger was that the image of one beloved may not suffice. Although Florence apparently accommodated herself to his unusual thought, hers was not the only image that moved him. He conducted for years a chaste but intimate affair with his work associate Phyllis Jones. Other women who sought him for counsel he treated similarly. These relationships were chaste, but unique. Love was to him a way of achieving a more intimate knowledge of God.

3. Charles Williams, *The Figure of Beatrice: A Study in Dante* (1943; reprint Cambridge: D. S. Brewer, 1994). He also wrote *Outlines of Romantic Theology* but could get no publisher to receive it. It was edited by Alice Mary Hadfield and published by Eerdmans in 1990.

It was when Williams joined the Inklings at Oxford that his closest friends became men. They saw him as a rare individual and tended to praise his person over his many works. The latter they esteemed but did not always understand. C. S. Lewis's recorded reactions were both enthusiastic and critical. He said Williams's rich imagination "could be saved from turning silly or even vulgar in print only by a severe early discipline which he never had" and criticized him for obscurity and occasional "errors in taste." But he also felt Williams saw further into spiritual reality than he did. [4] Lewis was responsible for arranging Williams's lectures at Oxford, and was so impressed with his discourse on Milton he avowed Oxford had not heard anything so genuinely wise since the great medieval or Renaissance lectures. [5] His fellow Inkling, J. R. R. Tolkien, given to composing poems, wrote a playful but sincere tribute to Williams:

> When your fag is wagging and spectacles are
>   twinkling,
> When tea is brewing or the glasses tinkling,
> Then of your meaning often I've an inkling,

4. "But I am convinced that both the content and the quality of his experience differed from mine and differed in ways which oblige me to say that he saw further, that he knew what I do not know. His writing, so to speak, brings me where I have never gone on my own sail or steam; and yet that strange place is so attached to realms we do know that I cannot believe it is mere dreamland." C. S. Lewis, "The Novels of Charles Williams," *Of This and Other Worlds*, ed. Walter Hooper (London: Collins, 1982), 52.

5. Carpenter, *Inklings*, 115–19.

> Your virtues and your wisdom glimpse. Your
>   laugh
> In my heart echoes, when with you I quaff
> The pint that goes down quicker than a half,
> Because you're near . . . [6]

Though Tolkien complained of being unable to understand his writing (Williams was reading his Arthurian poetry to the Inklings at the time), he warmly praised his person and genuinely enjoyed his company.

Nor was it only members of the Inklings who praised him. T. S. Eliot, a man rather sparing with his tributes, wrote that it would be misleading to call Charles Williams a mystic, but he seemed to him "to approximate, more nearly than any man I have ever known familiarly, to the saint." [7] And W. H. Auden credited Williams's influence in his conversion to Christianity. He wrote that when he met him, he felt for the first time in his life "in the presence of personal sanctity. I had met many good people before who made me feel ashamed of my own shortcomings, but in the presence of this man—we never discussed anything but literary business—I did not feel ashamed. I felt transformed into a person who was incapable of doing or thinking anything base or unloving." [8]

6. Carpenter, *Inklings*, 126.

7. T. S. Eliot, "The Significance of Charles Williams," *The Listener* XXXVI (Dec. 19, 1946): 894–95.

8. From James A. Pike, ed., *Modern Canterbury Pilgrims*, as quoted in Charles Osborne, *W. H. Auden: The Life of a Poet* (London: Macmillan, 1982), 202.

THE WAY OF EXCHANGE AND
OTHER THOUGHTS

To Williams the image of woman was not alone in nurturing virtue; all images may convey grace. This he called the Way of Affirmation. In the history of the Christian church the Way of Affirmation and the Way of Negation have been the two basic mystical approaches to God. Each concerns one's attitude towards images. The individual following the Way of Negation attempts to obliterate all images from the mind and wait before God in worship and trust. T. S. Eliot's persona in *The Four Quartets* expresses the requisite attitudes:

> I said to my soul, be still, and wait without hope
> For hope would be hope for the wrong thing; wait
> without love
> For love would be love for the wrong thing; there is
> yet faith
> But the faith and the love and the hope are all in the
> waiting [9]

The mind must be made an empty vessel for the Spirit of God to fill. While honoring this approach, Williams championed the opposite way.

The Way of Affirmation insists that all things in life, if seen rightly and with purity of heart, convey to the viewer some suggestion of their Creator. It is not

9. T. S. Eliot, "The Four Quartets," *Complete Poems and Plays* (New York: Harcourt, Brace & World, 1952), 126.

the easier way, for it demands one affirm unpleasant images as well as attractive ones.

> It is not to be rashly assumed that the Way of Affirmation is much easier than the Way of Rejection. To affirm the validity of an image one does not at the moment happen to like or want—such as that of one's next door neighbor—is as harsh as to reject an image—such as oneself as successful—which one does happen to like and want. "To fashion this ability" is a personal, secret, and arduous business. [10]

All human relationships become opportunities to bestow love.

In his writings Williams insists on the necessity of both ways. His most frequently quoted phrase is "This also is Thou; neither is this Thou." [11] It defines a sacramental vision and is the proper Christian attitude for addressing all aspects of experience. To participate in it is to acquire a mythic vision. While nothing in life is to be equated with God, nothing exists apart from Him.

Life is an immensely intricate pattern of interrelationships and interdependencies. Williams invites us to consider the interconnectedness of people much like a web or chain linked together; all that we do effects a

10. Charles Williams, *The Figure of Beatrice: A Study in Dante*, 13.

11. He writes in the preface to *The Descent of the Dove*: "A motto which might have been set on the title-page but has been, less ostentatiously, put here instead, is a phrase which I once supposed to come from Augustine, but I am informed by experts that it is not so, and otherwise I am ignorant of its source. The phrase is: 'This also is Thou; neither is this Thou.' As a maxim for living it is invaluable, and it—or its reversal—summarizes the history of the Christian Church." He apparently never identified the source.

myriad of people. Exchange, of which money is the symbol, is the law of life, and the substitutionary death and resurrection of Christ for all people is the ultimate Exchange. The obligation of those who profess to follow Christ is to try in all their daily affairs to exchange good for evil. The power to do so lies in love, in the Way of Affirmation. Christ coinheres in all Christians and they in Him. When this is practiced, interpersonal relationships are redeemed and godlikeness is realized.

Williams derived his beliefs from the Bible, in the nature of the Fall and the Divine Covenants that follow. [12] As the Persons of the Trinity coinhere each in the other, so do humans coinhere in Adam: "Whatever ages of time lay between us and Adam, yet we were in him and we were he; more, we sinned in him and his guilt is in us." [13] Adam and Eve's desire to know both good and evil was impossible without falling into evil, for they could only know by experience. In wanting to know evil they not only denied the goodness of good but they also turned good into evil. [14] God responded by devising a way, through a series of covenants with humanity, whereby evil could be turned into good. The

---

12. Charles Williams, *He Came Down From Heaven* (London: William Heinemann Ltd., 1938; reprinted Grand Rapids, Mich: Wm B. Eerdmans, 1984) is a succinct presentation of his doctrinal position. Charles Hefling, ed., *Charles Williams: Essential Writings in Spirituality and Theology* (Cambridge, Mass: Cowley Publications, 1993) is an anthology of passages from Williams's works which gives a good sampling of his views.

13. Charles Williams, *Descent of the Dove* (Grand Rapids, Mich.: Wm. B. Eerdmans, 1947), 69.

14. Hefling, *Charles Williams: Essential Writings in Spirituality and Theology* , 22, 23.

first was with Noah, and established the principle of exchange. Williams explained: "It proclaims a law: 'At the hand of every man's brother will I require the life of man.' It is a declaration of an exchange of responsibility rather than of joy, but the web of substitution is to that extent created, however distant from the high end and utter conclusion of entire interchange." [15]

In the history of Israel, humanity's plight again fell prey to its disobedience, and God announced a new covenant: "I will put my law in their inward parts, and write it in their hearts. . . . for I will forgive their iniquity, and I will remember their sin no more (Jer. 21:33–4)." This is possible because of the complete exchange effected by Christ, the suffering servant of Isaiah 53. In Him the kingdom of heaven has appeared. In it "a new knowledge arises. Men had determined to know good as evil; there could be but one perfect remedy for that— to know the evil of the past itself as good, and to be free from the necessity of the knowledge of evil in the future; to find right knowledge and perfect freedom together; to know all things as occasions of love." [16] Through love, any evil now can be redeemed.

Williams's convictions shape his fantasies. At their heart is the certainty that the Incarnation opens "all potentialities of the knowledge of the kingdom of heaven in and through matter." [17] They are mythic in

15. Williams, *He Came Down*, 24. See Gen. 9:5.
16. Williams, *He Came Down*, 77.
17. Williams, *He Came Down*, 101.

that they create a comprehensive vision of spiritual reality within the physical world. The quotidian world of sense experience is spiritually momentous; the potential for both good and evil in all aspects of human behavior is enormous.

Thomas Howard writes of Williams's worlds:

> The ordinary stuff of our experience seems both to cloak and to reveal more than itself. Everything nudges our elbow. Heaven and hell seem to lurk under every bush. The sarcastic lift of an eyebrow carries the seed of murder since it bespeaks my wish to diminish someone else's existence. To open a door for a man carrying luggage recalls the Cross since it is a small case in point of putting the other person first. [18]

In this study we will look at six of Williams's seven novels: *The Place of the Lion, Descent into Hell, The Greater Trumps, Many Dimensions, War in Heaven,* and *All Hallow's Eve.*

THE PLACE OF THE LION

In this impressive early work (1931), Williams presents definitively the true nature of spiritual power, the range of its possible perversions, and its divinely intended function in life. C. S. Lewis loved *The Place of the Lion.* Shortly after discovering this book (the first one of Williams's works he read), the two met in London and

18. Thomas Howard, *The Novels of Charles Williams* (New York: Oxford University Press, 1983), 5. Howard presents a very helpful series of essays on the novels.

a close friendship followed. Lewis wrote to Arthur Greeves: "I have just read what I think a really great book . . . . Do get it, and don't mind if you don't understand everything the first time. It deserves reading over and over again. It isn't often now-a-days you get a *Christian* fantasy." [19]

The concept at the heart of the fantasy is difficult, but Williams develops it with daring imaginative verve and plausibility. Creation as we know it took place when angels, celestial powers, entered into matter. The various powers deeply resident in the created world—strength, subtlety, beauty, speed, balance, and gentleness—are themselves angels. They are also the Platonic archetypes; Plato's transcendent forms, or ideas, which inform all material things.

They also may become beasts. In this novel, Williams's imagined structure of the created universe represents a fascinating synthesis of Platonic and Christian concepts. This entire structure of spiritual reality may become upset when people try to appropriate power to their own self-gratifying ends. Beasts incarnating such qualities as strength or beauty appear and draw their power back into themselves. For

19. Lewis to Greeves, *They Stand Together: The Letters of C. S. Lewis to Arthur Greeves (1914–1963)*, ed. Walter Hooper (London: Collins, 1979), 479. For Lewis's esteem of Williams's person, see the preface to *Essays Presented to Charles Williams* (Oxford University Press, 1947), and for his novels in general, see "The Novels of Charles Williams," *Of This and Other Worlds* (London: Collins, 1982), 46–54. One may conjecture Lewis's inspiration for Aslan in the *Chronicles of Narnia* came from this fantasy, and perhaps as well his handling of the theme of matrimonial love in *That Hideous Strength*, a work remarkably like one of Williams's. The character of Ransom in that novel may well have been modeled on Williams.

instance, the lion of strength appears on earth, drawing strength out of the world, and buildings collapse. Images of lions, snakes, butterflies, horses, eagles and lambs appear as mythological types throughout the story, symbolizing such Platonic archetypes as subtlety, beauty, swiftness, and so forth.

Of central interest among the characters are the two young men with whom the fantasy opens, close friends whose sighting of a lion on the lawn evokes in each radically diverse reactions. Anthony Durrant, who epitomizes Williams's spiritually ideal man, is a true son of Adam. He stares at the natural world and wonders what it is he is truly seeing. Possessed by a "passionate desire for intellectual and spiritual truth and honesty," Anthony is curious but not frightened. In strong contrast to his confident reactions are those of his friend Quentin Sabot, who is unnerved by the sighting and quickly degenerates into a trembling and cringing babbler who snatches a revolver from Anthony and fires several shots into the lion, to no effect. He typifies man "in this lost and imbecile" twentieth century, to whom the world is chaotic and meaningless; hence, he sees himself as standing alone against it. When he confronts what appears to be the world's irrational behavior, he is reduced to a frenzy.

The gallery of characters presents an array of differing responses to the mythical manifestations that occur throughout the fantasy. Another commendable character is Richardson; he provides one key to the book as a Christian who follows the Way of Negation. Other characters illustrate several warped responses in their desire to wield power for self-centered ends, or to surrender one's humanity in the absurd worshipping of power for its own sake.

Berringer, a cult figure, is responsible for beginning the catastrophic drawing of this world into the world of the Celestials. His intense concentration creates the image of the lion that Anthony and Quentin see in the opening scene. The lion embodies the angel of strength.

We learn little of Berringer as a man, inasmuch as his feat sends him into a coma, and he, together with his house, perishes in a supernatural conflagration which burns but appears not to consume. The intense burning is generated by his having triggered the start of what threatens to be a general drawing of this world into the world of the Celestials. Although Williams does not directly say as much, the raging fire suggests the fire of the New Testament end-time prophecies.

In the middle of the story, as Anthony accompanies a doctor to attend the comatose Berringer, he acquires the further insight and spiritual orientation that makes him embody Williams's ideal man. In the house burning with supernatural flames, he receives a vision of a great pit from which a strong wind begins to blow, threatening his balance, until he comes to understand that if he were to throw himself upon its strength and "be one with that power. . . nothing could oppose or bear up against it and him in it." [20] It is a vision of the nature and availability of true spiritual power to a person like himself; as complete man, it is his right and prerogative to be in harmony with this power.

Of particular interest is Damaris Tighe, Anthony's fiance. She is an aspiring academic; her quest is for intellectual power. The mythological manifestation appropriate to her is the pterodactyl; it appears outside her window accompanied by a stench which suggests spiritual death. She has been working feverishly to complete her doctoral dissertation on Abelard, a medieval French philosopher and theologian, and is engrossed in the contemplation of ideas from Plato and certain Church fathers. Her spiritual aberration is that she has come to attribute such reality to this abstract construct of ideas that she ignores and disdains the real world, scorning even her own father. Cutting herself off from concrete reality and depreciating human relationships, she is thus severed from the channels of spiritual energy. Williams clinches his point by quoting one of Abelard's couplets:

> Truth is always in the thing;
> Never in the reasoning.

Damaris is rescued by Anthony's love for her—which refuses to be discouraged by the Lilith-like dimensions

20. Charles Williams, *The Place of the Lion* (Grand Rapids, Mich.: Wm B. Eerdmans, 1980), 114.

of her personality. As in many of Williams's novels, his conviction as regards the effect of romantic love again shapes the story: the love relationship properly experienced is a means of enhancing the spiritual lives of both partners.

In the myth-bathed scene that concludes the fantasy, Anthony stands like Adam commanding and controlling creation. Ideal man's rightful power extends over the earthly manifestations of angelic beings: "By the names that were the Ideas he called them, and the Ideas who are the Principles of everlasting creation heard him, the Principles of everlasting creation who are the Cherubim and Seraphim of the Eternal. In their animal manifestations, duly obedient to the single animal who was lord of the animals, they came."[21] As a mythic figure, he epitomizes the person of moral stature and control whom God intended man to be.

DESCENT INTO HELL

Descent into Hell, though a difficult and challenging work, clearly shows the pattern of substituted love, along with Williams's compelling vision of the nature of hell in relation to this life and to time.

In this story the paragon of Christian maturity is a famous playwright, Peter Stanhope. He lives on Battle Hill, an upper middle-class settlement some thirty miles north of London, an area rich with the history of

21. Williams, *The Place of the Lion,* 202.

battles from ancient British wars. It symbolizes death permeating life, the terrible wrongs of the past awaiting atonement. His latest play, a masque which he intends as "an experiment in a different kind of existence," is being given its debut by the local drama club, but is attracting national attention. The well-developed plot concerns for the most part the spiritual states of the various men and women associated with the event.

Stanhope is an intriguing figure: magnanimous and deferential, graciously submitting to the opinions and desires of the producer and cast who tend to consider his play an amorphous affair upon which they could readily improve. The Kingdom of God, "which fulfilled itself in the remote recesses of his spacious verse," channels to him through his art the grace that enables him to "laugh and enjoy and assent" to their emendations and also infuses him with "the willingness to fulfill the moment as the moment." [22]

He befriends Pauline Anstruther, a timid, troubled young woman who has a minor role in his masque. She confides to him her distress: she has hallucinations of her meeting at unexpected times a person the exact image of herself, and she is seized with fear. [23] In compassionate understanding, he insists that she allow him

22. Charles Williams, *Descent into Hell* (Grand Rapids, Mich.: Wm B. Eerdmans, 1980), 145.

23. In her schooling she was made to learn the lines from Shelley: "The Magus Zoroaster, my dead child, / Met his own image walking in the garden." It is the same passage that T. S. Eliot uses to such powerful effect in his drama *The Cocktail Party*. Given Eliot's high esteem of Williams's work (See, for instance, his Introduction to *All Hallows' Eve*), one could surmise he lifted the idea from Williams's novel.

to bear completely her fear, so that she may be freed from it. She consents, he assumes her distress, and she is delivered. The episode is definitive in illustrating Williams's view of the nature of substituted love.

Lily Sammile, an aged, nondescript woman ubiquitously promising help, offers Pauline the largest temptation to deter her from true deliverance. Her first name suggests Lilith, and, true to the Jewish legend, she is dissatisfied with what God has ordained, offering as substitutes various refuges from distress such as the world affords: "she broke again into gabble, in which Pauline could dimly make out promises, of health, of money, of life, or their appearances, of good looks and good luck, or a belief in them, of peace and content. . . ." [24] Ironically, Lily is found at the end of the fantasy living in a hut by the cemetery, a ramshackle affair that collapses as the story draws to conclusion. Hers is the way of death and destruction.

The pattern of substituted love brings deliverance to the sufferer, but also salvation—and joy to—the one who loves. Among the episodes of British history with which Battle Hill is rife is the martyrdom of an ancestor of Pauline's. He was burned at the stake as he quoted to his persecutors "To him that hath shall be given," and, the one who has not "shall lose all that he hath." (See Matt. 13:12, KJV) As he is consumed with fire he shouts, "I have seen the salvation of my God." Pauline is

24. Williams, *Descent into Hell*, 208.

obsessed with her imagined version of the scene, the horror of her ancestor's demise and also the puzzle of his triumph in joy. Her aged aunt, who like Stanhope has achieved an understanding of the workings of Omnipotence, remarks to her niece, "Salvation is quite often a terrible thing—a frightening good." [25]

Pauline encounters the image of her suffering ancestor later in the story and, in a scene of intense mythic perception, she asks to bear the burden of his agony. As she participates in it and he knows relief, he experiences the true nature of salvation as substitution; the mystery of his final words is then made plain. Pauline is now able to face the apparition that is her double, and sees it glowing with supernatural beauty:

> Joy had filled her that afternoon, and it was in the power of such joy that she had been brought to this closest propinquity to herself. It had been her incapacity for joy, nothing else, that had till now turned the vision of herself aside; her incapacity for joy had admitted fear, and fear had imposed separation. She knew now that all acts of love are the measure of capacity for joy. . . ." [26]

She is subsequently released from the bondage of timidity and fear into the liberty of love.

In both transcending and telescoping time, Williams's vision of deliverance illustrates kairos time.

25. Williams, *Descent into Hell*, 56.
26. Williams, *Descent into Hell*, 171.

To God there is no before or after, and a thousand years are as a day. Pauline's encounter with her ancestor of centuries earlier was not determined by any action of human will, but rather by Omnipotence in the interests of her salvation. Omnipotence, we are told, has such "economy of means" that at least "two time schemes" exist: each person has one's own, and outside it there is a "general world of time." The past has "its own present beside our present"; from it its inhabitants can "either retire to their own mists or more fully invade the place of the living." In select scenes, therefore, the narrative freely merges individuals from the past into the present.

While Pauline's entrance into the world of complete coinherence illustrates the nature of full salvation, much of the fantasy details its opposite, damnation. Lawrence Wentworth is a distinguished authority on military history, whose counsel is sought concerning the costumes of the play. He is in love with Adela Hunt, a self-centered and ambitious young actress in Stanhope's masque. When she spurns Wentworth, he withdraws into a world of illusion in which he creates an image of her more satisfying to him than her flesh and blood person. In withdrawing into a world of complete illusion, of solitude and silence, he is repudiating the Way of Affirmation, replacing it with the vacuity of self-absorption. He diminishes his person towards nothingness, which is the essence of damnation.

A good portion of the action takes place on Battle Hill, suggesting how the life of man in the present rests upon the sufferings and deaths of the past. Stanhope's and Wentworth's residences are there, implying the poles of human destiny. These eventuate in one of two cities, Zion—the city of salvation and complete coinherence—or Gomorrah, the city yoked in the Bible with Sodom, here epitomizing the ultimate human perversion of vacuous egotism. Stanhope explains:

> We know all about Sodom nowadays, but perhaps we know the other even better. Men can be in love with men, and women with women, and still be in love and make sounds and speeches, but don't you know how quiet the streets of Gomorrah are? . . . . The lovers of Gomorrah are quite contented. . . They aren't bothered by alteration, at least till the rain of the fire of the Glory at the end, for they lose the capacity for change . . . .There's no distinction between lover and beloved; they beget themselves on their adoration of themselves, and they live and feed and starve on themselves, and by themselves too, for creation . . . is the mercy of God, and they won't have the facts of creation. [27]

Williams's version of the hell within, suggested by Milton in *Paradise Lost*, is stark and intense. We saw the theme in MacDonald; we will see it again in Lewis.

27. Williams, *Descent into Hell*, 174.

Williams's concern with the ultimate destinies of people focuses upon the mysterious loci of spiritual power, both for good and for evil, and how people of a variety of spiritual orientations relate to them. His knowledge of occult practices and cabalistic lore is extensive, and many of his characters make sinister attempts to command evil power and realize demonic intentions. Some readers are disturbed. T. S. Eliot puts it in helpful perspective:

> Williams seemed equally at ease among every sort and condition of men, naturally and unconsciously, without envy or contempt, without subservience or condescension. . . . Had I ever had to spend a night in a haunted house, I should have felt secure with Williams in my company: he was somehow protected from evil, and was himself a protection. He could have joked with the devil and turned the joke against him. To him the supernatural was perfectly natural, and the natural was also supernatural. And this peculiarity gave him that profound insight into Good and Evil, into the heights of heaven and depths of Hell, which provides both the immediate thrill, and the permanent message of his novels. [28]

Williams sees God as Omnipotent Love, and His love is the ultimate spiritual power. God, who is in absolute control of all of life, invites whoever will to

28. T. S. Eliot, Introduction, *All Hallows' Eve* by Charles Williams (Grand Rapids, Mich.: Wm. B. Eerdmans, 1963), xiii–xiv. This essay should be read in its entirety by all students of Williams.

colabor in love harmoniously with Him. In Williams's fantasy world, God is mysteriously both everywhere and nowhere; the reader is not directly made aware of His presence, but His love is incarnate in select characters such as in Peter Stanhope, or as in Sybil Coningsby in *The Greater Trumps*. Williams's vision echoes that of Isaiah, "Truly, thou art a God who hidest thyself." (45:15, RSV).

While his knowledge of the occult is patently wide, his handling of it is not that of the facile magician, but rather of that of the adept mythmaker with a profound vision of higher things. It is a necessary aspect of his vision: Zion would lack depth and plausibility without his startling images of the authority and power of evil. He has no simplistic illusions concerning the pernicious nature of evil, but he ultimately allows it no ground. Characters possessed of evil seek to wrest control and command evil power to self-centered ends; they enjoy a frightening momentary success. But they are overcome by those rare individuals who find complete repose in their adoration of God as Omnipotent Love and have come into league with His ultimate power and workings. Their lives are characterized by an equanimity of spirit balanced by daring, a meekness intermingled with authority; their involvement springs from their joyous participation in the patterns of exchanged love.

THE GREATER TRUMPS

In three of the fantasies, *The Greater Trumps*, *Many Dimensions*, and *War in Heaven*, Williams concentrates spiritual power in a talisman. In *The Greater Trumps*, a metaphysical thriller, the talisman is a deck of tarot cards and a mysterious game board of golden figures. According to gypsy legend, whoever controls a particularly rare deck of tarot cards may command the elemental forces of the universe and see accurately into the future. The mythic strength of this fantasy lies not in the cards but in the force of visionary love.

A gypsy family, the Lees, are determined to possess the cards. Henry Lee learns the deck is in the possession of Lothair Coningsby, to whose daughter, Nancy, he is engaged. A pompous, no-nonsense Brit who lives with his sister Sybil, Coningsby is unaware of the value of the deck he has recently acquired. It is from his standpoint of commonsensical outrage that much of the action of the fantasy is viewed. A warden of a mental hospital, he tends to see the conduct of people in general as skewed.

Henry schemes with his grandfather, Aaron Lee, to seize the cards. Aaron, a practitioner of black magic, has an ancient collection of tiny figures (like the ones on the tarot deck) he keeps secretly on a table in an inner room of his home. The figures move in a perpetual dance, suggesting the central dance of the universe. At their center is the figure of the Fool, who seems immobile and highly intriguing to all but Sybil, who sees it dancing everywhere.

Foremost among the tarot symbols are the Greater Trumps, those cards that exist above the four suits and consist of a series of elaborate figures: the Juggler, the Lovers, the Hanged Man, and, beyond them, the Fool. Theirs is "the meaning of all process and the measure of the everlasting dance." [29] Several years earlier the tarot cards had become separated from the figures. Only the cards can interpret the strange Dance. Aaron desperately wants to find the lost pack so that he may control the universe itself and know the future.

The Lees gain temporary use of the deck by inviting the Coningsby family to spend Christmas at Aaron's home, bringing the deck with them. Discovering that Nancy has a natural gift for handling the cards, Henry involves her in certain experiments to discover more precisely how they may be used to command the images. But when Lothair refuses any more than to lend the much coveted cards, Henry uses them himself to conjure up a turbulent blizzard. He directs its violent energies upon Coningsby, who goes out for an afternoon's walk on Christmas Day.

Henry's efforts in self-aggrandizement and personal power are foiled by the superior potency of love

29. Charles Williams, *The Greater Trumps* (Grand Rapids, Mich.: Wm B. Eerdmans, 1980), 21.

working effectively through the principle of exchange. Sybil and Nancy are the exemplars; Sybil is perhaps the most convincingly drawn and pleasing of Williams's saints. No cardboard qualities about her, she is free from pietist attitudes and conventional Christian cliches. True to her name, she sees people and situations with perfect clarity, [30] and she loves others with imaginative grace. Not only does she manifest a genuine spirit of worship at the Christmas service the family attends, but as her mind fixes upon the line from a carol, "Rise to adore the mystery of love," her ensuing actions convincingly show such adoration.

She rescues her brother from perishing in the storm, and, amidst the fear and heightened confusion of the household as the turbulence violently swirls through the house itself, she nurses the fear-possessed Aaron, who has fallen and injured his ankle, exchanging her love for his fear:

> Her hand closed round the ankle; her mind went inwards into the consciousness of the Power which contained them both; she loved it and adored it: with her own thought of Aaron in his immediate need, his fear, his pain, she adored. Her own ankle ached and throbbed in sympathy, not the sympathy of an easy proffer of mild regret, but that of a life habituated to such intercession. She interceded; she in him and he in her. . . . She throbbed for an instant not with pain

30. Howard, *The Novels of Charles Williams*, 124.

but with fear as his own fear passed through her being. It did but pass through; it was dispelled within her, dying away in the unnourishing atmosphere of her soul, and with the fear went the pain. [31]

Because Sybil believes so completely that the purposes of Omnipotent Love unlock all of the enigmas of life, she is not mesmerized, as are the others, with fear at the power of the tarot deck working in yoke with the mysterious golden figures. She is not even concerned whether some supernatural power is responsible for the storm. Her business lies with the welfare of suffering individuals, to whom she calmly ministers with fearless self-abandon. She sees the storm as the property and instrument of Love.

In the midst of its fury she affirms: "I know the dance, and the figures that make the dance. . . . Do you suppose that storm can ever touch the Fool?" [32] Thus the Fool becomes an effective surrogate for the mystery of God as Terrible Good. Only such people as Sybil can see him "leaping and dancing for joy." The Fool's presence in the tarot deck also suggests that the occult does not exist beyond the ultimate power of God. Sybil knows the secret that Nancy is learning.

Throughout the story Nancy is growing into a knowledge of the true power of romantic love. She demonstrates Williams's romantic theology. At the

31. Williams, *The Greater Trumps*, 219.
32. Williams, *The Greater Trumps*, 139.

beginning of the story she is presented as a young girl very much in love with Henry, but possessed with immature and self-serving attitudes. Her passion is, nevertheless, genuine, and matures into redeeming energy. The pivotal moment occurs for her at the Christmas service as she, standing beside her aunt with her mind fleetingly fixed upon the Incarnation, whispers to her "Is it true?" Sybil challenges her, "Try it, darling." The instance marks Nancy's spiritual transformation. Williams's rendition of the mysterious mental process of conversion is deft and convincing. Like her aunt, she not only begins to "adore the mystery of love" in the Christmas service, but she also soon has momentous opportunity to participate in Love's redeeming purposes.

Momentarily shocked upon learning that Henry's passion for the cards had driven him to attempt her father's murder, she, nevertheless, determines to use her gift in using the cards to see if she can still the storm. As she joins Henry in the effort, her love for him is not only renewed but increased because it is now a love "for something greater than him." In seeing her love in practical expression his own is deepened, and, gripped by his fear of the storm and his awe at Nancy's efforts, his attitudes begin to change for the better. The incident illustrates vividly how Williams saw life as existing on two levels, distinct but telescoped and interdependent: the passion of genuine love between the sexes has behind it the paradigm of the ideal, and as such is a powerful ally in the effecting of virtue.

Perhaps more than any of our other writers, Williams makes plausible his vision that true life is taking place on another plane, one comprehended only by people whose spiritual perception has been awakened by their participation in self-effacing acts of love. A person may compare T. S. Eliot's vision in his dramas *The Family Reunion* or *The Cocktail Party*, in which action transpires on two levels: that of spiritual reality, or myth, and that of the everyday. His gift lies in convincing his readers of the truth of this dual character of events. He makes us feel the momentousness of the mythic level and the frail and inconsequential nature of that "quality which has to be cast out," even though it is only the latter that most people see. One may think of the writer of Hebrews exclaiming that God will remove all that can be shaken in the world, that "what cannot be shaken may remain. Therefore, let us be grateful for receiving a kingdom that cannot be shaken . . . for our God is a consuming fire" (12:27–9; RSV). MacDonald, creating a sense of this duality in *Lilith*, focused our attention on the higher world; Williams makes us see its coincidence with the world we know.

MANY DIMENSIONS

Among the three novels whose plots are built around a talisman, *Many Dimensions* is the least successful. The symbol of power in *Dimensions* is a stone engraved with the tetragrammaton, [33] the Hebrew word YHWH used in the Old Testament for the unutterable name of God. It is presented as granting the one who possesses it seemingly unlimited fantastic powers. Williams apparently wants an image that can be made to suggest all the enormous power of which the imagination can conceive, power that is essentially amoral and as such can be commanded by either occult or mystical means to both good or evil ends. His concept sustains some apt comparisons to that of J. R. R. Tolkien in his use of the ring as a symbol for power in *Lord of the Rings*. But Tolkien handled his talisman with a mastery Williams failed to achieve. Williams seems to have seen power as morally neutral in character, available alike to people with good or evil motives, whereas in Tolkien the power the ring symbolizes diminishes all who command it; its use is repudiated by the characters who possess highest knowledge of the good, such as Gandalf.

In Williams's universe, talismans may be commanded by anyone possessing them, no matter the moral quality of their motives. Ultimately, power belongs to God and is in its most potent expressions at the behest of love. But evil characters, oblivious to the nature and authority of love, are desirous to achieve self-aggrandizement by exercising power over others, and are

33. Due to the sacred character of the tetragrammaton, the ancient Jews reading the Scriptures would substitute "Adonai" and later "Jehovah." The AV and RV use the term "the Lord" for the tetragrammaton.

ready to use base means to achieve this end. All attempts to command power other than those made in full harmony with the divine purposes are eventually self-destructive.

The tarot deck works in this manner. It is not an altogether happy symbol because it brings with it the baggage of strong occult connotations. The Grail in *War in Heaven* is weak for the opposite reason: it is too strongly associated with the divine. One would think a stone would be the most fortunate choice, as it is, so to speak, spiritually neutral. But the problem in *Many Dimensions* is that Williams allows it to veer too near to the merely sensational and magical, and, thereby, loses the authenticity of myth.

WAR IN HEAVEN

War in Heaven, the third of the talisman fantasies, is a murder mystery whose plot revolves around a conspiracy to obtain the Holy Graal (Williams's spelling) for evil purposes. In this book Williams evokes the Arthurian myths, a body of story that held deep fascination for him and—to a substantial but perhaps a lesser degree—for C. S. Lewis. [34] According to the legend, the cup with which Christ instituted the

34. See the discussion below on Lewis's *That Hideous Strength*. Williams, a poet of considerable talent, wrote *Taliessin Through Logres* and *The Region of the Summer Stars*, impressively long poems in which he made his own contributions to the Arthurian legends. These, together with his essay "The Figure of Arthur" and C. S. Lewis's essay "Williams and the Arthuriad," are all contained in a one volume edition with an introduction by Mary McDermott Shideler (Grand Rapids, Mich.: Wm. B. Eerdmans, 1974).

Eucharist was brought by Joseph of Arimathea to Britain, secretly deposited in an unknown castle there, and became the object of quest for knights of Arthur's Round Table. In *War in Heaven* the Graal is discovered at a small parish church in the village of Fardles.

The archdeacon at Fardles is one of three characters who become aware of its location; he recognizes its immense historical value to the Church because of its direct association with Christ. Aside from that, he views it as no more important than any other chalice. Nor is he perturbed when in the course of the plot he encounters evil characters indulging in occult practices. The forces of true spiritual good are not commanded by magic. Composed and unflappable, he holds that "one shouldn't be put out of one's stride by anything phenomenal and accidental," since "a just man wouldn't be." [35] To him, the occult is "a result of the lack of true religion in these days and a wrong curiosity," an attitude one can safely take to be Williams's own.

Sir Giles Tumulty and Gregory Persimmons, two characters who lack true religion and possess perverse curiosity, also become aware of the Graal's location at Fardles. They assume the chalice is invested with great spiritual power which they desire to command. Sir Giles is an "explorer and antiquarian" deeply versed in occult lore, and in this fantasy (he also appears in *Many Dimensions*) has submitted for publication a manu-

35. Charles Williams, *War in Heaven* (Grand Rapids, Mich: Wm. B. Eerdmans, 1980), 21.

script in which he conjectures that the Graal is at Fardles. In fact, the archdeacon becomes aware of the Graal's being in his church by his chance seeing of Sir Giles's manuscript. Tumulty's publisher is the firm of Gregory Persimmons, who has for years been deeply fascinated by the occult. When Persimmons learns of the Graal's location, he steals it; the archdeacon responds, and the action of the story largely consists in the two men vying for possession of the Graal. Their skirmish is viewed in terms of their respective character's attitudes and purposes.

As spiritually antithetical characters, the archdeacon and Persimmons represent the two spiritual poles, the righteous and the wicked. The end of the first is union with God; of the second, destruction. In the final scene of the story, the Eucharist is being celebrated by a small group of characters, with the Graal in its appointed place and the archdeacon in his stall. The lesson is read; the words "And God said: Let us make man, in Our image, after our likeness. . . in the image of God created He him, male and female created He them," rivet the attention of the participants. At the same time the archdeacon,

> hearing all these words, trembled a little as he knelt. The thoughts with which he approached the Mysteries faded; the Mysteries themselves faded. He distinguished no longer word from act; he was in the presence, he was part of the Act which far away

issued in those faint words, "Let us make man"—creation rose and flowed out and wheeled to its august
return—"in Our image, after Our likeness"—the
great pronouns were the sound of that return.[36]

He gently collapses and his spirit, along with the
Graal, departs at the foot of the altar. Williams is suggesting that the act of creation reaches its acme in the
completion of the genuinely godly man. He quotes
earlier a favorite passage of his from the Athanasian
Creed that affirms that the divine end is achieved "not
by conversion of the Godhead into flesh, but by taking
of the manhood into God"; the archdeacon illustrates
the principle. The "steady movement of creation" flows
through the Graal; that is, the purpose and end of God
in creation is the lifting of people into holy union with
Himself; the Eucharist symbolizes the union that is
experientially effected in the godly life.

Because they are seen primarily in their spiritual
dimensions, Williams's characters move on the level of
myth. He carefully avoids pietist descriptions of the
good, emphasizing instead their confident attitudes
and virtuous actions. The evil manifest perverted religious attitudes; evil is a perversion of the good. They
have a strong attraction to occult practices, and in their
dedicated pursuit of these sacrifice whatever vestiges of
virtue and humanity they yet have; Gregory
Persimmons is a good example of this type.

36. Williams, *War in Heaven*, 253.

[H]e was the only one who had a naturally religious spirit; to him only the unknown beyond man's life presented itself as alive with hierarchical presences arrayed in rising orders to the central throne. To him alone sacraments were living realities; . . . the Black Mass, the ritual and order of worship. He beyond any of them demanded a response from the darkness; a rush of ardent faith believed that it came; and in full dependence on that faith acted and influenced his circumstances. Prayer was natural to him as it was not to Sir Giles. . . and to the mind of the devotee the god graciously assented. Conversion was natural to him, and propaganda, and the sacrifice both of himself and others, if that god demanded it. He adored as he lay in vigil, and from that adoration issued the calm strength of a supernatural union. [37]

His god is Satan, to whom he duplicates attitudes quite like those Christians should exercise towards God in Christ. To the nominal Christians in the story he seems quite amiable and exemplary, and in the unregenerate world at large he is respected and emulated.

In his worship of Satan, Gregory concludes that in addition to the Graal he needs a child sacrifice. Much of the plot develops around his attempt to seduce for his diabolic purposes little Adrian Rackstraw, the only child of a worker at Persimmon's publishing firm. Dramatic energy is generated by the degree to which he nearly

37. Williams, *War in Heaven*, 174.

attains his diabolic end. The particular achievement of this novel lies in the degree to which Williams invests his characters with mythic dimensions, intensifying the reader's sense of the moral and spiritual momentousness of seemingly ordinary human actions.

ALL HALLOWS' EVE

In a progression up the hierarchy of spiritual evil, above Gregory Persimmons stands Father Simon, the powerful necromancer and Antichrist figure in Williams's final novel, *All Hallows' Eve*. This work thematically contrasts love versus hate, self versus selflessness, false spirituality versus true. Much of its strength as myth derives from the convincing growth in virtue that occurs in the two main characters, Lester Furnival and Betty Wallingford. We see these women becoming loving people and, in so doing, acquiring true selves. They, together with their respective men companions, form a community of the redeemed that contrasts sharply with those characters whose course, due to their own self-centered actions, is downwards to destruction.

As Antichrist, Father Simon is a pathetic but, nevertheless, frightening similitude to God. He is his own god, consumed with himself and preoccupied with acquiring power over others. A great religious leader in the eyes of the world, he has two counterparts in Asia and the Far East, forming a diabolical trinity. Preaching love, joy, and peace, he conceives of these as a sort of patronage extended to people whom he sees as vastly inferior to himself, in whom he would create a stupor of contentment, and from whom he expects absolute submission and worship (parallel in many ways to Dostoyevski's Grand Inquisitor). Simon even exercises power to the extent of creating a "human" body for the incarnation of two spirits; the best he can do, however, is an inept and wretched caricature of a true incarnation. Desiring to extend his domain of power to include the world of departed spirits, he begets and raises a child, Betty Wallingford, whom he devises to send into that nether world in order to achieve, by means of the reversed tetragrammaton, a devilish exchange for one of the departed there.

At the beginning of the narrative, we are given an intriguing depiction of the nether world of recently departed souls, a realm of transition in which the soul is enroute to either heaven or hell. Two young women, Lester Furnival and Evelyn Mercer, are newly arrived there (an airplane had crashed upon them). The atmosphere is mythic, its nature appropriate to their spiritual states. They move through the streets of a City of the Dead—a replica of London—composed of facades and empty of people, a world in which "all meaning had been left behind," [38] yet a place where

38. Charles Williams, *All Hallows' Eve* (Grand Rapids, Mich.: Wm. B. Eerdmans, 1981), 16. Williams's nether world bears interesting comparison to C. S. Lewis's in *The Great Divorce*, a fantasy published in 1945, the year of Williams's death. The subject evidently fascinated them both, and no doubt formed a part of their many conversations during those years when Williams was a integral part of the Inklings.

words have a startling exactitude and finality.

Wandering in this haunting loneliness, Lester and Evelyn reveal their true selves; neither seems admirable to the reader. Lester, who in life had been more interested in gadgets and material things than in people, has nevertheless a modicum of concern for Evelyn, who through ceaseless chatter shows herself consumed by self-pity and hatred. Recently married to Richard, Lester had made some effort to make their marriage a success. As the story progresses, she grows in virtue through more loving deeds, acts that illustrate Williams's convictions of substitution and exchange.

Richard, bereft of his wife, seeks the companionship of his friend, Jonathan Drayton, an artist of considerable talent who is engaged to Betty. In his paintings he purposes to achieve "common observation and plain understanding"; in other words, he feels that the function of art is to discover and reveal something of the glory that really resides in the objective world. Two of his paintings that are on display in his studio become central symbols in the novel. They capture with compelling force the spiritual qualities of their subjects. The one is of a City, the buildings of which are of heightened colors and powerfully emit light from a hidden source; it suggests the glory of reality truly seen. The other is of his future father-in-law, Father Simon, revealing him to be the harbinger of spiritual death.

In the scene in which Father Simon ruthlessly attempts to send the physically weak and timid Betty into the nether world in exchange for a spirit who will bring him the knowledge of the dead, he tries to exercise the power of the reversed tetragrammaton. By his doing so Betty and Lester meet, and Simon's effort is defeated by the greater power of love exercised between the two women. Lester confesses and Betty forgives her the wrongs she had previously committed, and in an act of joyous exchange Lester enables Betty to resist successfully Simon's sinister machinations.

Together with these exchanges, romantic love also performs its spiritual functions. Lester and Betty both act in a Beatrician role to their respective lovers. Richard is reborn, and Jonathan, admirable throughout the narrative, is strengthened through Betty in his serious artistic purpose. At the climax of the narrative, as this foursome is seated in a room with Jonathan's picture of light flooding a City, the light from the picture is "within the room also and vibrated there," and they seem to participate themselves in it. [39] In a mythic culmination, their purified acts are seen to merge with the acts of the City; that is, they are seen to be deeds of the true spiritual nature. Lester then is received into Zion by the triumphant dead on this All Hallows' Eve, while Evelyn is left in "that other City, there to wait and wander and mutter till she found

39. Williams, *All Hallows' Eve*, 234.

what companions she could." [40] In the end Father Simon sinks into the hell of himself.

In *All Hallows' Eve*, Williams presented with startling clarity his convictions of how eternity permeates time and human acts have eternal consequences. An active participation in the Way of Exchange, together with the substitutionary love it entails, is essential to mythic discernment and becomes an integral part of what it means to live a complete life.

Charles Williams's keen and thoughtfully crafted theological vision, caught in the epigram "This also is Thou; neither is this Thou," shaped both his life and his writings. In his novels, he achieved an authoritative depiction of the spiritual reality by which both human beings and the entire created world coinhere. He built upon the work of Chesterton and MacDonald, insisting that to see life rightly is to see it as sacred, but went beyond them in developing a convincing mythical vision of the unseen world.

---

40. Williams, *All Hallows' Eve*, 269.

6

J. R. R. Tolkien
Myth and Middle Earth
(1892–1973)

If men were ever in a state in which they did not want
to know or could not perceive truth (facts or evidence),
then Fantasy would languish until they were cured. If
they ever get into that state (it would not seem at all
impossible), Fantasy will perish, and become Morbid
Delusion. . . . Fantasy remains a human right: we make
in our measure and in our derivative mode, because we
are made: and not only made, but made in the image
and likeness of a Maker. [1]

Here we meet. . . the motive (to become dominant in
Hobbits) that the great policies of world history, 'the
wheels of the world', are often turned not by the Lords
and Governors, even gods, but by the seemingly
unknown and weak—owing to the secret life in

1. J. R. R. Tolkien, "On Fairy Stories," *The Tolkien Reader* (New York: Ballantine
Books, 1966), 75. This essay was first given as the Andrew Lang Lecture at the
University of St. Andrew's in 1938. It appeared in print in *Essays presented to Charles
Williams* (Oxford University Press, 1947); and then in *Tree and Leaf* (London:
George Allen & Unwin, 1964). It is a classic statement on the nature of fairy tales
and contains provocative assertions on the relation of the Gospels to them. For a
fuller discussion of this subject, see chapter 7 on Lewis.

creation, and the part unknowable to all wisdom but One. . . . [2]

n order to explore the "secret life in creation," J. R. R. Tolkien cast his art in the literary type termed fairy tales. While fairy tales are not automatically mythical, they create an atmosphere that is especially suited to the character of myth. Tolkien also saw that fairy tales were perfectly suited to Christian theology. Both fairy tales and Christianity demand belief in other worlds, and, while those of Christian conviction exist quite beyond the reach of the imagination, those envisioned in fairy tales (defined as he defines them) can offer insights unavailable to any other mental activity.

The atmosphere of fairy tales yields enchantment, the charm people feel when they glimpse something of the benign mystery of the universe. "Faerie itself may perhaps most nearly be translated by Magic—but it is magic of a peculiar mood and power, at the furthest pole from the vulgar devices of the laborious, scientific, magician," he explained. [3] It excites the human spirit to the point of deep-seated delight. This magic differs from ordinary magic in that it possesses an organic or natural air. The magic of the magician is manipulative and crude, motivated by the desire to

2. Humphrey Carpenter, ed., #131, *The Letters of J. R. R. Tolkien* (Boston: Houghton Mifflin, 1981), 143.
3. Tolkien, *Reader*, 39.

wield power over nature; that which enchants induces an exultation in the rightness of life, creates joy, and issues in humility. The atmosphere of myth is indispensable to portraying it. Fantasies that evoke this sense take us into a secondary world in which we experience escape, recovery, and consolation.

Tolkien was charmed by an anecdote he found while reading one of Chesterton's essays, about how Charles Dickens was seized with a strange feeling when on a dark London day he saw MOOREEFFOC written upon the glass door of a coffee room, and then realized he was viewing it from the inside. [4] Tolkien felt that one must look beyond the every day sameness and discover new perspectives from which the familiar look odd. When we experience the pleasant shock of entering a plausible fantasy world, we briefly escape from the dehumanizing and degrading aspects of our mechanized (and now computerized) society. This effect—which he calls recovery—is positive and exhilarating: we recover a sense of the preciousness of things. We begin to see them apart from possessiveness and self-advantage. Myth enables us to see the world with fresh attention, prompting us to cease taking things for granted and discover their full integrity. [5]

The result is humility and consolation. In the world of fairy tales, goodness has its proper beauty and

4. Tolkien, *Reader*, 77.

5. For a fuller discussion of recovery, see C. S. Lewis, "Tolkien's *The Lord of the Rings*," *Of This and Other Worlds* (London: Collins, 1982), 112-21.

certain deep and ancient desires—such as conversing with animals or traveling backwards through time—are satisfied. Perils and dire threats are real; failure and sorrow exist in all their startling momentousness, but beyond them is the consolation of the happy ending. The story concludes with that sudden and marvelous grace of happy resolution, and "we get a piercing glimpse of joy, and heart's desire, that for a moment passes outside the frame, rends indeed the very web of story, and lets a gleam come through." [6] Tolkien's understanding of his craft is immensely helpful, but more satisfying still is the degree to which his stories fulfill its promise.

DISCOVERING MYTH

The foundations for Tolkien's achievement were laid in his childhood, when he felt a prodigious interest in languages, the vehicles of myths. Orphaned at the age of twelve, he attended King Edwards (a distinguished grammar school in Birmingham) on scholarship, where he not only studied requisite Latin, Greek, French, and German, but soon delved into Anglo-Saxon, Middle English, and Old Norse, and then began inventing languages of his own. [7] His interest was especially piqued by the epic poems and myths he encountered in the

6. *Reader*, 87.

7. Humphrey Carpenter, *Tolkien: A Biography* (Boston: Houghton Mifflin Company, 1977), 22–37. This is the standard biography, to which I am indebted for biographical details.

remote past, exuding as they did that aura of antiquity that so fascinated him. He later studied comparative philology at Oxford, but his work was interrupted by a stint in the army during World War I. While there he contracted trench fever. During his long convalescence he began composing myths of his own. These myths were the beginning of *The Silmarillion*, which was edited and published posthumously by his son, Christopher, nearly six decades later. [8]

After marrying Edith Bratt, a fellow orphan and his adolescent sweetheart, he began his career as a teacher of Anglo-Saxon. In the early years of his creative output, two types of stories formed in his imagination: one type was built around grand and heroic themes (such as "The Lost Road," with its father and son quest for the ideal kingdom of Númenor); the other type composed for amusement, mostly to tell to his four children as evening entertainment. In 1945 he was elected the Merton Professor of English Language and Literature at Oxford University; this election allowed more time and opportunity to pursue his writing as a private hobby.

J. R. R. Tolkien and C. S. Lewis were both academics who met at Oxford in the 1920s. Tolkien was a devout Roman Catholic, Lewis an atheist. Helped by Tolkien's convictions as to the nature of myth, Lewis

8. First published in London by George Allen and Unwin in 1977, and in Boston by Houghton Mifflin. Christopher has also edited and published posthumously his father's other stories.

was soon converted to Christianity. [9] They were drawn together by their mutual interest in what they termed "northernness," or the mythic aura that arose from Norse myths and legends. It created within both strange longings. Each in his teens had undertaken to compose stories of his own in an attempt to capture that fascinating, elusive quality of desire. Their creative activity as adults was an extension of these early endeavors. Tolkien recalled in a letter: "L[ewis] said to me one day: 'Tollers, there is too little of what we really like in stories. I am afraid we shall have to try and write some ourselves.' We agreed that he should try 'space-travel', and I should try 'time travel.'" "What we really like in stories" he defines in another letter as "discovering Myth." [10]

Tolkien's view of the nature of myth, which Lewis was subsequently to develop and make a cornerstone in many of his writings, affirms that the mythologies of ancient peoples occasionally glimpse "something really higher. Divinity, the right to power (as distinct from its possession), the due worship, human inventions though they may be." This "something really higher" came to full historical realization in the Incarnation of Christ and the consequent salvation of which Christians partake. Amidst the complex narratives of

9. See Humphrey Carpenter, *The Inklings: C. S. Lewis, J. R. R. Tolkien, Charles Williams, and their friends* (Boston: Houghton Mifflin, 1979), 24–45 for a detailed account of their early friendship and Lewis's subsequent conversion.
10. Carpenter, *Letters*, 378, 29.

myth, certain realities are adumbrated which the Christian scriptures reveal to be historical fact. The myth of the dying and rising god, for instance, existing in various forms in so many mythologies, is an adumbration of the historical reality of the death and resurrection of the Son of God.

The historical account in the Gospels of the incarnation, death, and resurrection of Christ is the central eucatastrophe of history. *Eucatastrophe* is Tolkien's term for the essence of consolation—the "happy ending" that affords a joyous sense of conflicts resolved and justice achieved. "There is no tale ever told that men would rather find was true," he states concerning the Incarnation. [11] The pattern portrayed in the life of Christ expresses the complete paradigm upon which successful fantasies draw.

OWEN BARFIELD'S INFLUENCE

Tolkien's view of the nature of mythology and its meaning was directly related to his interest in languages. Language, after all, is the vehicle of myth. Tolkien was influenced by Owen Barfield, [12] a seminal thinker who occasionally contributed to the intellectual dynamic of the Inklings. Barfield came to the group through Lewis; they had been close friends during

11. Carpenter, *Letters*, 72.

12. See especially Owen Barfield, *Poetic Diction* (1928; reprint Middleton, Conn.: Wesleyan, 1973). Verlyn Flieger, *Splintered Light: Logos and Language in Tolkien's World* (Grand Rapids, Mich.: Wm. B. Eerdmans, 1983), 35–87, offers a helpful summary of Barfield's influence on Tolkien's thinking.

their undergraduate days at Oxford. It was the combination of Barfield's and Tolkien's influence that moved C. S. Lewis away from his early atheistic rationalism towards the acceptance of the supernatural and the function of the imagination in perceiving it.[13]

Barfield's work was chiefly in semantics, or the science of meaning. He argued that language in its earliest stage was not metaphorical, as so many students of language have argued, rather it was mythical. Myths present a distinct apprehension of reality. People expressed in their myths the living spiritual presences they perceived in natural phenomena. Languages originally sprung from such mythical perceptions. The languages we know in all their multiplicity are fragmented from ancient tongues of great simplicity and unity, tongues characterized by a deep richness of mythical awareness. The earliest words, therefore, were imbued with an abundant fullness of meaning.

Myths may appear today as "corpses," and even to some (such as the linguist Max Muller) as a kind of disease of language,[14] but in reality

> [T]he myths, which represent the earliest meanings, were not the arbitrary creations of "poets," but the natural expression of man's being and consciousness

13. For a quick summary of the nature of what Lewis called the "great war," the astute intellectual exchanges between himself and Barfield, see Carpenter, *The Inklings*, 36–37.

14. Tolkien, *Reader*, 48. Tolkien is especially incensed by this view.

at the time. These primary "meanings" were *given*, as it were, by Nature, but the very condition of their being given was that they could not at the same time be apprehended in full consciousness; they could not be *known*, but only experienced, or lived. . . . Not man was creating, but the gods—or, in psychological jargon, his "unconscious." [15]

When the "full consciousness" began to "know" what was given, to contemplate it rationally and imaginatively, metaphors followed. The perceived relationships among and between objects gave birth to figurative language; logical processes multiplied vocabularies and inevitably fragmented languages. "Created" meanings took the place of "given" or mythical meanings. Contrary to the accepted idea that words do not mean anything in themselves, but rather it is people who invest words with meaning, Barfield insisted that words came into being as a conveyance of the living meaning in the outer world. Successful "poetic diction," the language used by true poets, recovers something of the original richness of meaning, vestiges of which still reside in words themselves.

One can quickly see the influence of such thinking upon Tolkien. He was such a lover of languages that he invented new ones as a pastime, and his fantastic worlds were created to answer to the mythological power that resided in them. His elaborate appendixes,

15. Barfield, *Poetic Diction*, 102.

in which he presented in meticulous detail the characteristics of elven languages, attest to the vital role he saw these languages as having in forming the nature of his fantastic worlds. "A language requires a suitable habitation, and a history in which it can develop," he explained to an inquirer. [16]

The power of a language is the power of its mythological energies. Tolkien undertook to replicate this situation in *The Silmarillion*, creating a mythology strongly analogous to the Christian. He proceeded in *The Hobbit* and *The Lord of the Rings* to show life shaped by and responding to its mythological past. *The Silmarillion* gives the pure mythology of the Elder Days; the hobbit stories are set in a subsequent, more realistic period. Prompted by a breathtakingly comprehensive vision, he did on a finite level what God did on an infinite: speak entire worlds into being.

ART AS SUBCREATION

Tolkien's term for artistic composition is "subcreation." Divine reality was his model, myth his mode. Human beings, because they are made in the image of God, though fallen, have in their artistic creations the possibility of envisioning truth. "Fantasy remains a human right: we make in our measure and in our derivative mode, because we are made: and not only made, but made in the image and likeness of a Maker." [17]

16. Carpenter, *Letters*, 375.
17. Tolkien, *Reader*, 55.

He summarized his theory of artistic creation in a poem composed for Lewis:

> The heart of man is not compound of lies,
> But draws some wisdom from the only Wise,
> And still recalls Him. Though now long estranged,
> Man is not wholly lost nor wholly changed.
> Dis-graced he may be, yet is not de-throned,
> And keeps the rags of lordship once he owned:
> Man, Sub-creator, the refracted light
> Through whom is splintered from a single White
> To many hues, and endlessly combined
> In living shapes that move from mind to mind.
> Though all the crannies of the world we filled
> With Elves and Goblins, though we dared to build
> Gods and their houses out of dark and light,
> And sowed the seed of dragons—'twas our right
> (used or misused). That right has not decayed:
> We make still by the law in which we're made. [18]

What is of especial interest in Tolkien's poem is the metaphor of art as refracted light, "splintered from a single White," and "endlessly combined / In living shapes that move from mind to mind." Language is composed of living shapes, words charged with mythical light. People, as speaking beings, are conduits of that light. Here he is echoing Barfield.

The light and word imagery, and the "law in which we're made," also resonate with the thought of St. John:

18. See Flieger, *Splintered Light*, pp. 43ff, for a discussion of the presence of Owen Barfield's thought in this poem.

Christ, the Logos, the Creator, is the "true light that enlightens" everyone (cf. John 1:1–9). Both light and *logos* (to the extent this term signifies words) are the prime agents of perception. Light illumines, words shape and communicate conceptions of reality. When the imagined worlds of literary art properly harmonize with the world God has made, they possess a significance quite beyond themselves. One may recall with renewed insight the psalmist's affirmation, "In thy light do we see light" (Ps. 36:9).

The tone of the poem suggests not only an assurance of the worth of what "we" were doing, but an obligation to do so. In his epilogue to "On Fairy Stories" he explains:

> The Evangelium has not abrogated legends; it has hallowed them, especially the "happy ending." The Christian has still to work, with mind as well as body, to suffer, hope, and die; but he may now perceive that all his bents and faculties have a purpose, which can be redeemed. So great is the bounty with which he has been treated that he may now, perhaps, fairly dare to guess that in Fantasy he may actually assist in the effoliation and multiple enrichment of creation. All tales may come true; and yet, at the last, redeemed, they may be as like and as unlike the forms that we give them as Man, finally redeemed, will be like and unlike the fallen that we know.

The art of the Christian artist can be redeemed and itself be redemptive.

THE SILMARILLION

Although it was not published until after his death, *The Silmarillion* was virtually complete before Tolkien began his hobbit stories. When his publishers asked for a sequel to *The Hobbit*, he offered them *The Silmarillion*, only to have it turned down. He then composed *The Lord of the Rings*, a tale that quickly grew to epic proportions. Having shaped its imagined world directly upon the mythology of *The Silmarillion*, he felt the two really composed an integrated whole and sought to persuade his publisher to publish them together, making one extended "Saga of the Jewels and the Rings." The publisher, however, did not want to financially risk publishing so much material at once.

Readers today greatly profit from experiencing the two together. If one comes to the reading of Tolkien as an adult without having encountered as a child his hobbit stories, the place to begin is with his initial body of mythology contained in *The Silmarillion*. The result will be a still greater appreciation for the mythological foundation of Middle Earth and the role of myth in the action. The genealogical, geographical, and historical allusions that may otherwise seem obscure and, at times superfluous, will become an indispensable part of the whole.

The text of *The Silmarillion* is a compilation of accounts purported to emerge out of ancient dreamtime by means of a long oral tradition, finally written by various unknown scribes and bards. Therefore, one should not expect a full consistency among the various retellings of the myths. The text consists of five different sections, the "Questa Silmarillion" being the first and largest. The complexity of the nomenclature and the geography of Beleriand, that country in Middle Earth where most of the action is set, is augmented by the addition of a glossary, maps, and genealogical tables.

Tolkien created with dexterity that aura of myth he and Lewis both so highly prized. The mythic atmosphere does more to keep one reading than does plot, action, or even the development of themes. Precisely what moments in the text excite the sense that something ineffable beyond the walls of the known world is being communicated will vary from reader to reader. Among the finest moments may be those in which the reader catches glimpses of the glory emitted from the Blessed Realm, Aman, the home of the Valar who dwell by the Outer Sea. The depictions of the radiance shining from the trees of Valinor and instilled by the elfish artist Fëanor in the Silmarils is a prime instance.

A full recounting of Tolkien's elaborate plots and the myriad of characters and episodes that pertain to Middle Earth would not directly serve the purpose of

our study. Indeed, there is no substitute for the
delightful task of immersing oneself in the vigorous
and trenchant realism of his imagined worlds.
Creation, and its consequent subcreation, is a primary
theme of *The Silmarillion*: first, the creation by Ilúvatar,
or God Most High, of the various echelons of supernatural beings and earthly inhabitants. On earth the
First-born are the elves, immortal until men arrive;
their fate is to fade away from Middle Earth and
become a secret people.

Those whom Ilúvatar created may in their turn sub-
create. The "Quenta Silmarillion" not only presents an
authentic mythology of the origins of the world, elves,
and men; the imagery also composes a sort of allegory
on the nature of subcreation with an emphasis upon
misuse. Various subcreators work with "splintered
Light," beginning with the supernatural Valar, continuing with Yavanna, spouse of the Valar Aulë, and then
Fëanor, a talented elvish craftsman. Yavanna creates the
resplendent Trees of Valinor from whose fruit the sun
and moon are made. They emit such supernatural light
that all who see them are filled with awe and wonder.
Fëanor takes some of the wondrous light and creates
the Silmarils, jewels which in turn emit awesome light.
The works of Yavanna and Fëanor are examples of subcreation, and are blameless. Because the elves create
their art through magic, it is untainted by human lim-
itations: "more effortless, more quick, more complete

(product and vision in unflawed correspondence)." [19]
Such art, as a type of subcreation, possesses a high spiritual and moral quality.

ART AND EVIL

While a proper attitude toward art has its rewarding
place in the eternal order of things, improper attitudes
have dire consequences. The fall of the elves occurs
when they abuse their artistic gifts. Melkor—the Valar
who is Tolkien's surrogate for the biblical Lucifer—
becomes consumed with desire to possess the Silmarils.
His covetousness not only issues in discontent, lust,
self-will, arrogance and greed, but it also eventuates in
the destruction of the First Age of Middle Earth. The
"Quenta Silmarillion" presents the earliest story of his
seizing of the Silmarils and the ensuing struggle of
elves and men against him and his chief henchman
Sauron to retrieve them; this struggle is known as the
War of the Jewels.

The war, however, is not cast simply as a struggle of
good versus evil inasmuch as both sides are culpable.
Melkor takes the jewels to Angband, his stronghold in
the far North. Various elves then desire to repossess
them, and in their passion fall into similar sins. Most of
the tales that follow involve attempts to recapture the
jewels by sundry of the elven lords, detailing their

19. Tollien to Milton Waldman," *Letters*, 146. This letter, written in response to his
prospective publisher asking for a "sketch" of his imaginary world, contains a wealth
of statement as to Tolkien's thematic intentions.

strategies and bravery. The desire to have and to control these products of elven magic is a corrupting force, and the outcome of the War of the Jewels is disaster. Melkor and Sauron are overcome but not destroyed. The Silmarils are lost to the elves, being cast into the depths of earth, sea, and sky, and the Elder Days or First Age of Middle Earth comes to its conclusion. As men, called the Followers, come increasingly into the saga, the elven population begins to dwindle.

Yoked with the theme of creation is that of the fall and its consequences: "there cannot be any 'story' without a fall," Tolkien explained. "All stories are ultimately about the fall." [20] Creation and the fall are themes central to myth. Tolkien shows how they are inextricably coupled with the nature of art, underscoring the mythic potential that resides in artistic creation—a concept far removed from today's prevailing confusion as to the nature of art.

The power of high art is frustrated when it is appropriated for self-serving ends. The proper response to its power is a renunciation of all personal ambitions in its regard, of self-abnegation in its presence—in short, humility. Wrong attitudes in its regard: ambition, greed, attempts to use it for self-aggrandisement, are all seriously destructive. An overarching theme in Tolkien's fictional universe is that of the paradoxical relation of renunciation to all moral and spiritual

20. Carpenter, *Letters*, 147.

power: this power is achieved only through denial of self-centered and personal aims. Although *The Lord of the Rings* is not concerned with the nature of artistic endeavor, renunciation is essential to Frodo's heroic quest.

Magic, characterized as essentially "good" in Tolkien's world, may be appropriated to evil purposes. Rather than allowing the art it produces to be an autonomous source of delight, evil beings try through it to secure power for "the tyrannous re-forming of Creation,"[21] a direct affront to Ilúvatar. Such attempts seem to occur in cycles: after one is quelled by the forces of good, another soon arises.

THE SECOND AGE OF MIDDLE EARTH

The Second Age, briefly chronicled in the "Akallabêth"— the fourth section of *The Silmarillion*—continues to develop Tolkien's vision of the nature of radical evil. It is the land of Númenor (akin to our fabled kingdom of Atlantis), a land awarded by the Valar to the Dúnedain, men who played an important role in the defeat of evil in the War of the Jewels. They become proud and, discontented with their mortality, rebel. Sauron, who has regained strength after his defeat in the War of the Jewels, beguiles them into the worship of Melkor. He draws them into a war against the Valar; the men are defeated and their land vanishes into the sea. Elendil,

21. Carpenter, *Letters*, 146.

who did not side with Sauron, escapes and founds the kingdoms of Arnor and Gondor in Middle Earth.

Sauron is again defeated and stripped of his power, but he is not annihilated. His continual regaining of power and posing dire threats in succeeding eras embodies Tolkien's vision of the radical and seemingly perpetual existence of evil in time. It is capable of constant renewal of its horrendous reality and dire threats. Each generation must rise to oppose its protean expressions, expending heroic efforts upon the task.

The nature of the heroism necessary for the defeat of evil is one of the great themes of *The Lord of the Rings;* it lies not in acquisition, great physical prowess, or great cunning, but in self-abnegation and renunciation. All personal advantage must be denied, all personal aggrandizement forsaken, all sacrifices must be made. Renunciation is a principle found throughout the Bible, from Abraham's renouncing his homeland to make a journey into the unknown to Christ's humiliation and death. It is neither natural nor easy, it makes little sense to the worldly wise, but the theme commands great mythic power. It arouses an instinctive awe and admiration in all who observe it in action. Reading *The Silmarillion* lays the foundation for a greater appreciation of the theme of renunciation explored in *The Lord of the Rings.* But between the myth and the epic lies the classic children's story, *The Hobbit.*

THE HOBBIT

One day, sitting in his study grading examination papers, Tolkien discovered one student had turned in among his essays a blank sheet of paper. He wrote across it: "In a hole in the ground there lived a hobbit," and the newly coined name began to generate a story in his mind. When his children and the Inklings delighted in his reading *The Hobbit* to them, he offered it for publication. The invention of this race of Little Folk [22]—perhaps more than any other of his many creations—is the measure of Tolkien's imaginative achievement. *The Hobbit* is an excellent volume to introduce young people to fantasy and myth—it displays his understanding of a child's world and his ability to engross their minds imaginatively.

The Hobbit shows that acts of renunciation are of superior heroic stature to those of acquisition. The latter alone cannot overcome evil. After the hero Bilbo is introduced and his hobbit nature established, he is enlisted by the wizard Gandalf to accompany a party of dwarves as their "burglar" on an expedition to retrieve their treasure, stolen by the dragon Smaug. The object of the dwarves' mission is the repossessing of their rightful riches. After many harrowing adventures, in which the party is opposed by such creatures as goblins,

22. I am indebted to Robert Foster, *The Complete Guide to Middle Earth* (New York: Ballantine, 1978) for checking my own recollections of Tolkien's immensely complex world.

wolves, and giant spiders, and helped by others, such as eagles, men and elves, they approach the Lonely Mountain and the dragon's den.

After Bilbo is successful in enabling the dwarves to recover their cache, he secretly takes for himself the fabulous white Arkenstone as part of the share he has been promised for his work. He reaches the zenith of his heroism, however, when he renounces the Arkenstone. When the elves and the dwarves are about to go to war over the treasure, Bilbo heroically offers the elves the Arkenstone to settle their claim. Gandalf suddenly reappears to commend Bilbo for his renunciation. When he is finally offered his share of the treasure, Bilbo, disillusioned, again declines wealth, taking home with him only what he can carry on his pony. The theme of renunciation is at the climax of the tale. In keeping with the "there and back" journey of quest romance, he returns to his home in the Shire.

THE LORD OF THE RINGS

The Hobbit was an immediate popular success with children, but Tolkien was dissatisfied. He began to feel he had betrayed the genre of fairy stories by implying they were only children's fare. In the year following its publication, he delivered the Andrew Lang Lecture at the University of St. Andrews. His lecture, "On Fairy Stories," shaped a definitive apologetic for the genre he regarded as perhaps the highest type of literature. "If

fairy story as a kind is worth reading at all it is worthy
to be written for and read by adults." [23]

Tolkien's publisher was clamoring for a sequel to
The Hobbit, but he launched instead into the immense
task of composing the massive *Lord of the Rings*.
Although for convenience it was published in three
volumes, it is not a trilogy, but rather a modern saga
divided into six books (two in each volume). It is an
impressive attempt to embody the highest qualities of
the genre he loved.

Scholars have remarked concerning the similarity
among the adventures of *The Hobbit* and *Lord of the
Rings*: the latter can be viewed as a rewriting of the former, many episodes being similar but reworked for the
adult mind; further, the patterns of events established
early in Frodo's journey are repeated as the tale progresses. The scheme is, in other words, cyclic, as on the
highest level are the three ages of Middle Earth. The
most characteristic expressions of the cycle are the
rhythmic recurrences of good and evil events. The history of the rings, recounted by Gandalf to Frodo and
later enlarged upon at the council at Rivendell, reaches
back into the dream-time of the Elder Days. The
struggle between good and evil, having its origins in
the creation myths recounted in *The Silmarillion*,
perennially recurs.

23. Tolkien, *Reader*, 67.

The original rings were created when Sauron convinced the elves that through their art they could establish a paradise on earth. The series of rings they crafted gave their possessors certain powers, chief among them the means to retard change. The rings were distributed among elves, dwarves, and men. Learning from their craft, Sauron shaped in the Mountain of Fire One Ring that enabled him to wield control over the others, granting himself absolute power.

In moving from the Silmarils to the Ring for his central unifying symbol, Tolkien shifts the readers' attention from the mythic glory of high art to the threat of sheer power. The Ring inevitably issues evil in the hands of all who lack the wisdom and goodness to exercise it; only One possesses these requisites and has the right to power. For all others, to presume to know what is good for others and to wield power to impose it upon them is to sin. The Ring is imbued with great mythic potency; it also is a symbol suggesting a vital moral significance.

In *The Lord of the Rings*, Tolkien successfully created a world that blends realistic and mythic elements with a greater sense of realism than the world of *The Silmarillion*. Much of the presentation of the rugged terrain through which Frodo and his party travels is described in detail, and the characters are presented with emotions—loves, desires, and fears—that easily invite reader identification. At the same time, this world is

permeated with a compelling quantity of myth, investing everything with a momentousness quite beyond that
of simple realism. One result, as Lewis pointed out in his
review of *The Lord of the Rings*, [24] is that we as readers
experience recovery; our fascination with this imagined
world enriches our appreciation for the world we live in.
While the world of *The Lord of the Rings* is less mythic
than that of *The Silmarillion*, it brings the power of myth
more forcibly to bear on us.

THE WIZARDS

Wizards form one of the links between *The
Silmarillion* and *The Lord of the Rings*. Much of the
mythic atmosphere derives from them, both because of
the magic powers they command and because of the
way they illustrate the theme of self-advantage vs.
renunciation. They were given their powers for the
purpose of opposing the machinations of Sauron:

> [I]t is said among the Elves that they were messen-
> gers sent by the Lords of the West to contest the
> power of Sauron, if he should arise again, and to
> move Elves and Men and all living things of good
> will to valiant deeds. In the likeness of Men they
> appeared, old but vigorous, and they changed little
> with the years, and aged but slowly, though great
> cares lay on them; great wisdom they had, and many
> powers of mind and hand. [25]

24. Lewis, *Of This and Other Worlds*, 112–21.
25. Tolkien, *The Silmarillion* (London: George Allen and Unwin, 1977), 372.

During the Third Age of Middle Earth, they are chief among those who effect magic, both good and evil. Among them are Gandalf—one of Tolkien's most engaging creations—and Saruman (not to be confused with Sauron, the Maiar who serves Melkor). Saruman succumbs to the desire for personal power and in *Lord of the Rings* tempts Gandalf to seize the Ring with him and employ its powers for "good." Although to use the Ring for good seems reasonable and proper, it is insidiously wrong, because the good is unknowable to all wisdom but Ilúvatar's. He alone will realize ultimate good through his "secret workings" in creation.

Possessed of great wisdom, Gandalf labors in full harmony with these workings, even though he does not himself fully understand them. He is enveloped in mystery: he is often absent from the narrative, combating evil on a level and in a manner never fully explained. The reader, whose curiosity is piqued but not satisfied, becomes more aware that the cosmic moral struggle has dimensions extending far beyond human understanding. When early in the story Gandalf refuses the Ring offered him by Frodo, his vehement rejection of it dramatically underscores not only its powerful appeal but also Gandalf's strength of resolve and the moral grandeur of his refusal:

> "No!" cried Gandalf, springing to his feet. "With that power I should have power too great and terrible....

I do not wish to become like the Dark Lord himself.
Yet the way of the Ring to my heart is by pity, pity
for weakness and the desire of strength to do good.
Do not tempt me! I dare not take it, not even to keep
it safe, unused. The wish to wield it would be too
great for my strength." [26]

That Gandalf renounces power because he does not
trust his own wisdom and instincts—even though he
seems to be the epitome of all that is good, wise, and
admirable—establishes a strong precedent for Frodo's
renunciation that results in his long quest.

ARCHETYPAL IMAGES

The archetypal images that we have noted provide the
basic structure in mythic literature—the journey, trial,
deliverance and renunciation—permeate *The Lord of
the Rings* in tight combination. Early in the narrative,
Frodo repeats the resolve Bilbo has made before him:
"The Road goes ever on and on / Down from the door
where it began, / Now far ahead the Road has gone, /
And I must follow, if I can. . . ." Life, as a journey, is
shrouded in mystery. In terms of the resolve necessary
to stay upon it and the trials of the way, it is as narrow
a road as Bunyan's. The force of destiny is balanced
against freedom of choice and commitment to duty: he
"must follow," if he can. Frodo is one of the "seemingly
unknown and weak" who, "owing to the secret life in

26. Tolkien, *The Fellowship of the Ring* (New York: Ballantine, 1995), 95.

creation," help turn the wheels of the world. After the Ring is destroyed, the long concluding section is filled with the rewards proper to heroic achievement, offering a fitting sense of consolation.

The journey undertaken by Frodo and his helpers is beset with a series of trials. The journey is also an inner one: as Frodo's retiring hobbit-qualities and early hesitation are overcome, his outlook broadens, and his pluck deepens by the events occurring on the Road. The nobility of servanthood—a frequent theme in the fantasies we have been considering—is forcibly presented in the self-effacing constancy of Sam, Frodo's inseparable friend. It is indispensable to effecting the deliverance of the entire cosmic scheme from the dire threat of enthrallment to Sauron's evil power.

TYPICAL EPISODES

Tolkien employs three types of images to create the atmosphere of enchantment. He maintains a sense of the glory that surrounds the good throughout the narrative, but its majesty and its preeminent desirability is perhaps most apparent in the images of women, languages, and landscapes (especially trees). Escape, recovery, and consolation result from them, all working to suggest something of the secret life of creation. Occurrences of these images are often preceded by horrendous encounters with evil, instances when Frodo and his party are exposed to the severity of evil, its subtle entrapping power, its vicious aggressiveness, and the desolation and death it proffers.

After Frodo's initial encounters with the Black Riders and Barrow-wights, he and his party meet Tom Bombadil, one of the most intriguing episodes in the entire saga. Strongly mythic, he represents an immense antiquity, the "Master" over whom the Ring has no power and to whom it has no appeal. Tom is a force for good that predates and transcends evil; he even expresses an indifference towards the Ring. His mythic consort is Goldberry, the first of Tolkien's women that move in an atmosphere of mythic wonder and seem to bestow a benediction upon all that surrounds them. She exudes confidence and joy as she administers hospitality to the wonder-struck Frodo and his party:

> "Fair lady Goldberry!" said Frodo at last, feeling his heart moved with a joy that he did not understand. He stood as he had at times stood enchanted by fair elven-voices; but the spell that was now laid upon him was different: less keen and lofty was the delight, but deeper and nearer to mortal heart; marvellous and yet not strange. [27]

Later, as the party leaves Bombadil's house and Lady Goldberry escorts them on their way, they survey in her presence the valley of the Brandywine and beyond it, the far horizon. All seems invested with mythic glory: it speaks to them "out of memory and old

27. Tolkien, *Fellowship*, 173.

tales, of the high and distant mountains," and they momentarily feel that they, like Tom, could leap over the intervening hills straight upon them.

Not unlike the women figures in the fantasies of George MacDonald, Tolkien's most readily appear shrouded in myth. There are also shades of Charles Williams's thinking here. These women characters are Beatrician, not so much in beckoning directly to heaven, but in creating a desire to achieve great goodness, a sensation of exhilaration and capability, and an inspiration towards the realization of high destiny. Another instance of such a woman occurs at Rivendell. When Frodo first sees Elrond's daughter Arwen, he beholds a greater loveliness than he had ever "seen before nor imagined in his mind"; the image contributes to the mythic depth of that scene. Her great elven beauty retains something of the resplendence of her mythic ancestor Luthien, the most beautiful of all the Children of Ilúvatar. After the War of the Rings, she becomes consort to Aragorn; her beauty is united with his heroism. She does much to create the consolation Tolkien achieves in that scene.

The episode at Rivendell offers an instance of the mythic power of language. Tolkien's love of language and his view of its mythic power is evident numerous times in the story. We have noted above how his thinking on the mythological character of language is derivative of the semanticist Owen Barfield. At a

moment during the music and camaraderie that follows
the meal in Elrond's house, Frodo is momentarily left to
himself while Bilbo consults with Strider (Aragorn)
concerning the song he is composing. As Frodo overhears the conversation in elven tongues that surrounds
him, he becomes enchanted to the point of swoon:

> At first the beauty of the melodies and the interwo-
> ven words in the Elven-tongue, even though he
> understood them little, held him in a spell, as soon as
> he began to attend to them. Almost it seemed that
> the words took shape, and visions of far lands and
> bright things that he had never yet imagined opened
> out before him; and the firelit hall became like a
> golden mist above seas of foam that sighed upon the
> margins of the world. Then the enchantment became
> more and more dreamlike, until he felt that an end-
> less river of swelling gold and silver was flowing over
> him, too multitudinous for its pattern to be compre-
> hended; it became part of the throbbing air about
> him, and it drenched and drowned him. Swiftly he
> sank under its shining weight into a deep realm of
> sleep. [28]

Through the elven language he has caught sight of a
high, ethereal reality, one more appropriate to dream
than waking, that envelopes his entire being. He has
been enchanted by something whose essence exists at
the heart of language, a mythic reality momentarily
glimpsed. In his swoon he hears Bilbo reciting a poem

28. Tolkien, *Fellowship*, 307.

of mesmerizing rhythms and melodic diction that relates the myth of the Eärendil.

Preeminent among Tolkien's mythic women figures is the elvish queen Galadriel who reigns in Lothlorien, the kingdom at which the party arrives near the end of book 2. The episode provides perhaps the strongest delineation of mythic goodness in the saga. It conjoins a woman of great mythological beauty with a landscape unblemished by evil, and it provides a context of heightened reality for an important act of renunciation.

Lothlorien is an unfallen elvish kingdom; in entering it Frodo feels as though "he had stepped over a bridge of time into a corner of the Elder Days, and was now walking in a world that was no more." [29] It represents Tolkien's strongest attempt to translate mythic glory into the more realist setting of *The Lord of the Rings*, an effort that stands in instructive contrast to the descriptions of the mythic in *The Silmarillion*. Readers may feel that here the mythic has more force and arouses greater desire simply because of the way it is framed between episodes of dire threat and danger: those of Moria that precede it and of the River Anduin to come.

Lothlorien is a land that does "not fade or change or fall into forgetfulness," kept by a "secret power that holds evil" from it. Nevertheless, the man Boromir, concerning whose character the reader has come to be

29. Tolkien, *Fellowship*, 453.

wary, sees it as a "perilous land," and receives Aragorn's rebuke: "Perilous indeed, fair and perilous; but only evil need fear it, or those who bring some evil with them."[30] Goodness itself is a terror to anyone who clings to any evil intent—as we later learn is the case with Boromir— but it also is feared by normally good people. As the story progresses and the hobbits tell others of Lothlorien, many think of it with apprehension, and call it "perilous." This scene offers another version of the theme of terrible good that we have already noted in George MacDonald's work and will examine again in that of C. S. Lewis.

The purely good can discern some of the secrets of the hearts of others. The charming queen of Lothlorien, Galadriel, possesses a mythic goodness and beauty that has a piercing effect upon those who see her: each feels as though their inner motives are laid bare in her sight. The fact that she already possesses one of the three rings originally crafted for elven-kings accounts for her queenly stature and her successful resistance to Sauron's opposition; she can read his mind but not he hers. The glory of her appearance matches the moral purity of her wisdom; she refuses the Ring when Frodo offers it to her, realizing, as did Gandalf at the beginning of the saga, that even she is not wise enough to wield the power the Ring would afford her. Her refusal is gripping, inasmuch as it involves her

30. Tolkien, *Fellowship*, 455, 439.

acquiescing to the fate of the elves; they are destined to diminish and fade away in the passing of time. Galadriel's wisdom, moral purity, and self-discipline enables her to refrain from grasping a power of which even she is not worthy, and anticipates Frodo's crowning action of renouncing the Ring by destroying it.

Although the text nowhere states as much, the discerning reader may legitimately infer that only God is worthy to wield absolute power over the universe for its ultimate good. The Ring must be destroyed. As the party leaves Lothlorien, Galadriel's gifts to the various members later prove indispensable to the success of their mission, especially the lembas, or elvish waybread that sustains them, and (to Frodo) the crystal phial containing some of the mythic light of Eärendil, to be used to illumine the "dark places" ahead. Through these talismen of her glory and righteous power, the enchantment the entire scene creates has a continuing presence as the story progresses.

FRODO'S HEROIC RESOLVE AND RENUNCIATION

Galadriel resists the lure of the Ring, but Boromir does not. As the party leaves Lothlorien and moves down the River Anduin, the burden of decision for which direction to go rests upon Frodo. As he goes off by himself to decide, Boromir attempts to force him to do what he has long advocated: they should go to Minas

Tirith in Gondor and there enlist the power of the Ring to defeat the Enemy. In short, it is the temptation already refused by Gandalf and Galadriel, to "trust in the strength and truth of Men," marshaling power to effect a human concept of the good. The confrontation precipitates not only Frodo's inner struggle but also his valiant decision:

> "I will do now what I must . . . . This at least is plain: the evil of the Ring is already at work even in the Company, and the Ring must leave them before it does more harm. I will go alone. Some I cannot trust, and those I can trust are too dear to me. . . ."[31]

When Sam insists on joining him, they set off on the last stage of their quest together, and volume 1 closes.

Their epic journey, replete with horrendous trials and heroic exploits, culminates in book 5 with the destruction of the Ring. As Frodo and Sam near their destination, suddenly Gollum appears and attacks Frodo in a last desperate attempt to possess the Ring. As they grapple, Frodo is imbued with mythic splendor and, momentarily standing over Gollum as a being of supernatural strength—"stern, untouchable now by pity, a figure robed in white" holding at its breast a wheel fire—rebukes Gollum to "trouble" him no more.[32]

Frodo stumbles on to the Crack of Doom, a spent creature. Just as we expect him to throw the Ring into

31. Tolkien, *Fellowship*, 519, 20.
32. J. R. R. Tolkien, *The Return of the King* (New York: Ballantine Books, 1995), 272.

the volcanic depths to its complete destruction, he fails
to do so, announcing in a clear voice: "I do not choose
now to do what I came to do. I will not do this deed." [33]
Then suddenly Gollum seizes the Ring and, dancing in
a frenzy of glee at the very brink of the Crack, topples
over the edge to the doom of both.

The scene is significant for it embodies moral
extremes—a person's best intentions versus the inability
of his will to follow through. Frodo provocatively represents human nature, for people have both aspects
within. He is like people who have before them an Ideal
to which they journey but yet cannot realize, whether
through lack of ability or lack of resolve. Frodo both
fails and succeeds in his quest. His failure is certain, but
in such failure lies triumph. For without his quest the
Ring would not have been destroyed. Because it symbolizes power that is evil, the Ring is consumed along
with its victim (who was consumed by it). Evil has
within itself the seeds of its own destruction. With the
doom of the Ring, the entire empire of the Dark Lord
disintegrates. Within the context of myth, Tolkien
explored the nature of good and evil with a purity and
power that realistic literature is hardly able to do.

Another hero emerges in *The Lord of the Rings:* Sam
Gamgee, Frodo's loyal and unfailing servant. He epitomizes the ideal of servanthood, which, in Christian
terms, is the epitome of heroism. He is a foil for Frodo

33. Tolkien, *Return*, 274.

as regards the theme of renunciation. On numerous occasions he sacrifices his own desires, such as those to return to the peace of his garden in the Shire, and, with no thought to his own advantage, continues to think only of the good of his Master and their mission. The character of Sam demonstrates how attractive and desirable goodness incarnate is. The moral beauty and power of self-effacing service for the greater good, therefore—as over against the ghastliness of Sauron's intentions to use power to subdue others to his own advantage—is the most basic theme of *The Lord of the Rings*. In portraying it, both Frodo and Sam are true heroes. Both are exemplary in avoiding pride, the besetting sin of heroism.

Above and beyond the intentions and purposes of all the characters in the saga stands an overarching Power whose purposes will not fail, but whose workings quietly exist outside the conscious awareness of created beings. Its greatest strength is realized through human weakness. The presence of such Power is glimpsed in the text, such as the one contained in Gandalf's statement when he first explains to Frodo that he was meant by a Higher Power to possess the Ring.[34] The sudden transfiguration of Frodo in his struggle with Gollum just prior to the Ring's destruction further attests to the presence of the supernatural in league with the good. Nowhere in the text are decisions freely made by either

34. Tolkien, *Fellowship*, 88.

individual characters or groups abrogated. The One honors without exception the set of the will and works completely through human endeavor. It is, therefore, hardly accurate to call it Fate, as some scholars tend to do. It is the power and purpose of God.

THE JOY OF CONSOLATION

In "On Fairy Stories," Tolkien stressed the importance of consolation: the "imaginative satisfaction of ancient desires" and the joy of the happy ending. He devotes much attention to it in his long ending to *The Lord of the Rings*. The joys of eucatastrophe begin immediately upon the destruction of the Ring. Frodo and Sam are transported to the Land of Ithilien, where Gandalf in gladness and laughter announces the world cleansed of this threat of the Dark Lord. The spirit of relief, freedom, and elation is strongly mythic:

> "A great Shadow has departed," said Gandalf, and then he laughed, and the sound was like music, or like water in a parched land; and as he listened the thought came to Sam that he had not heard laughter, the pure sound of merriment, for days upon days without count. It fell upon his ears like the echo of all the joys he had ever known. But he himself burst into tears. Then, as a sweet rain will pass down a wind of spring and the sun will shine out the clearer, his tears ceased, and his laughter welled up. . . . [35]

35. Tolkien, *Return*, 88.

The highest heroism is that of the human spirit in virtue; the highest honor comes from those who have earned the right to give it.

Continuing in joy, the love that blossoms between Aragorn and Arwen—and Faramir and Éowyn—depicts the beauty of the union of man and woman quite apart from the direct reference to sexual attraction found in realist stories. As their spirits find delight in communion each with the other, a sense of appropriateness and completeness brings the reader delight. Both couples have through their virtuous endeavors earned the right to power, something occasionally glimpsed in the highest myths. [36]

Against the backdrop of the ending of the Third Age of Middle Earth, with its corollary fading of the elvish peoples and the inevitable partings of all members of the Fellowship of the Ring, stands the bliss of the hobbits returning "home" to their beloved Shire. But, alas, all is not well there. Culprits have seized power and a moral blight is corrupting all. The theme of power exercised by unworthy people is here repeated in microcosm, a curse the hobbits repel, but not without effort and cost. Given the date of the composition of the saga, when Hitler's power and threat to Britain was at its height, Tolkien may well be interpreted as warning his fellow Brits that corruption of power could happen even in their beloved "Shire," England. In the

36. Tolkien, *Return*, 283.

new mill that appears in the Shire, with its "rules" posted ubiquitously to govern every aspect of life, he manages to suggest the threat to the quiet freedom and peace of ordinary life posed by industrialism and the managerial mentality. Tolkien's handling of these themes bears interesting comparison to the threats to social well-being that C. S. Lewis depicts in *That Hideous Strength*, a fantasy that was being composed at roughly the same time and read aloud at the Inklings' meetings.

Bilbo, old and decrepit, sails with Frodo and the elves from the Grey Havens out upon the unknown sea to the Far Shore. Here Tolkien attempts the final consolation, that of death as triumphant conclusion to heroic endeavor. They depart under Gandalf's benediction "Go in peace." Tolkien maintains in "On Fairy Stories" that the highest type of story offers "escape from Deathlessness," in marked contrast to the ideal of "endless serial living" offered in inferior works. [37] He is, of course, as a Christian writing a Christian work, [38] not contemplating death as extinction, but rather as escape into life on a higher plane. It is a triumphant escape for all who have been heroic in virtue.

---

37. Tolkien, *Reader*, 85.

38. "*The Lord of the Rings* is of course a fundamentally religious and Catholic work; unconsciously so at first, but consciously in the revision. That is why I have not put in, or have cut out, practically all references to anything like 'religion,' to cults or practices, in the imaginary world. For the religious element is absorbed into the story and the symbolism." Carpenter, *Letters*, 172.

THE IMPORTANCE OF MIDDLE EARTH

The concept of two planes of existence, the historical and the mythical, permeates Tolkien's fantasy writings. In recommending that *The Silmarillion* and *The Lord of the Rings* be published together, he evidently wanted his readers to experience imaginatively these two levels and the relationship between them. At one point in their arduous journey, Frodo and Sam pause to rest and eat. In their conversation, Sam begins comparing their present plight to the "brave things in the old tales and songs," that is, to the mythic level of experience. As regards the tales of adventures that "really" matter, he remarks:

> "Folks seem to have been just landed in them, usually—their paths were laid that way, as you put it. But I expect they had lots of chances, like us, of turning back, only they didn't. And if they had, we shouldn't know, because they'd have been forgotten. We hear about those as just went on . . . . I wonder what sort of tale we've fallen into?" [39]

Against the peril of turning back, Sam emphasizes the possibility of achieving highest honor. The prize—that of participating in the higher, more intense, and unfading reality of myth—is reserved for those who persist and endure. The tenacity of purpose and consistency of action required echoes that demanded of Bunyan's pilgrim.

39. J. R. R. Tolkien, *The Two Towers* (New York: Ballantine Books, 1995), 407.

All tales have a teller. In a letter discussing the alleged "failure" of Frodo, Tolkien makes this provocative remark:

> Frodo deserved all honour because he spent every drop of his power of will and body, and that was just sufficient to bring him to the destined point, and no further. Few others, possibly no others of his time, would have got so far. The Other Power then took over: the Writer of the Story (by which I do not mean myself), "that one ever-present Person who is never absent and never named" (as one critic has said). [40]

In a footnote he identified the Writer as "the One." The Divine Presence is composing a great myth out of history, an eternal narrative of all the Triumphant Dead. Later, as Frodo and Sam watch with great relief the final eruption of Mount Doom, Sam sighs: "What a tale we have been in, Mr. Frodo, haven't we? . . . I wish I could hear it told." [41]

Among the writers in our study, Tolkien extends our sense of the cosmic inclusiveness of myth. A more comprehensive mythological understanding of the universe is difficult to conceive. It issues in a profound Christian vision of the immensity of evil, the mystery of its grip on created beings, and the pernicious quality of its disintegrating and destructive nature. At the

40. Carpenter, *Letters*, 253.
41. Tolkien, *Return*, 281. Cf. Heb. 12:1: "Therefore, since we are surrounded by so great a cloud of witnesses, let us also lay aside every weight, and sin which clings so closely, and let us run with perseverance the race that is set before us."

same time, he develops in his readers a fuller vision of the moral purity, or glory, of the Divine Power whose will will be realized, not at the expense of man, but for his greater good.

Tolkien's most enduring imaginative impact is perhaps his presentation of hobbithood, embodying as it does the virtues that make life most endearing. By depicting the anagogic dimension of life, he presents a fuller vision of human experience than pure realistic fiction can achieve. In choosing to work within the genre of the fairy tale, he paradoxically achieves an intensified realism. Middle Earth, with its maps, elven languages, and its incredibly complex mythology, is as fully and convincingly real as is the fictional world of the most acclaimed of writers. The qualities which Tolkien felt indispensable to success in this genre are themselves characteristics of the mythic vision. Myth arouses desire for escape into a higher reality, generates a recovery of appreciation for the world we know, and entices with the ultimate consolation of a just, eternal reward.

7

C. S. Lewis
Myth and Sehnsucht
(1898–1963)

And this brings me to the other sense of glory—glory as brightness, splendour, luminosity. We are to shine as the sun, we are to be given the Morning Star. I think I begin to see what it means. In one way, of course, God has given us the Morning Star already .... Ah, but we want so much more—something the books on aesthetics take little notice of. But the poets and the mythologies know all about it. We do not want merely to see beauty, though, God knows, even that is bounty enough. We want something else which can hardly be put into words—to be united with the beauty we see, to pass into it, to receive it into ourselves, to bathe in it, to become part of it. That is why we have peopled air and earth and water with gods and goddesses and nymphs and elves—that, though we cannot, yet these projections can, enjoy in themselves that beauty, grace, and power of which nature is the image. . . . For if we take the imagery of Scripture seriously, if we believe that God will one day give us the Morning

Star and cause us to put on the splendour of the sun, then we may surmise that both the ancient myths and the modern poetry, so false as history, may be very near the truth as prophecy. [1]

ewis entitled his account of his conversion from atheism to Christianity, *Surprised by Joy*, a phrase taken from one of Wordsworth's sonnets. He related various experiences beginning with earliest childhood memories and culminating during the Trinity Term in 1929 at Magdalen College, Oxford, when, alone in his quarters he "gave in, and admitted that God was God, and knelt and prayed." [2] The story of his spiritual odyssey is one of being driven by a deep, compelling yearning—he could not tell for what—which he had mysteriously felt on certain specific occasions: as a small child he had stood by a blooming currant bush (which sparked an even earlier memory of a toy garden, a plaything given him by his brother) and felt "an enormous bliss;" on another occasion he had sensed an ineffable charm from the description of autumn in Beatrix Potter's *Squirrel Nutkin;* and on still another, upon reading of the death of Balder, the Norse god of beauty, goodness and wisdom, he had "desired with almost sickening intensity something never to be described." [3] The longing kept recurring, and nothing

1. C. S. Lewis, "The Weight of Glory," in *The Weight of Glory and Other Addresses* (Grand Rapids, Mich.: Wm. B. Eerdmans Publishing Co., 1965), 12-13.
2. C. S. Lewis, *Surprised by Joy* (London: Geoffrey Bles, 1955), 215.
3. Lewis, *Surprised*, 22, 23.

would quench it.

Lewis called this inmost emotion, which drives people to ever new quests which never satisfy, *Sehnsucht*, a German term for yearning or a wistful longing. In the quotation above, he describes it as a desire "to be united with the beauty we see, to pass into it, to receive it into ourselves, to bathe in it, to become part of it." It echoes St. Augustine's well-known statement to God: "You have made us for yourself, and our heart is restless until it rests in you." [4] Lewis's apologetic writings tend to be built upon this desire, and his imaginative works depict many incidents of it. He felt it to be the shaping motive behind the ancient myths, and he was especially impressed with the way those myths stimulated this desire.

MYTH: THE VEHICLE OF REALITY

Like his close friends Charles Williams and J. R. R. Tolkien, Lewis was fascinated with the nature of myth and mythopoeia throughout his career. The largest single influence upon him was that of George MacDonald, whom he hailed as the "greatest genius" in mythmaking that he knew. He freely acknowledged his debt in the preface to his anthology of MacDonald's writings: "I have never concealed the fact that I regarded him as my master; indeed I fancy I have never

4. St. Augustine, *Confessions*, trans., Henry Chadwick (Oxford: Oxford University Press, 1991), 3.

written a book in which I did not quote from him." His greatest fascination with MacDonald, however, was not directed towards what is quotable, nor towards the plots to his stories, but towards the "souls" of his fantasies, that "something inexpressible" which he identified as myth.[5]

As a sixteen-year-old pupil privately tutored in England, he happened to see a copy of MacDonald's *Phantastes* in a bookstall in a railway station and purchased it.[6] Encountering its mythic quality initiated the change in his life that culminated years later when, on a memorable night at Magdalen College, J. R. R. Tolkien convinced Lewis that myth was the very language of truth, and he was soon converted.[7]

With Tolkien's help, Lewis came to see ancient pagan mythologies as conveying vestiges of divine power, true indications of the working of the eternal in time. He no longer viewed them as "lies in silver," unfounded and false in substance (in accordance with the more traditional Christian attitude); they came to be stories that not only suggest the spiritual condition of people but also manifest something of supernatural reality—or mythic truth. One can imagine the excitement Lewis must have felt the night on

5. C. S. Lewis, *George MacDonald: An Anthology* (New York: Macmillan, 1948), 16, 20.

6. C. S. Lewis, *The Great Divorce* (New York: Macmillian, 1946) 58–59.

7. Cf. accounts of Lewis's conversion, such as in Humphrey Carpenter, *The Inklings* (Boston: Houghton Mifflin, 1979), 41–45, and George Sayer, *Jack: C. S. Lewis and his Times* (London: Macmillan, 1988), 129–35.

Addison's walk when Tolkien brought that thought to bear upon him and they talked late into the night. The mystery that had aroused his yearnings since his boyhood was not enticing lies, but Reality itself.

Lewis at various times attempted, in both prose and fiction, to define the nature of myth. [8] While he was often concerned with myth as story, he also saw it as containing something quite distinct from story. In his essay "On Stories," he explained that what he really liked in stories was not the pleasure generated from exciting adventures, but rather, that derived from intuitive encounters with " 'the only real other world' we know, that of the spirit. . . ." One of the functions of true art is to present glimpses of "what reality may well be like at some more central region." [9] The emanations of this higher, essential reality that reach to earth, the very atmosphere of glory which is the inevitable concomitant of all supernatural manifestations of the Real, was what Lewis called myth.

Lewis's concept of myth, therefore, was markedly different from that of many in the literary community at large, who saw it as simply a literary genre, an effort of the human imagination. With Lewis, myth was a

8. Among his many remarks on the nature and function of myth, see especially his essays "On Stories," "Myth Became Fact," and "Religion without Dogma," *God in the Dock* (Grand Rapids, Mich.: Wm. B. Eerdmans, 1970); "On Science Fiction" and "Tolkien's *The Lord of the Rings*," *Of This and Other Worlds*, ed. Walter Hooper (London: Collins, 1982); his preface to *George MacDonald: An Anthology* (New York: Macmillan, 1948); "On Myth," *An Experiment in Criticism* (Cambridge: Cambridge University Press, 1965); and *The Pilgrim's Regress* (1933; Grand Rapids, Mich.: Wm. B. Eerdmans, 1989), 151–57; 170–71.

9. Lewis, *Of This and Other Worlds*, 36, 39.

vehicle by which supernatural reality communicates to man; hence, he emphasized the extraliterary aspect of his concept. "What flows into you from myth is not truth but reality (truth is always *about* something, but reality is that *about which* truth is), and, therefore, every myth becomes the father of innumerable truths on the abstract level." [10] The flow of energy is from Ultimate Reality to the individual, not from the individual imagination upwards.

In *The Great Divorce,* a certain quality of being is necessary for an individual to respond positively to Higher Reality, and, hence, to the mythic atmosphere it exudes. Myth is measured by the effect an encounter has upon receptive readers: "We feel it to be numinous. It is as if something of great moment had been communicated to us." [11] It follows that a given story may be mythic to one person and not to another. Nevertheless, to be a conduit for myth is the highest function of art. Literature that effects such mythic moments conveys to the reader a religious experience. The allegorical account of Lewis's own spiritual journey, *The Pilgrim's Regress,* speaks directly to the point.

THE PILGRIM'S REGRESS

While *The Pilgrim's Regress,* Lewis's first published work after his conversion, was inspired by Bunyan's famous work, John (Lewis's pilgrim) is driven by a

10. Lewis, "Myth Became Fact," *God in the Dock,* 66.
11. Lewis, *An Experiment in Criticism,* 44.

compelling desire, rather than by the obsessive fear that drives Christian from the City of Destruction. John sets out from Puritania, the country of his youth, compelled by his burning determination to find the Island he has seen in the distance. In his preface to the third edition Lewis reaffirmed his earlier conviction that this "dialectic of Desire, faithfully followed, would retrieve all mistakes, head you off from all false paths, and force you not to propound, but to live through, a sort of ontological proof." He remarked: "The only fatal error was to pretend that you had passed from desire to fruition, when, in reality, you had found either nothing, or desire itself, or the satisfaction of some different desire." [12] Such confidence may seem remarkably close to that Goethe suggests in *Faust*, that one may be saved by striving, so long as one does not say to any inferior satisfaction the fatal words: "Abide, you are so fair." The arena for John's striving, however, as opposed to Faust's plunging into sensuous experience, is almost exclusively that of the mind as it confronts various philosophical positions. The regions both to the North and the South of John's narrow way are allegorically redolent with spiritually fatal intellectual errors.

In *The Pilgrim's Regress* Lewis suggested that God

12. C. S. Lewis in his preface to third edition, *The Pilgrim's Regress: An Allegorical Apology for Christianity, Reason and Romanticism* (Grand Rapids, Mich.: Wm. B. Eerdmans, 1989), 10. See Kathryn Lindskoog, *Finding the Landlord: A Guidebook to C. S. Lewis's Pilgrim's Regress* (Chicago: Cornerstone Press, 1995) as a helpful companion for Lewis's difficult work.

had been working throughout ancient history to prepare for His final revelation in Christ. When John
meets the allegorical Father History, he explains that
the Landlord (God) had in earliest times sent the
human race both rules and pictures: the rules of moral
law to the Jewish peoples and the pictures of myth to
the pagan world. Both are calculated to arouse the
desires of humanity for the coming of Christ and the
Christian Way of grace; both are inadequate of themselves and have been rendered dangerous by the efforts
of the "agents of the Enemy" to pervert them to wrong
ends. Nevertheless, "the Landlord succeeded in getting
a lot of messages through." [13] Such gracious divine
efforts continue throughout history: the images of
woman in chivalric times and those of nature in the
early nineteenth century, John is told, are two further
instances of divine workings through myth.

The characters John meets all promise him satisfac-
tions that he finds to be false, mistaken, or inadequate—
until he bows to the wisdom of Mother Kirk, repudiates
all alternatives, and abandons himself to the conversion
she prescribes. He now discovers that his desire for the
Island finds fulfillment in his newfound perception of
the Landlord, whose true character stands in marked
contrast to the one so dreaded in his childhood and
maligned by those whom he had met on the road.

His vision of the Island across a vast sea is revealed

13. Lewis, *Regress*, 153.

to him to be the backside of the mountains of the Landlord; he has come "half-round the world" only to glimpse the place he started. But he has to cross the brook to reach the ultimate object of his desire—the brook in his own childhood country of Puritania. His companion Vertue comments that it seems they have "crossed the brook"—dealt with Death—already in their conversion experiences. "You will meet the brook more often than you think: and each time you will suppose that you have done with it for good," a guide tells him. "But some day you really will." The brook reminds one of Bunyan's river which Christian must cross to attain the Celestial City, the river of death; Lewis emphasized the ongoing need to die in life spiritually.

John must now live the spiritual life, imaged in the fantasy by his essentially retreading his former journey—hence, the "regress" of the title. Although John now finds the way "twice as narrow and twice as dangerous" as formerly, all appears altered. Mr. Sensible's house is no more because, in terms of the Christian realities John now sees, there are no sensible alternatives to Christian commitment. Mr. Sensible now appears "so near to nonentity . . . that he is now invisible." The Valley of Wisdom, once so impressive, now appears to be "the twilight porches of the black hole."

John's adventures conclude by his slaying the dragons of North and South, images for the opposing mental attitudes of cold intellectual Stoicism on the one hand and hot sensual perversions of emotional experience on the other. From the slaying of the dragons he inherits certain qualities: from the breath of the slain dragon of the North he gains a fortitude and keenness of mind, and from sinking his teeth deeply into the heart of the dragon of the South he gains a passionate courageousness. The allegory closes with John and Vertue returning to Puritania and crossing the brook for the final time.

The final portion of the allegory, following John's submission to Mother Kirk, is less vivid and convincing than the earlier scenes of John's desperate attempts to cross the Great Chasm by any means other than that offered by Mother Kirk. Lewis's forte is his keen-minded ability to expose the shortcomings of all attempts of the soul—no matter how sophisticated—to avoid or ignore the claims of Christian truth. His clever allegorical presentations of them lends imaginative verve to his devastating refutations.

The allegory may be felt to be uneven and sometimes tedious in its complexity (are three pale men really necessary?), but many of his characters are neatly individualized (e.g., Vertue, Mr. Enlightenment) and the descriptions of nature along the journey pervade the atmosphere of the abstract with that of felt reality. These features, together with the spirited depiction of John's childhood in Puritania, mark the artistic strength of this fantasy. Lewis not only convincingly recreated at the beginning the world as a child perceives it, but he also handled impressively the dramatic irony whereby John learns in the end that, after all, considerable truth did exist beneath the mesh of inconsistencies and curious contradictions that characterized the religious views of the adults inhabiting his childhood world.

CHRIST AND REASON

Plainly, conversion was to Lewis, at this juncture of his Christian life, an intellectual transaction in which the will is forced to capitulate to the superior demands of Truth. The role of Christ as the One who makes salvation available is disturbingly muted in John's experience: he is simply "the Man" who mysteriously appears to offer John aid in his sincere efforts to hurdle a particular portion of the Great Chasm, and to give him some pertinent advice. John's experience lacks any counterpart to that of Christian's great burden which Bunyan depicts weighing so heavily upon his back until he finds respite by leaving it at the foot of the cross. Indeed, in terms of this fantasy, the Cross seems quite peripheral to Lewis's concerns.

The absence is the more noteworthy because Lewis in the totality of his writings paid ample homage to Christ and Calvary. On the basis of this work, however, one may conclude that early in his career his realities were almost exclusively intellectual. To be sure, the text indicates that Mother Kirk will give John needed

instruction, but nothing adequately indicates the cen-
trality of Christ in Christian salvation.

As the early Lewis delineated the pattern of
Christian conversion from using his own as a model, he
viewed it as an intellectual affair, seemingly convinced
that a sincere, clear-sighted and informed intellectual
striving, motivated by the deep compulsions of desire,
will lead one to Christian orthodoxy. In *The Allegory of
Love*, he approved of Albertus Magnus's view that:
"The real trouble about fallen man is not the strength
of his pleasures but the weakness of his reason"; [14] and
in *Perelandra* he has the Green Lady equate Christ to
Reason: "Since our Beloved became a man, how should
Reason in any world take on another form?" she asks.
Such thinking strongly echoes Milton's equation of
Christ and Right Reason in *Paradise Lost*.

But Lewis's faith in the efficacy of reason diminished
later in his life, when he came to recognize the larger
privilege of the imagination in the perception of Higher
Reality, and to place yet a stronger emphasis upon myth.
He increasingly acknowledged the importance of complete humility in the presence of the Person of Christ. [15]
In the conclusion of *Till We Have Faces*, published in
1956, Orual's devastating intellectual humiliation before

14. C. S. Lewis, *The Allegory of Love* (New York: Oxford University Press, 1958)), 15.

15. The conviction of the ability of reason to penetrate into the highest reaches of
Truth seems pretty well to dominate Lewis's thinking until he felt himself defeated
in his famous debate with Elizabeth Anscombe, a philosopher of Roman Catholic
faith, which took place in 1948. On this watershed experience, see Carpenter,
Inklings, 216–217; Sayer, *Jack*, 186–187; and A. N. Wilson, *C. S. Lewis: A Biography*
(New York: W. W. Norton, 1990), 210-20.

the gods, her affirmation of the supreme efficacy of self-abandoning love, her desire that her work be read in "Greece," and the humbling of the Fox, all stand as Lewis's final comments on the matter.

THE GREAT DIVORCE

In *The Great Divorce,* Lewis placed less emphasis upon "right thinking" and more upon the quality of being as a result of conversion. He gave high tribute to MacDonald both by making him a prominent character in the fantasy and also by shaping the episodes in terms of certain spiritual principles he found in his writings. The fantasy enlarges upon a medieval legend that the damned are periodically afforded holidays in heaven, if they choose to take them. Lewis joins the "bus tour" as the narrator. Their destiny is not "Deep Heaven," but rather its outskirts, the "Valley of the Shadow of Life." The denizens of hell with whom he rides exhibit self-centered attitudes, complaining and cynical. "The one principle of Hell," MacDonald wrote, "is, 'I am my own.' " [16]

By portraying these visitors as deeply pained and revolted by their fleeting introduction to the outskirts of Reality, Lewis achieved a strong mythic effect. Their confrontations with the spiritually Real immediately exposes their true spiritual states. The narrator (Lewis)

16. George Macdonald, "Kingship," *Unspoken Sermons: Third Series* (London: Longmans, Green, 1891), 102.

meets the sainted MacDonald who acts as his mentor and guide, not unlike Virgil did to Dante in *The Divine Comedy*. MacDonald explains the metaphysics that pertain: "Hell is a state of mind. . . . And every state of mind, left to itself, every shutting up of the creature within the dungeon of its own mind—is, in the end, Hell. But Heaven is not a state of mind. Heaven is reality itself. All that is fully real is Heavenly. For all that can be shaken will be shaken and only the unshakable remains." [17]

In chapter 4 of *The Great Divorce* Lewis made clear that one acquires a proper acclimation to Heaven not simply by changing one's manner of thinking but by means of the free gift of God's grace. The narrator overhears a conversation between Len, a denizen of heaven (called Solid People), and the Big Ghost from hell. In his pride and self-righteousness the ghost insists upon his "rights" and, refusing the joy he cannot understand, proudly determines to return to hell. Len, who in his earthly life had committed a murder, had also come to the end of himself and found spiritual transformation and joy in divine forgiveness. "'I'm not asking for anybody's bleeding charity,'" the Big Ghost avows. "'Then do. At once. Ask for the Bleeding Charity. Everything is here for the asking and nothing can be bought,'" Len counsels, but to no avail.

The pattern of the above incident recurs in the

17. Lewis, *The Great Divorce*, 69.

many incidents that follow. The visitors from hell, seriously unprepared for the enjoyment of heaven, look with displeasure and final disdain upon the environment in which they now find themselves. In their pride and self-centeredness all but one choose to return to the environs more appropriate to their states of mind. The redeemed try ineffectually to reason with the damned who, in their obstinacy, are shown steadily diminishing in their very beings toward nothingness. Sin not only renders its victims incapable of enjoying Reality, but it also destroys the very beings of all who embrace it.

Many incidents affirm one of Lewis's most provocative themes: corrupt love exerts a subtle but terrible tyranny over the beloved. Any potentially beautiful human relationship—such as between parents and children or husband and wife—can be perverted into a hellish one by the self-centered appropriating of its victim to the lover's own gratification.

In this exploration of the nature of heaven and hell, Lewis is examining spiritual principles; he has not the slightest intention of anticipating the palpable actuality of the world to come. In the preface he writes:

> I beg readers to remember that this is a fantasy. It has of course—or I intended it to have—a moral. But the transmortal conditions are solely an imaginative supposal: they are not even a guess or a speculation at what may actually await us. The last thing I wish is

to arouse factual curiosity about the details of the after-world.

Nevertheless, the "transmortal conditions" which he imagined do go beyond the presentation of a moral, in that they are redolent with the aura of myth. Making heaven attractive and stimulating a desire for it among readers (as fallen beings, no one can fully appreciate goodness) affords a large challenge to any artist's imaginative abilities. In this fantasy, Lewis avoided overt statements of *Sehnsucht*, undertaking rather to show heaven as the place of gratified longings. The quality of his brief but poignant descriptions, together with the assuring attitudes of complete satisfaction and delight on the part of the Solid People, work effectively in this regard. As the Solid People approach the visitors:

> The earth shook under their tread as their strong feet sank into the wet turf. A tiny haze and a sweet smell went up where they had crushed the grass and scattered the dew. Some were naked, some robed. But the naked ones did not seem less adorned, and the robes did not disguise in those who wore them the massive grandeur of muscle and the radiant smoothness of flesh. Some were bearded but no one in that company struck me as being of any particular age. . . . [18]

The same blades of grass that, when crushed by the feet of the Solid People yield enticing odors, are sharp as diamonds to the narrator's feet. The visitors scream

18. Lewis, *Great Divorce*, 30.

and run away in fright, then huddle together, cowering.

THE SPACE TRILOGY:
OUT OF THE SILENT PLANET

The theme struck in *The Pilgrim's Regress* of the nature and role of myth in human experience continues through the space trilogy. The initial fantasy, *Out of the Silent Planet*, published in 1938, was Lewis's first effort after his making a compact with Tolkien, in which they agreed he would compose myths of space and Tolkien myths of time. Read in installments to the Inklings, it gained their enthusiastic approval. Composing a fantasy in which fallen humans are taken to the planet Malacandra (Mars) offered Lewis precisely the opportunity he desired to create a mythic atmosphere—a sense of a higher, unfallen reality—in comparison to which he could imaginatively highlight human inadequacies. As in *The Great Divorce*, he showed this unfallen world as ministering to the gratification of *Sehnsucht*. Clyde Kilby remarked:

> The novels *Out of the Silent Planet* and *Perelandra* are among Lewis's own myths to suggest worlds in which the unity of being sweetly and desperately longed for are in some measure attained. One of the most significant things Ransom learned on his journeys to Mars and Venus was that "the triple distinction of truth from myth, and of both from fact was purely terrestrial—was part and parcel of the

unhappy division between soul and body which resulted from the Fall. Even on earth the sacraments existed as a permanent reminder that the division was neither wholesome nor final. The Incarnation had been the beginning of its disappearance. In Perelandra it would have no meaning at all. Whatever happened here would be of such a nature that earthmen would call it mythological." Myth— the Christian element of myth at least—is therefore something like the Eucharist itself, a symbol of man's relationship to God and of his glorious return to paradisal fellowship with the uncreated, unconditional Reality Himself.[19]

Myth is integral to the completeness of our being. The challenge Lewis felt is that of creating an imagined world more immediately and directly satisfying to human desire, one in which a redeemed person would rejoice, feeling more completely his belonging to it.

In *Out of the Silent Planet*, three types of characters portray three different spiritual states. Ransom, the first type, is a professor of philology on a walking holiday somewhere in England, a man basically good, with rather normal curiosities and inclinations. His life is spiritually changed for the better when he is captured and transported to a utopian planet, Malacandra, and is fully exposed to unfallen life there. His captors, Weston and Devine, represent the second type, virulent

19. Clyde S. Kilby, *The Christian World of C. S. Lewis* (Grand Rapids, Mich.: Wm. B. Eerdmans, 1964), 82. Kilby's work remains a valuable commentary on Lewis's achievement.

scientific humanists, epitomizing the secular spirit that Lewis was convinced is the chief threat to true life on this planet, and which he exposed throughout the trilogy. He may also have had in mind the mentality represented by Nazism, which was rising at the time he was writing. In contrast to Ransom, their reactions to the creatures on the planet of Malacandra serve only to intensify their vices.

The unfallen Malacandrian creatures compose the third type. These *hnau* can be divided into three groups: the *sorns*, or intelligentsia; the *hrossa*, or lovers of both action and language (they sing and hunt); and the *pfifltriggi*, or craftsmen. One may be reminded of Plato's three classes of people in *The Republic*. Each is distinguished by its distinctive character, and a hierarchy exists among them. Each group is ruled by those above it and is responsible to rule those below. Lewis's thought is derivative of the Great Chain of Being, the concept developed in the Renaissance that saw all of life arranged in a huge hierarchical pyramid with God at the top and all gradations of being extending downward to the least significant. Life on Malacandra is highly ordered, a very reasonable and sensible affair. In its attractive simplicity it is blessedly free from the perverse complexities brought about by the selfishness, greed, and sensuality that possess humankind.

At the top of the Great Chain of Being is the Old

One, God Most High. The hierarchy extends downward from Him, helping to explain relationships among groups. The hrossa hunt and kill the hnakra; the event is justified because sport and danger are necessary to keep life from becoming tedious, death is a transition to a higher life, and superior beings have full rights over lower ones. The *sorn* explains to Ransom: "There must be rule, yet how can creatures rule themselves? Beasts must be ruled by hnau and hnau by *eldila* and eldila by Maleldil." [20] Maleldil is a type of Christ. Lewis's imagination is especially captivated by heavenly beings, or eldila, whom he envisions in a series of ranks. Each planet is ruled by its archangel, with Oyarsa ruling Malacandra and the Bent One, or Satan, ruling Thulcandra, or Earth. Although the Bent One's evil rule isolates Earth from the other planets in the galaxy—hence its designation as the "silent" planet—Maleldil has a plan to wrest it out of his control.

The scene in which Weston and Devine are marshaled before Oyarsa to explain themselves and receive his judgment forms the climax of the fantasy. The blatant inconsistencies and follies of Weston's scientific humanism are brilliantly exposed, with Lewis commanding both logic and humor to make his point very clearly. In unflinching seriousness Weston undertakes to defend his ready willingness not only to sacrifice,

20. C. S. Lewis, *Out of the Silent Planet* (New York: Macmillan, 1965), 102.

Hitler-like, an unlimited number of lives, but also to disrupt their present happy order. He self-righteously justifies himself by professing to serve human posterity. His heroic self-image stands in absolute antithesis to the flagrant sacrifices of other lives his deeds effect, rendering him both hilarious and horrifying. Oyarsa, now understanding the full nature of human fallenness, sends them all, Ransom included, back to earth with a stern prohibition against their ever returning.

Once at home, the three travelers each have different reactions to their adventure. Weston and Devine sink more deeply into their perversity; Ransom becomes more spiritually mature. Lewis is imaginatively applying the principle announced by Christ: To the one who has more shall be given; from those who have not shall be taken away even that which they have (Matt. 13:12). Acting as an interpreter between Oyarsa and Weston has helped Ransom think carefully through all the issues at stake; right reason is all on the side of Oyarsa, and it prevails. The effect on Ransom, however, is much more than intellectual. Having experienced the higher mythical reality—the environment more appropriate for man—his imagination is haunted by its recollection and his spirit frustrated by his inability to express the ecstasy he has known. The more immediate knowledge of the Real that myth has afforded him is incommunicable.

PERELANDRA

In the second volume of the trilogy, *Perelandra*, Lewis further undertook to depict the nature of mythical Reality by recreating Eden and imaginatively recasting the story of the Fall. Like Malacandra, Perelandra is a planet answering to human yearnings. He explored the deceptive nature of temptation, together with the viciously disintegrating effects that disobedience to the divine will has on human nature, a theme basic to *The Great Divorce*. Published in 1943, *Perelandra* was Lewis's favorite among his imaginative works, even though he felt *Till We Have Faces* to be the superior achievement. [21] Lewis was deep within a study of Milton's works during this period, his *Preface to Paradise Lost* having appeared the year before. One can readily draw many parallels between this fantasy and *Paradise Lost* and *Comus*.

Lewis established immediately the sense of the mythic: the physical world is permeated with spiritual reality. As the story opens, the narrator, "Lewis," walking towards Ransom's cottage, is inexplicably possessed by fear and dread; something about the atmosphere is ominous and oppressive. The fallen eldila who have the earth in bondage are trying to prevent his mission.

Having arrived, Lewis learns that Ransom is being summoned—he is uncertain why—by Oyarsa to the

21. C. N. Manlove, *C. S. Lewis: His Literary Achievement* (New York: St. Martin's Press, 1987), 45.

planet Perelandra, or Venus. Lewis is told to encase him in a coffin-like vehicle (death is the means to higher life) in which the eldila are to transport him through space. Following Ransom's departure and return, the narrator relates to us Ransom's story. The elaborate point of view enables the reader to feel, with the narrator, a certain sense of discomfort and dread in the presence of the ' "otherness" of mythic goodness. This feeling is quite different from Ransom's who upon his return now feels desire and fascination.

The reader's dread is transformed into desire in the presence of Lewis's narration of Ransom's first impressions of Perelandra. The descriptions of higher mythic reality, both alien to people and yet somehow at the same time answering to their deepest desires, have appreciable imaginative power. Having quickly been transported there, Ransom is all but overwhelmed with elation and delight: "a strange sense of excessive pleasure which seemed somehow to be communicated to him through all his senses at once. . . ." He wonders, "Were all the things which appeared as mythology on earth scattered through other worlds as realities?" [22]

Ransom soon learns he was not transported to Perelandra simply to savor mythic reality. Soon after he meets the Green Lady, a type of Eve, his old enemy Weston appears in his space ship. A twentieth-century Satan, he proceeds to tempt the Green Lady to disobey

22. C. S. Lewis, *Perelandra* (New York: Macmillan, 1965), 37, 45.

Maleldil's decree that she and her "King," a type of Adam, not take up residence upon the Fixed Land of Perelandra. While they are allowed momentary excursions to it, their abode is to be upon any of the numerous Floating Islands. The reason for the prohibition, the reader later learns, is that living on the Fixed Land would establish within them an undue sense of independence from Maleldil, lessening their love and trust.

Weston tries to convince the Green Lady that Maleldil is really not wanting to enslave them to literal obedience; rather, he is desiring that they demonstrate their greater maturity by choosing freely and independently to live there. By ushering their species into a new and higher phase of spiritual growth and progress they would be considered heroes. Weston's spurious reasoning is powerfully and plausibly presented. The reader sees how near to truth the most vicious of lies can be. Weston is himself pathetic and despicable. Ransom's dawning awareness that he was brought to Perelandra to help foil Weston's attempt and to defeat him underscores the truth that divine power continually works through weak and seemingly negligible vehicles to accomplish its purposes. Nevertheless, Lewis's presentation of Ransom's masochistic killing of the vile and reprehensible Weston is somehow dramatically weak, almost sadistic. The reader must remember that Lewis was writing during World War II; evil enemies should be destroyed.

In the final scene of the fantasy, Lewis ventured an eschatology, together with firm affirmations of the wisdom of the divine government and eternal purposes. The King, now reunited with the Green Lady (his absence during the temptation scene is explained in terms of his having been called away to receive higher instructions concerning their future), now assumes his throne and instructs Ransom. The great good, which Maleldil intended in creating Thulcandra and which was lost because of the Fall, is in Perelandra to be realized. It is not a greater good than that of Eden—Lewis has his doubts about the doctrine of *felix culpa* [23]—but an alternative one. After the evil that possesses Thulcandra is obliterated, the Great Dance will proceed. Lewis's vision of Ultimate Things is sweeping and exhilarating.

THAT HIDEOUS STRENGTH

While *That Hideous Strength* does not present another journey into space, it is rightly related to its two predecessors by its further exploration both of the nature of human fallenness and the character of myth. Lewis integrated with these themes his views on gender and their implications regarding marriage. In the climax of

23. Trans.: "O happy sin." The doctrine was suggested by Augustine and advocated by, among many others, John Milton (cf. *Paradise Lost*, XII. 451–78). It has never been accepted as a part of orthodox theology.

Perelandra, as the Oyarsas of Malacandra and Perelandra appear to Ransom as male and female figures respectively, yet without sexual characteristics, Lewis remarks that gender differences compose a fundamental polarity in reality, of which sexual differences are but one of the dissimilarities. The last novel of the trilogy more fully examines the concept: humanity's relationship to God is a paradigm for the relationship of wives to their husbands.

Modeled loosely on the fantasies of Charles Williams, the narrative concerns the political life of a small British university that is in the process of selling a wooded tract of land adjacent to its campus to the National Institute of Co-ordinated Experiments—ironically shortened N.I.C.E.—a futuristic organization whose social experiments are shaped by Weston's humanist philosophy, now dubbed "that hideous strength." In the midst of the woods are the ruins of Merlin's Well, a symbol of what Lewis considers the best from British antiquity, the mythic past of Arthurian legend. The well is also an image that suggests the proximity of mythic reality to daily life. The ancient wizard Merlin is buried there, to be resurrected by the eldila when he is needed.

Mark Studdock, a newly hired sociology professor at Bracton, is torn between his allegiance to the college and his attraction to N.I.C.E, located at Belbury. The latter is trying to allure him into joining their staff. His scholarly wife, Jane, unhappy in her marriage, has recurring dreams that eerily presage the future.

The N.I.C.E. illustrates the insidious nature of secular humanism, a philosophy that Lewis saw as mounting in the twentieth century and posing the most perilous spiritual threat to Western civilization. He expounds upon its character in *The Abolition of Man;* here he imaginatively projects it. His setting this fantasy upon earth rather than in outer space allows him to show how widespread the philosophy is and what form it presently takes. It represents "that constructive fusion between the state and the laboratory on which so many thoughtful people base their hopes for a better world"; hence, its prevalence. Lord Feverstone (the character Devine in *Out of the Silent Planet*) optimistically voices its outlook:

> "It does really look as if we now had the power to dig ourselves in as a species for a pretty staggering period, to take control of our own destiny. If Science is really given a free hand it can now take over the human race and re-condition it: make man a really efficient animal. If it doesn't—well, we're done." [24]

Such thinking is religious in the dedication it demands from its devotees, and in its "redemptive" intentions; it, in effect, deifies man. It represents, however, a self-deception; and were it able to realize fully its intentions, earth would be turned into hell.

24. C. S. Lewis, *That Hideous Strength* (New York: Macmillan, 1965), 41.

The community of scholars that compose N.I.C.E. sustain a cacophonous relationship with their fellow humans and to nature. Their particular type of intellectuality and their humanity-centeredness prevents them from seeing mythic reality. There are vestiges of mythic glory in the elements of ordinary experiences properly perceived, as there are in beautiful human relationships. These scholars indulge in abstract thinking that depreciates the value of the individual and ignores the preciousness of concrete reality.

Mark Studdock possesses this mentality:

> [H]is education had had the curious effect of making things that he read and wrote more real to him than things he saw. Statistics about agricultural labourers were the substance; any real ditcher, ploughman, or farmer's boy, was the shadow. Though he had never noticed it himself, he had a great reluctance, in his work, ever to use such words as "man" or "woman." He preferred to write about "vocational groups," "elements," "classes" and "populations": for, in his own way, he believed as firmly as any mystic in the superior reality of the things that are not seen. [25]

This is, it would seem, the besetting sin of academia. A certain goodness and grace resides in an individual's appreciation of specific elements in quotidian reality; abstract constructs, so absorbing to the academic mind, have no reality in themselves even though they create

25. Lewis, *Hideous Strength*, 87.

the delusion that they possess great worth. One may recall Charles Williams's developing this theme in the experience of Damaris Tighe in *The Place of the Lion*. Neither he nor Lewis is ridiculing the act of abstract thinking in itself—an activity indispensable to life and one at which both were most adept—but rather the act of divorcing thought from the real world.

Such error in thinking is opposed in the story by the little community of people at St. Anne's. Their leader is the hero of the trilogy, Ransom, who is now, by virtue of his having been victorious over the satanic Weston amidst the higher mythic reality of celestial spheres, a Fisher-King, the Pendragon of Logres. His wound, acquired in that clash, strengthens his image as keeper of the grail. To understand fully the significance of these titles, one has to consult the Arthurian myths, especially as they involve the grail legend. [26] The Fisher-King guarded the castle which contained the Holy Grail; hence, he symbolizes a keeper of spiritual mysteries, in whose power is the means of salvation, suggested by the grail. The quest for it—undertaken of old by Arthur's knights—symbolizes the deep yearning of the soul. In Arthur's time, Pendragon was a title given to a supreme head, and Logres was the name given to Britain. Lewis uses Logres to designate a spiritually ideal state: what human society ought to be.

26. For a succinct and helpful discussion of these aspects of the Arthurian legends, see David C. Downing, *Planets in Peril* (Amherst: The University of Massachusetts Press, 1992), 76–78.

Lewis's model for Ransom may have been Charles Williams, whose spiritual demeanor he much admired.

As Mark Studdock is being attracted to the N.I.C.E. community, Jane becomes acquainted with the community of people at St. Anne's. It is not a group of Christian believers as such; rather, it is a community of diverse, ordinary people, well-oriented to daily life, with Ransom as their spiritual head. Among them is MacPhee, a crotchety rationalist, modeled on Lewis's favorite tutor of his adolescence, William Kirkpatrick, and Mr. and Mrs. Dimble, a college tutor and his wife, who exemplify a rather ideal marriage relationship.

The conflict between these two communities is in essence a spiritual one, engineered by eldilic power. Lewis's conception of an hierarchy of angelic beings who govern the spiritual aspects of life on the various planets is elaborate and persistent throughout the trilogy. The evil eldila are controlling the actions of the people at Belbury; the "good" are over the community at St. Anne's. The difference lies in that the people of St. Anne's consciously and willingly obey their biddings, whereas those at Belbury are unaware they are being used. The most intriguing scenes of the fantasy are those in which the eldila come to St. Anne's in the form of classical gods and goddesses in order to hold counsel with Ransom and Merlin, and the scene in which they administer judgment upon the N.I.C.E. community.

Merlin is instrumental in both scenes. Both communities are interested in him; he represents an ancient power that, although the N.I.C.E. people do not understand, they feel they need, and the people at St. Anne's want to keep them from attaining. Merlin's magic is distinct from "what the Renaissance called magic," Lewis affirmed. [27] It is "something brought to Western Europe after the fall of Numinor and going back to an era in which the general relations of mind and matter on this planet had been other than those we know." [28] It is, in short, ancient mythological power, which now readily allies itself with the forces of good.

In Lewis's imagined world, the power of myth accompanies manifestations of the angelic or divine in human experience and may effect radical spiritual changes. Mark's conversion begins by his becoming aware of a certain mythic aura present in the "normal" aspects of life: "it was all mixed up with Jane and fried eggs and soap and sunlight and the rooks cawing. . . ." Something from beyond the "dry and choking" aspects of life had been "invading" him. [29] Echoes of Chesterton's insistence on the sacramental nature of ordinary reality reside in the scene.

27. Lewis's thinking is interestingly like Tolkien's concept of the "good magic" necessarily present in fairy stories. See Tolkien's discussion of good and evil magic in "On Fairy Stories," *The Tolkien Reader* (New York: Ballantine Books, 1966), 33–99.

28. Lewis, *Hideous Strength*, 200, 201. Lewis borrowed the concept of Numinor from Tolkien's mythology, such as in *The Silmarillion*. Tolkien was incredulous when he discovered Lewis spelled it with an "i" instead of an "e," attributing the mistake to Lewis's having heard but not seen the term (*Letters*, 224).

29. Lewis, *Hideous Strength*, 247.

A mythic quality is also present in objects Jane views at the moment of her conversion:

> Then, at one particular corner of the gooseberry patch, the change came. What awaited her there was serious to the degree of sorrow and beyond. There was no form nor sound. The mould under the bushes, the moss on the path, and the little brick border, were not visibly changed. But they were changed. A boundary had been crossed. She had come into a world, or into a Person, or into the presence of a Person. . . . [30]

These mythic energies exuding from the Divine Presence effect Jane's transformation; her "little idea of herself which she had hitherto called *me* dropped down and vanished." She now sees herself both as a person yet also "a made thing, made to please Another and in Him to please all others." The perception takes place in a moment of time, so that she contemplates it as a memory, but the visitation transforms her life and outlook.

Mythic power is also vividly present with Mark and Jane as they come together at the conclusion of the fantasy in an ideal relationship as husband and wife. Matrimony is the first word of the novel as well as its final subject; Lewis offers an explicit interpretation of the biblical paradigm for marriage. Mark and Jane have both been purged of the detrimental attitudes that had

30. Lewis, *Hideous Strength*, 318.

nearly destroyed their union. Mark now knows the "humility of a lover," while Jane has acquired "the humility of a wife." The mythological Venus stands at the door of their "bridal chamber" as they each approach it, and a sense of " 'Beauty too rich for use, for earth too dear' " invades their transformed matrimonial relationship. Lewis's high view of marital union no doubt enhanced his own later marriage.

Near the conclusion of the novel, when the gods of classical mythology descend to hold counsel with Ransom and Merlin and bring judgment upon Belbury, the aura of myth—"the packed reality of heaven"—so pervades St. Anne's that the behavior and condition of the occupants are radically altered. Their intellectual powers are heightened, evident in their sudden eloquence and wit. They seem repositioned into the heart of meaning itself, a shift immediately manifest in their full command of language:

> For Ransom, whose study had been for many years in the realm of words, it was heavenly pleasure. He found himself sitting within the very heart of language, in the white-hot furnace of essential speech. All fact was broken, splashed into cataracts, caught, turned inside out, kneaded, slain, and reborn as meaning. For the lord of Meaning himself, the herald, the messenger, the slayer of Argus, was with them: . . . whom men call Mercury. . . .[31]

31. Lewis, *Hideous Strength*, 322.

The scene answers to *Sehnsucht*: the individuals know the bliss of heightened reality. Theirs is not simply a perception, but a participation in fullness of life and cosmic design. They take "their places in the ordered rhythm of the universe" and blissfully join in the Great Dance.

Amidst this influx of transmuting mythic power are others of the classical gods besides Mercury—Venus, Mars, Saturn, even Jove. They form a vast hierarchy of angelic power, and are among the good eldila. Lewis's view of pagan deities differs from that of the more traditional Christian attitudes; the gods are a part of eternal reality.

In strong contrast, the denizens of Belbury sitting in banquet are visited with profound and sweeping judgments appropriate to their evil acts. They are held fully responsible for allowing themselves to be mastered by the evil eldila. The effects of judgment upon them are the antitheses of those ecstasies experienced at St. Anne's: their language is reduced to gibberish, their comradeship to murder, their regimental order to confusion and chaos. They commit ghoulish and grotesque acts and come to ignominious ends. Some become reincarnated as wild and vicious animals (shades of MacDonald and Williams), and attack one another.

A duality of images characterizes the entirety of the fantasy: two Merlins, two communities, two Directors, and so forth. The structure emphasizes the dichotomy of good and evil that permeates all of life. These moral realities are at the heart of existence, ultimately dividing people into two contrasting camps.

TILL WE HAVE FACES

In *That Hideous Strength*, Lewis defines his view of the nature and power of myth. But he is not done with his vision. In what well may be regarded as his masterpiece, *Till We Have Faces*, he explores the character of pagan mythology and suggests the presence in it of some essential religious truth and authentic mythic power. The setting is the imagined kingdom of Glome during the pre-Christian classical era and the narrative is a retelling of the myth of Psyche and Cupid. Lewis makes certain minor alterations in the standard version of the myth found in Apuleius, a Latin poet of the second century A.D., which he puts in an appendix at the back of the text. The reader should begin by reading this note giving the details of the ancient story.

The focus of the myth is on Psyche and her love for the god Cupid, her betrayal of him, the consequent judgments, and her final apotheosis. Psyche is a transliteration of the Greek word for soul; she is in Lewis's version the soul ideally conceived, displaying paradigmatic religious attitudes and experiences. Her rebel sister Orual, the "writer" who is relating her spiritual odyssey, expresses a range of negative reactions to her various encounters with mythic reality. The pun value of her name, "or-you-all," suggests that in terms of religious responses, hers is the most prevalent alternative to those of Psyche. Most of the other characters are conceived primarily in terms of their attitudes towards the gods and religious realities: the royal father of the sisters is a self-centered pragmatist and hypocrite, the Fox a representative of Grecian rationalism, Bardia an upright pagan who prudently chooses to keep the gods at a respectful distance, and Arnon a "modern" priest who would explain pagan mythology in humanist terms that emasculate it of its real religious value.

In her ideal religious attitudes, Psyche offers a model for all believers, not as a Christian, but as a model pagan. She may be taken as an example of Paul's observance that "when Gentiles who have not the law do by nature what the law requires . . . they show that what the law requires is written on their hearts. . ." (Rom. 2:14, 15; RSV). When Clyde Kilby wrote to Lewis shortly after the fantasy appeared asking about possible symbolic significance in the narrative, Lewis responded:

> Psyche is an instance of the *anima naturaliter Christiana* making the best of the Pagan religion she is brought up in and thus being guided (but always "under the cloud," always in terms of her own imagination or that of her people) towards the true God. She is in some ways like Christ not because she

is a symbol of Him but because every good man or woman is like Christ. What else could they be like?[32]

Being a good person, she inevitably conforms to the image of the One Perfect Person, even though her culture is a pagan one. Integral to her goodness is her longing towards the eternally Good. Lewis is invariably eloquent in his expressions of *Sehnsucht:*

> It was when I was happiest that I longed most. It was on happy days when we were up there on the hills, the three of us, with the wind and the sunshine . . . . And because it was so beautiful, it set me longing, always longing. Somewhere else there must be more of it. Everything seemed to be saying, Psyche come!
> . . . . The sweetest thing in all my life has been the longing—to reach the Mountain, to find the place where all the beauty came from—[33]

Her willing submission to the demands of her religion is motivated by her yearnings for more of whatever it is that delights her on earth and her faith that her destiny is to participate in an intensified reality.

Not only do the compelling beauty and attractiveness of her virtue and her high destiny to be a bride of a god establish strong analogies to Christian experience—her reversals do as well. She is by some resented

32. Lewis to Kilby, 10 February 1957, Marion E. Wade Center, Wheaton College, Wheaton, Ill.

33. C. S. Lewis, *Till We Have Faces* (San Diego: Harcourt Brace Jovanovich, 1956), 74–75. Compare Tangle and Mossy's longing "for the land from which the shadows come" in George MacDonald, *The Golden Key.*

for her goodness, and she is eventually rejected and sacrificed for her faith. Even so, she feels chosen for her trials; Job-like, she knows that having to experience adversity may be a mark of divine favor bestowed upon a righteous person.

Orual, on the other hand, is possessed by a whole range of rebellious attitudes that prevent her from seeing the realities that Psyche sees. Her will is set against the gods. She loves her sister and feels deep distress at her death, but her love is self-centered and possessive. In developing this aspect of Orual, Lewis brings to its acme the theme of perverted love he orchestrated in *The Great Divorce*. True love honors and respects the individuality of the beloved; it does not tyrannize nor seek its own gratification. But Orual determines to control Psyche and possess her for herself. The center of her personality is really her mind, not her heart. In her rationalism she dismisses the mythic moments which present themselves to her. When the world momentarily seems beautiful and she hears a voice asking, "Why should your heart not dance?" she stubbornly recounts to herself her negative experiences in "this god-haunted, plague-breeding, decaying, tyrannous world."[34] No one is so blind as one who will not see.

Her problem is one of perception: she is unable to see the mythic reality that Psyche sees because she

34. Lewis, *Till We Have Faces*, 96, 97.

refuses to see it. In struggling against joy she excludes herself from its domain. [35] When in chapters 10 and 11 Psyche undertakes to show Orual her god's palace only to discover that in Orual's repudiation of its reality she is unable to see it at all, the reader feels with full dramatic power the tragedy of spiritual blindness. One recalls the imaginative strength of similar scenes concerning spiritual perception in George MacDonald's Curdie stories.

Lewis succeeds in inducing the reader to sympathize with Orual's "case against the gods" throughout part 1; she gives eloquent expression to objections all thinking believers have felt at some time or other. In her demand that the gods work according to her expectations, not allowing for the divine initiative and otherness, she also typifies prevalent attitudes among unbelievers. Orual's disillusionment in part 2 is, therefore, the more imaginatively powerful, as the reader realizes the dramatic irony of the final reversal of her attitudes.

The reversal is achieved through the divine sentence pronounced upon Orual and Psyche. *Till We Have Faces* is perhaps most provocative in its exploration of the paradoxical nature of divine judgment: it is for the spiritual good of the judged. When Orual induces

35. She provides a sterling example of Christ's teaching in Matt. 6:22–23: "The eye is the lamp of the body. So, if your eye is sound, your whole body will be full of light; but if your eye is not sound, your whole body will be full of darkness. If then the light in you is darkness, how great is the darkness!" (RSV). See also 2 Cor. 4:3, 4.

Psyche to betray her god by lighting a lamp at night to view him, the cosmos itself is shaken, and the god pronounces the inevitable judgment upon them both. Psyche's sin was one of presumption and disobedience; the forgiveness of which she was confident does not cancel the necessary and certain consequences of her audacity. She is exiled; for her distrust and disobedience she "must hunger and thirst and tread hard roads." Concerning Orual, he exclaims, "You, woman, shall know yourself and your work. You also shall be Psyche." [36] Such knowledge, together with its final effects, is the foundation principle of all divine judgment.

All the events that henceforth befall Orual arise from this positive divine judgment. Contrary to all her expectations, the final effect is to purge her of her rebellious attitudes and bring true enlightenment. In the story the divine intention is realized with relentless and compelling dramatic irony. The events occurring in the final half of part 1, such as her becoming queen, defeating Argan, and receiving the homage of her people as a just and wise ruler, bring her no inner satisfaction, but they prepare her for her eventual spiritual transformation.

Orual acknowledges that "the Queen of Glome had more and more part in me and Orual had less and less," her true self growing "slowly smaller and less alive." [37]

36. Lewis, *Till We Have Faces*, 173, 174.
37. Lewis, *Till We Have Faces*, 226.

One recalls the shrunken souls of the damned in *The Great Divorce*. Unalarmed at her spiritual diminishment, she takes solace in recounting the political triumphs of her rule. All the while the divine mercy is working to bring an end to her rebellious self, in order that a true, redeemed self may emerge. Her actions present a penetrating and insightful study in the manner in which a soul stifles those aspects of life that are calculated by divine grace to bring spiritual enlightenment and health. The astounding paradox is that the divine intention will not finally be defeated; its triumph is presented in part 2.

Part 2 presents the process whereby she comes to repent of the folly of all her rebellion and perceives her true spiritual state. In Orual's final insight concerning herself and her complaint, Lewis turns the famous Socratic dictum "Know thyself" on its head. Orual comes to realize:

> The complaint was the answer. To have heard myself making it was to be answered. Lightly men talk of saying what they mean. . . . I saw well why the gods do not speak to us openly, nor let us answer. Till that word can be dug out of us, why should they hear the babble that we think we mean? How can they meet us face to face till we have faces? [38]

38. Lewis, *Till We Have Faces*, 294.

The entirety of part 1 consists of her "babble," which arises from her supposed self-knowledge. Her knowledge misses the true significance of her experiences, her sincerity notwithstanding. To come to know one's self truly is to come to know the impossibility of such knowledge; one cannot know oneself accurately so long as one is a fallen and incomplete person. The presumptions of rationalism are thus destroyed. Hence, the significance of the title, a phrase lifted from a scene in George MacDonald's *Lilith*. That fantasy acts as a source and prototype for much of Lewis's thinking. [39]

In part 2 Lewis undertakes to end his tale in a manner that reminds one of the ending of *The Pilgrim's Regress*, in which John, after his conversion, retreads his former journey with transformed attitudes. Now dying, Orual hastily recounts the steps that effected her change of heart, lest she "die perjured." The basic effect of her spiritual transformation is a change in perspective. Through a series of incidents her eyes are now opened to her former self-centeredness that prompted her to misperceive the nature of her experiences. She now sees herself to have been an unjust and tyrannous sister towards Redival and a consuming vulture towards Bardia. She dreams, and has dreams within dreams (shades of *Lilith*) that reveal to her the basic reasons why she must die to self. In the sinfulness of her human

39. See chapter 17. On the theme of coming to know oneself and one's work, see Lilith's experience in Mara's house, chapter 39.

nature she is herself Ungit: in the way she appropriated other people to herself she was in effect demanding sacrifices. Further, in wanting to possess for herself all things in her world, she is in reality determined to be her own god. In her complaint she bursts out against the gods, "There's no room for you and us in the same world"; in her illumination, her rebellious self is annihilated. Indisputably, "the complaint was the answer."

In the scene in which Orual identifies herself as Ungit, Lewis manages to suggest several things about such heathen deities. They are, in their demands for sacrifice, primarily projections of fallen human nature, rather than simply fertility gods associated with seasonal cycles, as prevailing wisdom would see them. But at the same time devout sacrifices to them, as illustrated by the humble peasant women bringing her pigeon to be offered, have a certain religious validity, a legitimacy that the intellectualized explanations of the "modernist" priest deny. The peasant woman is similar to Psyche in that she devoutly obeys the primitive truths which she sees and in obeying finds inner peace. The gods "will have sacrifice—will have man," the Fox, in one of Orual's visions, explains.

In the final chapter Lewis encapsulates a remarkable quantity of truths concerning the spiritual life. The Fox, who as the Grecian teacher has been the voice of rationalism and has a tendency towards a cynicism throughout the novel, confesses to the gods he is "to blame" for most of Orual's attitudes. Lewis's final assessment of a rationalist approach to life interestingly modifies that which he held early in his career. In the gallery of living pictures through which the Fox leads Orual, they contemplate Psyche in a series of scenes prototypical of spiritual experience. Psyche, whose beauty is again emphasized, is the religious soul facing temptations and spiritual pitfalls, together with the necessary sufferings, all of which must be endured and overcome in order to be "united with the Divine Nature." The final chapter swiftly depicts the range of extreme experiences through which the Redeemed of the Ages have had to pass. The passage echoes the gallery of the faithful in Hebrews, chapter ii.

Psyche tells Orual that the purpose of her "long journey" had been to fetch the beauty necessary "to make Ungit beautiful"—that is, to transform human nature. Orual, who has seen herself to be Ungit, now also is made to see herself as Psyche, fully as beautiful as her sister. The god's judgment "You also shall be Psyche" is fulfilled. The god of the Grey Mountain— both Ungit's son and Psyche's lover—whose judgment had sent Psyche on her long and arduous journey and had decreed that Orual would come to know both her self and her work, now has triumphed in the redemption of both.

Among the many achievements of Lewis's remarkable career, his literary myths are perhaps the most engaging, and *Till We Have Faces* his finest work. It gives definitive imaginative expression to his vision of the nature of life and the role of myth. In presenting myth within a myth, it possesses a compelling purity in its vision and authenticity in its tone.

There is a sense in which Lewis's writings are a pastiche of a great many writers whom he admired. Certainly his debt to all the authors we have considered in this study is evident enough. But no one who has read far in Lewis's writings would accuse him of merely imitating anyone. He was a superb stylist, one of the most articulate of twentieth-century writers, excelling in both logical, analytical adeptness and creative, imaginative expression. His apologetic for Christianity, based upon mortal restlessness and yearning for fullness of life, answers to something very deeply human.

His synthesis of creative and critical skills makes for an impressive breadth of accomplishment. But it was his appreciation for myth that invested his imaginative work with the stature it enjoys in the view of so many. His view is highly controversial in a secular age, when all alleged manifestations of the supernatural are explained in naturalist or humanist terms. But only the supernatural can explain the internal longing Lewis identified as *Sehnsucht*, the longing to be united with the beauty we see and to put on the splendor of the sun.

8

Myth Today
L'Engle, Wangerin,
Siegel, and Hurnard

The journey homewards. Coming home. That's what
it's all about. The journey to the coming of the
Kingdom. That's probably the chief difference
between the Christian and the secular artist—the
purpose of the work, be it story or music or painting,
is to further the coming of the kingdom, to make us
aware of our status as children of God, and to turn
our feet toward home.[1]

maginative writing most worthy to be called
art has within it something that furthers the
journey of humanity homeward. Following
the appearance in midcentury of the mythopoeia
created by C. S. Lewis and J. R. R. Tolkien, a great
many writers have undertaken to write similarly. Some
authors have seen science fiction—which appeals to

1. Madeleine L'Engle, *Walking on Water* (Wheaton, Ill.: Harold Shaw Publishers,
1980), 162–63.

many readers today—as a congenial context for the mythic vision. Madeleine L'Engle is perhaps the most noteworthy of these. Others, such as Stephen Lawhead, have retold with much embellishment the Arthurian legends, and still others, such as Robert Siegel, have written what may loosely be called beast epics. Hannah Hurnard has written allegories of spiritual odysseys. Sampling some of these works suggests the state of literary myth today.

Many authors have been inspired by Tolkien's *Lord of the Rings* and created fantasy worlds modeled on his. The reader is presented with queer creatures definitely divided into good and evil types, with the bad stealing some talisman and the good retrieving it. Many are well-told and provide imaginative escape into an interesting other world where novel events take place. But these authors fail to establish a genuine center in myth and their work tends not to rise beyond the level of entertainment. Mere gestures made towards the supernatural seem shallow and artificial. For Tolkien, the elaborate mythology of *The Silmarillion* provided a permanent reference for the action of *The Lord of the Rings* because he was concerned with the "secret life of the universe," showing it to be both mysterious and momentous. He succeeded in arousing a combination of fear and desire that a true encounter with myth evokes. As a result, the rings are true talismans, possessing supernatural power no reader doubts, and

Frodo's heroic quest is grippingly dramatic. If Tolkien had failed in establishing such a convincing center in myth, his work would have received little notice when it appeared and be forgotten today.

Reading widely in contemporary fantasies suggests what any worthy aspirant to mythopoeia will confirm, that the mythic dynamic may not be commanded. No particular literary style or finesse will automatically capture it, no religious zeal or knowledge in itself will effect it, no narrative formula will contain it, and no mere descriptions of a more ethereal reality will evoke it. Writers who intend myth may or may not be convincing. And, to an extent, not all sensibilities will agree as to the presence of true myth in any specific work. George MacDonald was right when he observed "Everyone . . . who feels the story, will read its meaning after his own nature and development: one man will read one meaning in it, another will read another." [2]

Madeleine L'Engle, who among contemporary writers is on occasion singularly successful in achieving the level of myth, muses upon how elusive anagogical significances are:

> What is this anagogical level? It's not easy to define, because it is out of the realm of provable fact. It is most easily discernible in the great works of fantasy, such as Dante's own *Inferno*. The best science fiction is

2. "The Fantastic Imagination," *The Heart of George MacDonald*, ed. Rolland Hein (Wheaton, Ill.: Harold Shaw, 1994), 425.

"anagogical." I do not believe that it is a level that is ever used consciously even by the greatest writers. It is that level of a book which breaks the bounds of time and space and gives us a glimpse of the truth, that truth which casts the shadows into Plato's cave, the shadows which are all we mortals are able to see." [3]

Eternal reality may at best be only glimpsed, not because God is capricious, but because, as Emily Dickinson observed, it is "too bright for our infirm delight," or, to quote T. S. Eliot, because "human kind / Cannot bear very much reality." [4] Just as Scripture tells us more than once that no human may look directly upon the living God and live, so we may only occasionally catch glimpses of His glory.

In her series portraying the adventures of the Murry family, *A Wrinkle in Time, A Wind in the Door, A Swiftly Tilting Planet,* and *Many Waters,* Madeleine L'Engle achieved the condition of myth by imaginatively breaking "the bonds of time." She took her readers out of *chronos* time (hours, weeks and years) into *kairos* time (time free from duration), from which she imagined it possible to visit different moments in the past. In *Many Waters,* for instance, her characters Sandy and Dennys Murry are transported back to the times of Noah,

---

3. Madeleine L'Engle, *A Circle of Quiet* (New York: Farrar, Straus and Giroux, 1972), 61–62.

4. See #1129, "Tell all the Truth but tell it slant—" *The Complete Poems of Emily Dickinson,* ed. Thomas H. Johnson (Boston: Little, Brown, 1960), 506; and Section I of "Burnt Norton" in "The Four Quartets," *T. S. Eliot: Complete Poems and Plays, 1909–1950* (New York: Harcourt, Brace & World, 1952), 118.

before the Flood, and there they have adventures with biblical personages. She, therefore, adds a dimension not present in Tolkien's *Lord of the Rings*, in that the time of Middle Earth is chronological time imagined in a prior era and we simply are there as the story opens. L'Engle's story transports us, making us feel the thrill of travel through time, but not allowing us to become intellectually preoccupied with the metaphysical problems involved. She simply ignores such concerns, quite aware that narrative plausibility does not depend upon solving all the philosophical dilemmas that may occur to those with rationalist obsessions. L'Engle coined the term *tesser*, by which she means to travel through time, not in a linear sense, but as though time were in folds or wrinkles, and one could step from one moment to another like one might step over a chasm without transiting the gully beneath; hence, the first title in the series.

A WRINKLE IN TIME

Like the Curdie stories of George MacDonald, the audience L'Engle envisioned is that of early adolescence, but the adult reader finds much to enjoy. She captured the world as seen by child characters who, because they have precocious abilities, are misunderstood and belittled by their peers: their need for acceptance, love, and understanding is strong, yet they feel independent and adventurous and require opportunities to express their unique abilities. Her protégés in the Murry family are Meg and her younger brother Charles Wallace, both of whom have problems at school fitting in with other children and are misunderstood by their teachers. A part of their uniqueness is their ability to *kythe*, which is an adeptness at silently reading each other's thoughts.

Their own needs and expectations are presented in such manner that one is prepared to accept the unusual and the fantastic when it occurs. When they meet fantastic experiences with an adolescent matter-of-fact air, not incredulous at their happening but rather mesmerized by the new feelings they experience, the reader meets these experiences in the same way. Our attention is focused, not upon the absurdity of such occurrences, but upon how new experiences of space and time would feel.

This in itself is not mythic, but the sense L'Engle created of the eternal permeating the temporal is. Her ability to make goodness attractive and the moral beauty of higher reality reminds one of George MacDonald. In *A Wrinkle in Time*, Meg and Charles Wallace, together with their friend Calvin, meet three mythical beings, Mrs. Whatsit, Mrs. Who, and Mrs. Which, who, it is later suggested, are messengers of God. They represent divine energies in the universe that help and enable people to do good. With their help, these children tesser to the planet Camazotz, where Meg and Charles Wallace's father is being held captive by the Forces of Darkness. Mr. Murry is a physicist on an experimental mission for the United States government. Enroute, on the planet Uriel, Mrs. Whatsit, who is personally transporting them, suddenly changes into a beautiful being, half human and half horse, similar to a Grecian centaur. We read:

> She was a marble white body with powerful flanks, something like a horse but at the same time completely unlike a horse, for from the magnificently modeled back sprang a nobly formed torso, arms, and a head resembling a man's but a man with a perfection of dignity and virtue, an exaltation of joy such as Meg had never before seen. [5]

The centaur's perfection of being comes from virtue infused with joy; goodness is beautiful. They soon come upon a company of such creatures, all participating in an ethereal music emanating from their very movements, a music with meaning quite beyond the power of words to capture. The children understand something of its meaning because of their ability to kythe, combined with Mrs. Whatsit's talent to translate the music to song:

> The resonant voice rose and the words seemed to be all around them so that Meg felt that she could almost reach out and touch them: "Sing unto the

5. Madeleine L'Engle, *A Wrinkle in Time* (New York: Dell, 1976), 63.

Lord a new song, and his praise from the end of the earth, ye that go down to the sea, and all that is therein; the isles, and the inhabitants thereof. Let the wilderness and the cities thereof lift their voice; let the inhabitants of the rock sing, let them shout from the top of the mountains. Let them give glory unto the Lord."

Throughout her entire body Meg felt a pulse of joy such as she had never known before. . . . joy flowed through them, back and forth between them, around them and about them and inside them. [6]

Considerably more is involved in this scene than simply an encounter with the singing of scriptural sentiments. We are made to feel a fleeting participation in the inner nature of the universe itself.

L'Engle's universe is not, however, free from evil. We feel its horror as strongly as its basic glory. Being allowed to view their home planet, the young people see it shrouded in the shadows of evil. As we participate in Meg's perplexity, she is overwhelmed with a terror beyond words, too deep for screaming, too pervasive for quavering. One may recall Lewis's depiction of our "bent planet" in the Space Trilogy, but L'Engle makes us *feel* the horror of evil, in contrast to Lewis's more intellectualized vision. The children watch as a shaft of light clashes with the Darkness and momentarily disperses it, but is consumed in the process. "It was a star,"

6. L'Engle, *A Wrinkle in Time*, 66.

Mrs. Whatsit said sadly. "A star giving up its life in battle with the Thing. It won, oh, yes, my children, it won. But it lost its life in the winning." [7] The ongoing battle against evil extracts severe cost.

Camazotz, the planet upon which their father is held captive, is entirely Dark, held more completely than earth under the domination of the evil power, IT. IT, we learn, is a pure, disembodied brain, situated in the Central Intelligence Agency of the planet, exercising utter control over every aspect of life. The result is the complete obliteration of all wills but its own, so that monotonous rhythm and sterile conformity is everywhere, with the inhabitants being reduced to mindless automatons. Children skipping rope or playing ball do so to a terrible sameness of rhythm and pattern. All hearts beat uniformly. When Charles Wallace, with a tinge of hubris, undertakes to overcome IT and free his father by feigning submission, he is himself trapped. Even so, Mr. Murry, imprisoned because he will not submit, is freed by Meg with the aid of mysterious glasses lent to them by Mrs. Who. A radically different way of looking at things and approaching experience, it is implied, will free one from such enslavement.

But they are forced to flee Camazotz and leave Charles Wallace behind. Finding themselves on the planet Ixchel, they are restored to health by the help of

7. L'Engle, *A Wrinkle in Time*, 86, 87.

a variety of planetary life-forms whom Meg terms "the beasts." Frantic, Meg rails against her father, until Mrs. Whatsit appears and makes it clear that only she can save her brother. They are bonded through their mutual ability to kythe. The task is hers; supernatural power can magically do it for her. Our lives, Mrs. Whatsit explains, are like the poet's sonnet, a very strict literary form within which the poet has freedom to work. What a sonnet says is completely up to the poet. The analogy defines helpfully the relationship between divine power and human will.

As Meg undertakes the mission, Mrs. Whatsit gives her her love and reminds her of the biblical assurance, "The foolishness of God is wiser than men. . ." [8] Meg goes, and accomplishes the release of her brother, not by hating IT, but by the power of her loving Charles Wallace. Attempting to image forth such themes as the power of love and hate is dramatically difficult, and L'Engle's attempt in this fantasy does not seem as happily successful as one could wish, in that it rests too much on Meg's telling her brother she loves him. The affirmation frees him. The scene is swiftly completed, and the party returns to earth and home within two short paragraphs. The effect, though not completely satisfying, nevertheless clinches her point.

The story mounts a strong imaginative attack against a demonic rationalism. L'Engle suggests the

8. Mrs. Whatsit quotes extensively from I Corinthians 1:25-8.

danger confronting any society is mindless conformity
to pure intelligence divorced from all else that makes
people fully human: emotions, intuition, imagination,
common sense, humane judgment, and above all faith.
Evil has ultimately a mythic source that preys powerfully upon the human will; it may be successfully
opposed only by a combination of will and the enabling
perceptions of Christian faith. Completeness of being
is oriented both to time and eternity. She states her
position directly in *A Circle of Quiet:*

> [M]y intellect is a stumbling block to much that
> makes life worth living: laughter; love; a willing
> acceptance of being created. The rational intellect
> doesn't have a great deal to do with art. . . . With my
> naked intellect I cannot believe in God, particularly
> a loving God. My intellect is convinced that any idea
> of the person's continuing and growing after death is
> absurd; logic goes no further than dust to dust.
> Images, in the literary sense of the word, take me
> much further. [9]

The faith that rejoices in one's being created by a
loving God in whose hands one's destiny lies is not
opposed to reason, but transcends it, resting upon a different foundation than a purely intellectual one.
L'Engle quietly invested the story with an orientation
to Christian truth, not by direct statements, but by
conveying through the story itself and its images that

9. L'Engle, *A Circle of Quiet,* 40–41, 194.

ultimate power resides in the prerogatives of divine purpose and goodness.

These ultimate truths are bathed in the aura of myth. Mr. Murry, who makes no announcements of Christian faith, simply affirms in a moment of crisis: "We were sent here for something. And we know that all things work together for good to them that love God, to them who are the called according to his purpose." [10] The strange ministering creatures on the planet Ixchel who help them in rescuing Charles Wallace, when asked how they do what they do, explain: "Good helps us, the stars help us, perhaps what you would call *light* helps us, love helps us. . . . We look not at the things which are what you would call seen, but at the things which are not seen. For the things which are seen are temporal. But the things which are not see are eternal." [11] Such affirmations, biblical though they are, seem quite naturally and almost inevitably to originate from the images themselves, strengthening the mythic sense that the ultimate reality is that of spirit.

THE WIND IN THE DOOR

By cloaking it in myth, L'Engle handled the theme of the redeeming power of love with deft artistic skill in the second fantasy in the series, *The Wind in the Door*.

10. L'Engle, *A Circle of Quiet*, 157.
11. L'Engle, *A Circle of Quiet*, 169.

We are made to see the inextricable relationship of love to the ability to name accurately our world and the people in it. It is of primary importance that one sees things accurately—valuing them as God values them—that is, giving them their proper name. L'Engle showed it cannot be done without love. She presents love, not simply on the level of rhetorical affirmation, but on that of experience itself. We are made to feel with Meg, her protagonist, the struggle to effect love, the spiritual perceptions which are indispensable to its proper expression, and the beauty of its redeeming efficacy.

True to her metier, L'Engle rested the story upon a scientific hypothesis. Living within the human cell are mitochondria, organisms so infinitesimally small the most powerful of microscopes cannot detect them, and, within them are other diminutive organisms known as farandolae. Although so minute they may only be postulated, if something happens to them, we die. Mr. and Mrs. Murry, experimental scientists, are worried about an inexplicable destructive force that seems to be working in the universe. They ponder a phenomenon recently detected in our galaxy: certain stars seem to be vanishing completely. On earth, irrational violence seems unleashed in the cities. They hypothesize that there is some connection between the destruction of stars in space to the effect farandolae have upon mitochondria.

The chief characters are again Meg, Charles Wallace, and Calvin. The precocious Charles Wallace is having difficulties in school adapting to "normal" children and teachers, and he is mysteriously ill. Meg is frustrated not only because she is struggling with her studies but also because the principal, Mr. Jenkins, seems perversely to misunderstand her. Mrs. Murry theorizes that her son's strange malady is due to his having contracted mitochondritis: something is wrong with his farandolae, and he appears to be dying.

In the story, both problems are set right through love. Meg, Charles Wallace, and Calvin are called to help. They are met at night by supernatural creatures: Blajeny, a supernatural Teacher in human form, and Proginoskes, a cherubim, delightfully described as a feathered dragon with a multitude of eyes and wings in constant motion. He commissions Meg as a Namer and they kythe. He shows her that the destruction taking place in the universe—whether it be the annihilating stars into nothingness, the "unnaming" of people, or the attacking of farandolae within the human cell—is the work of Echthroi, or fallen angels, whose very being is hate. Hatred destroys; love, its opposite, enables true Namers to give accurate names. Love alone makes people know who they are.

Blajeny assigns each of the children tests; successfully passing them results in the spiritual growth each need. Meg is confronted with not one, but three Mr.

Jenkins, and her test is to name the right one. Each of
the effigies has traits repugnant to her, but she identifies the real Mr. Jenkins through discerning the precise
nature of his repulsive traits. In imaginatively comprehending his true nature, she begins to love him, not in
the sense of feeling any emotional attraction for him,
but by recognizing the modicum of good that is in
him—he once gave a pair of much-needed shoes to
Calvin—she is willing to give of herself to help him
become a better person. This truth is dramatically
presented in their making a trip to Metron Ariston,
which is a postulate or an idea, rather than a planet,
and there Meg has to give of herself through kything
in order to make Mr. Jenkins understand and have a
part in their mission of self-giving.

The trip takes Meg and Calvin within a mitochon-
drion inside one of Charles Wallace's cells. Inside the
cell they find a mouse-like creature named Sporos, who
is immature and impudent. The next test Meg and
Calvin face is to help Sporos, unlikable as he is, to
"deepen," or mature. The cherubim Proginoskes
explains:

> When Sporos Deepens . . . it means that he comes of
> age. It means that he grows up. The temptation for
> farandola or for man or for star is to stay an imma-
> ture pleasure-seeker. When we seek our own pleasure
> as the ultimate good we place ourselves as the center

> of the universe. A fara or a man or a star has his place
> in the universe, but nothing created is the center. [12]

To deepen is to participate in the music of the stars, the harmony at the heart of all creation. If the children fail in their task of love, the Echthroi will have won and Charles Wallace will die.

It is such convincing insights into the anagogical level of reality that transform this fantasy into myth. The reader is made to feel that all created life is interdependent—not simply physically—but on the level of love. To bear the plights and problems of others is both spiritually beautiful and vitally necessary to the life of the universe. It works redemption. One is poignantly reminded of Charles Williams's doctrines of coinherence and substitution. In depicting imaginatively the nature of Christian love as that which gives of itself to help another become more completely and fully human, L'Engle revealed something of its mythic reality and power. In a day in which love is so shallowly treated and grossly misunderstood, her literary achievement stands out as genuine.

WALTER WANGERIN

Another presentation of the nature of love that commands the power of myth is Walter Wangerin, Jr.'s *The Crying for a Vision*. In this work Wangerin engagingly recast the folklore and legends of the Native American

12. L'Engle, *A Wind in the Door* (New York: Dell, 1976), 172.

Lokota tribe, revealing themes fundamental to all humanity in truly mythic style. By clothing them in his own fictional narrative, he illustrated that, while myth is not the same as the story that contains it, its power is enhanced by a story well-told. The themes are those of quest, renunciation, sacrifice, and reconciliation. They are, as the author affirmed in his preface, themes analogous to those present in real relationships among people, creation, and the Creator.

The several episodes of the unfolding narrative develop the tensions between the great and ferocious warrior Fire Thunder and the village orphan, Waskn Mani, whose father is unknown. Fire Thunder is the prototypical Indian warrior garbed in silent dignity, mighty in the hunt, dreadful in battle, and capable of great brutality when offended. His opposite in type and sensibility, Waskn Mani desires love and belonging. He is innocent and outgoing with a large capacity for delight and wonder, and humbly communes with nature and animals. Forced as a growing boy to learn how to hunt, he is deeply offended by the necessity to kill. Through a mystical relationship with a wolf he learns the principles that, while needless killing violates the holiness and coinherence of all things, needful hunting is holy, requiring a sacrifice which the victim freely makes. Giving up life for the good of another is a valiant exchange. The hunt is sinful only when it is conducted in the wrong manner, with wanton disregard for the basic sacredness of life.

Responding to the offense of being spurned in love, Fire Thunder violently lashes out, first against the animals of the forest in a vicious act of destruction, and then against other Indian tribes by leading his band of renegade warriors on killing raids. He precipitates a blight upon the land by breaking the sacred bond of interdependence of all creatures. Everything is turned into a wasteland and many of his own people die. Horror-stricken, Waskn Mani prays that God will have mercy on his people. He is apotheosized, and in a subsequent scene Fire Thunder believes he is dead, a willing sacrifice for the latter's sin, in order to restore the life and health of the Lakota people. Wangerin wrote with penetrating insight and sensitivity, tapping the imaginative power resident in these themes so central to myth.

ROBERT SIEGEL

Robert Siegel's *Whalesong* trilogy, an ecological myth, explores similar themes. His narrators are whales, with whom we travel through the sea, a vast unknown not unlike outer space.

They plunge into its depths, venturing into its caverns and exploring its arctic reaches. With appreciable imaginative strength Siegel recreated the thoughts and feelings of a whale, supposing they think and feel as do humans, plausibly presenting their

perspectives. We gain a keener comprehension of the
barbarities of whalehunting, the ironic finality of
sunken ships, and the nature-invading calamities of oil
spills. More realist authors could sustain our interest in
such material through one volume at best; by means of
myth, Siegel keeps us reading through three.

The ocean provides a context propitious to myth,
since both the depths of ocean and the reaches of myth
itself take us into the unknown, about which we are
intensely curious. The pod of whales with whom we
become familiar are strengthened in character and
community through their myths of origin and destiny.
These myths are communicated not only in story, but
also in a mysterious blending of underwater light and
whale song. Graphic descriptions of different qualities
of light filtered through water, together with the sense
of being surrounded by musical sound—prolonged
whale songs are said to travel immense distances—
achieve a compellingly eerie quality in the text. The
whales acquire an inner illumination of spirit. In the
extreme depths of the ocean some occasionally experience mystical encounters by penetrating into the far
reaches of ocean caverns.

The third volume of the trilogy, *The Ice at the End
of the World*, begins with such an encounter. The huge
white whale Hralekana, wounded during an heroic
deed (recounted in the prior volume) in which he
foiled an underwater nuclear explosion, must descend

into the legendary caverns for healing. There he is met by the Whale of Light, a supernatural being who commissions him to destroy the Kraken, a mountainous squid-like monster that inhabits the deep. To prepare him for his task, he is told the myth of the Kraken's origin, an account that echoes Christian myths of the origin of Satan as a fallen Son of the Morning. His heroic triumph is achieved through his obedience to such archetypal themes as self-sacrifice, self-abnegation, and the power of suffering.

Towards the end of the narrative, which relates the whale pod's harrowing encounters with the brutal prac- tices of whale hunters and the cataclysmic tragedy of underwater testing of nuclear bombs, Hralekana again plunges to his cavern in the Deep to meditate on his distressing experiences. There he is filled with a great longing as he hears the mystic song of mermen and mermaids. When he swims forth to find them, he is mystically illumined: "It was as if my eyes were open for the first time," he explains, and continues:

> From the green and blue hollows of the waves, shin-
> ing like gems, to the fiery radiance of the froth, to the
> glowing sky, light shone through all. . . And there on
> the rocks, almost too bright to look upon, reclined
> the mermen and mermaids—their tails lustrous with
> silver, or aquamarine, or lavender, shimmering as

they twitched and moved; their skin gold or white
shading to green; their hair pale, streaming down
their backs, or dark, clustered in deep green curls
about their shoulders. But their faces—I can't
describe their faces—for these were living light and
no words can do them justice. . . . [13]

After praising Hralekana for his heroic feats, the
mermen and maids affirm the precious nature of all
created beings, their mythic radiance underscoring the
point. They then issue a solemn warning concerning
human stewardship of the earth and sea: People must
learn to honor the complex mystery of interrelatedness
and live in harmony with the music of the worlds.

An undeniable truth, profoundly and simply put,
one that the contemporary world sorely needs to heed.
In evoking the aura of myth, Siegel invested the theme
with greater authority. The reader attuned to myth,
however, may expect a sense of consummation in a
higher, ultimate world. Siegel possesses the talent to
have given it, but he chose rather to let the emphasis
fall upon the welfare of contemporary society.

HANNAH HURNARD

In *Hind's Feet on High Places*, Hannah Hurnard fires
the reader's desire for the glory of such consummation.
It is somewhat ironic that our study, which began with
the achievement of John Bunyan, should conclude with

13. Robert Siegel, *The Ice at the End of the World* (San Francisco: Harper Collins,
1994), 185.

this provocative contemporary allegory. The general attitude nowadays seems to be that allegory is outmoded and is a literary style inadequate to appeal to our more sophisticated imaginations. Indeed, some of our authors openly objected to it. George MacDonald, for instance, asserted strict allegory to be a weariness to the spirit, and J. R. R. Tolkien studiously worked to avoid it in *The Lord of the Rings*. Hurnard wrote unabashedly in the allegorical tradition, with its prescriptive air. She succeeded because she baptized allegory in myth.

While her work can awaken in readers the desire for purity and full spiritual maturity, the emphasis falls upon the realization that such a life is not easily attained. She stimulates readers to pursue the goal while at the same time inducing them to contemplate the cost. Like Bunyan, her prose style strongly echoes that of the King James Bible, with its definite iambic rhythms and strong cadences. Her command of scriptural imagery, especially that found in the writings of the Old Testament prophets and poets, is knowledgeable and full. In addition, she exceeded her literary ancestor in her abilities as a poet. The text has many pleasing poetic renditions of passages from the Song of Solomon. Unfortunately, her narrating voice addresses the reader occasionally, breaking the illusion of imagined reality with an unpleasant sense of sermonizing, and the text may be thought to put an undue amount of emphasis upon the value of adversity and pain.

At the beginning of the story, Much-Afraid (Hurnard's pilgrim) leaves her dwelling in the Valley of Humiliation because of her compelling desire for the "high places." Remaining behind would ensure her marriage to Craven Fear, a fate that overwhelms her with horror. The seminal text is that of Habakkuk 3:19, "The Lord God is my strength, and he will make my feet like hinds' feet, and he will make me to walk upon mine high places" (KJV). The metaphor of climbing to the beckoning heights of the Kingdom of Love is nicely maintained throughout; as in Bunyan, the Narrow Way is beset with difficulties to be overcome and perplexities to be squelched by the acquiescence of faith. Perhaps the largest source of bewilderment to Much-Afraid is that the path seems so often to lead her away from—rather than in a discernibly straight path towards—her desired goal. Nevertheless, she has the unfailing availability of the Chief Shepherd, whom she has but to summon, and the constant wisdom of two companions, Sorrow and Suffering, upon whom she must rely.

Again as in Bunyan, the reader may feel occasional disagreement with the theology that shapes the allegory, especially when it seems to veer toward nurturing a martyr complex: suffering may seem at times to be valuable for its own sake. The imagined world shaped by Hurnard's convictions is, however, sacramental. In this she recalled other of her literary ancestors, such as George MacDonald and G. K. Chesterton. The reader's interest is frequently invigorated by her descriptions of the natural terrain through which Much-Afraid passes. In a manner that vaguely recalls Tolkien's achievement in Middle Earth, her natural scenes are both realistic and mythic. Cliffs and coves, oceans, flowers, and wastelands, all are made to live in their own natural right while at the same time—in her case—being invested with abstract significances.

Hurnard's art is disarming; it exhibits not only high talent and careful craftsmanship but also a depth and maturity of spirit. Too many authors of contemporary fantasy that aspire to the condition of myth seem inadequate to the task. Madeleine L'Engle remarked:

> The great artists, dying to self in their work, collaborate with their work, know it and are known by it as Adam knew Eve, and so share in the mighty act of Creation. . . . nothing is created without this terrible entering into death. It takes great faith, faith in the work if not faith in God, for dying is fearful. But without this death, nothing is born. [14]

When aspiring artists do not grasp this essential nature of artistic composition, their work quickly betrays their lack of comprehension. But those few in every generation who do, and who experience the requisite intellectual travail, contribute to humankind something that

14. L'Engle, *Walking on Water*, 195.

will endure as essential to the human spirit. The spiritual dying of which L'Engle spoke takes the artist deep within the self where exist the wellsprings of myth. The reader is convinced that the great archetypal images reside within the human imagination because of the nature of creation, the Fall, and redemption. One of the paradoxes of art is that each generation has need for its own authors freshly to explore these fundamental themes. In *Ulysses*, one of James Joyce's characters remarks that the supreme question about a work of art is out of how deep a life it springs. [15] The judgment should speak directly to all who would undertake to present a mythic vision, the most essential of all literary undertakings.

Myth is something people desperately need, cannot, in fact, live without. No other demand so profoundly defines our humanity. When true myths are absent, false ones rush in to fill the vacuum. Discursive statements, important as they are, will not satisfy the human spirit; mere intellectualization starves it. The imagination in its highest reaches must have myth; it is a bridge that spans the gap between man and the eternal.

15. James Joyce, *Ulysses* (London: Penguin Books, 1984), 152

GLOSSARY OF TERMS

All words set in small caps are referenced elsewhere in the glossary.

anagogical. That aspect of experience that is directly concerned with the presence in it of the eternal and the divine; pertaining to the spiritual significance of events or circumstances.

archetypes. Images, such as the journey or the sea, which are largely present in the ancient myths and keep recurring in literature; sometimes called primordial images.

coinherence. Charles Williams's term for the complete interdependence of all things. It characterizes the relationship among the members of the Trinity, in which each is completely present in the other while remaining distinct. It is to be consciously and thoroughly practised by Christians through acts of exchange, which effect the SUBSTITUTION that is the true spiritual life of a Christian community.

consolation. J. R. R. Tolkien's term for the joy and satisfaction experienced by the happy ending of fairy stories.

dyscatastrophe. Tolkien's term for failure and sorrow in a story, the possibility of which enhances the joy of the happy ending.

enchantment. Tolkien's term for the reader's absorbed reactions to a completely successful story of an altered world. It involves a purity of emotional response and a sense of profound satisfaction.

escape. Tolkien's term for the imaginative experience which fairy stories afford of a higher and better world, one more satisfying to the deeper desires of the human spirit.

fantasy. Stories that depart from realistic presentations and present happenings that do not occur in everyday life, but which nevertheless possess an air of reality.

eucatastrophe. Tolkien's term for the "good catastrophe" that effects the resolution in a fairy story, the "sudden and miraculous grace" that brings the reader deep joy and satisfaction.

exchange. Williams's term for the principle of interaction among people that effects SUBSTITUTION.

imagination. Generally defined by these authors in the tradition of Coleridge's thought. See *Biographia Literaria,* chapter 13. MacDonald sees it as that faculty of the mind which gives form to thought. Since all forms are created and upheld by God, the artist, working perceptively, can think God's thoughts after him and reveal them to the world.

kythe. Madeleine L'Engle's term for communicating without words, by intuitive concentration.

magic. The exercise of power to effect alterations in the normal aspects of the known world. Tolkien argues that the special magic that induces ENCHANTMENT is indispensable to fairy stories.

myths. Stories of a nation that arise from their primordial past and contain elements which seem to depict to them the ANAGOGICAL meaning and significance of life. In bringing the transcendent and eternal to bear upon life, they inspire awe, often affording imaginative glimpses that answer to deeply felt human desires, and generally address the question, How should we then live?

mythopoeia. Literary myths: those composed in historic time by known authors.

recovery. Tolkien's view for a renewing effect from reading fairy stories. Through them we perceive the mythic qualities of strangeness and wonder present in nature and the normal features of life, qualities to which we are oblivious because of our familiarity with everyday objects.

sacramental. A view of reality that sees all images as having the potential to be vehicles of divine grace because something of the divine is mysteriously present in them.

secondary world. Tolkien's term for the imagined world of a story, secondary because it necessarily must be created from images—or variations of images—occurring in the real world.

Sehnsucht. Spiritual yearning; a longing after a higher, unbroken and eternal world in which something that is adumbrated in the images of stories—and in life itself truly percieved—will be real, and a conviction that that world is one's true "home."

subcreation. Tolkien's term for artistic creation. The artist works with images that have been divinely created and composes by the same laws by which he himself has been made. Responsible art is, therefore, "refracted light" from God's "single white."

substitution. Williams's term for the essence of the Christian life. As Christ substitutes his life for that of each believer, so each Christian is through love to take complete responsibility for other lives.

tesseract. L'Engle's term for travelling through time and space. It is imagined possible because of a "wrinkle" in time or space, whereby a chronological movement through the centuries, or linear travel through space, is avoided.

The Way of Affirmation. The mystical approach to God that sees all images as SACRAMENTAL and therefore undertakes to discern God in all things.

The Way of Negation. The mystical approach to God that undertakes to obliterate all images from the mind, so that the Divine Spirit may fill the individual.

SELECT BIBLIOGRAPHY

(Works quoted, together with suggestions for further reading.)

Augustine, Saint. *Confessions.* Translated by Henry Chadwick. London: Oxford, 1991.

Barfield, Owen. *Poetic Diction: A Study in Meaning.* Middletown, Conn.: Wesleyan University Press, 1973.

Batson, Beatrice E. *John Bunyan: Allegory and Imagination.* Totowa, N.J.: Barnes and Noble, 1984.

Buechner, Frederick. *The Sacred Journey.* San Francisco: Harper San Francisco, 1991.

———. *The Longing for Home: Recollections and Reflections.* San Farncisco: Harper San Francisco, 1996.

———. *Telling the Truth: The Gospel as Tragedy, Comedy, and Fairy Tale.* San Francisco: Harper & Row, 1977.

Bunyan, John. *Grace Abounding to the Chief of Sinners.* 1666.

———. *The Holy War.* 1682.

———. *The Pilgrim's Progress,* 1684.

Brown, John. *John Bunyan: His Life, Times, and Work.* Revised by Frank Mott Harrison. London: Hulbert, 1928.

Carpenter, Humphrey. *The Inklings.* Boston: Houghton Mifflin, 1979.

———. *Tolkien: A Biography.* Boston: Houghton Mifflin, 1977.

———, ed. *The Letters of J. R. R. Tolkien.* Boston: Houghton Mifflin, 1981.

Dante. The Divine Comedy. 3 vols. Dorthy Sayers and Barbara Reynolds, trans. Penguin Classics/

Harrison, G. B. *John Bunyan: A Study in Personality.* Garden City, N.Y.: Doubleday, Doran, 1928.

Kaufmann, Milo. *The Pilgrim's Progress and Traditions in Puritan Meditation.* New Haven and London: Yale, 1966.

Chesterton, G. K. *Autobiography.* London: Hutchinson, 1969.

———. *Orthodoxy.* London and New York: John Lane Company, 1909. Ignatius Press, 1995.

———. *Manalive.* London: T. Nelson and Sons, 1912.

―――. *The Man Who Was Thursday.* 1908.

Dale, Alzina Stone. *The Outline of Sanity: A Life of G. K. Chesterton.* Grand Rapids, Mich.: Wm. B. Eerdmans Pub. Co., 1982.

Downing, David C. *Planets in Peril: A Critical Study of C.S. Lewis's Ransom Trilogy.* Amherst: University of Massachusetts Press, 1992.

Dickinson, Emily. *The Complete Poems of Emily Dickinson.* Edited by Thomas H. Johnson. Boston: Little, Brown, 1960.

Eliot, T. S. *Complete Poems and Plays.* New York: Harcourt, Brace & World, 1952.

Flieger, Verlyn. *Splintered Light: Logos and Language in Tolkien's World.* Grand Rapids, Mich.: Wm. B. Eerdmans, 1983.

Foster, Robert. *The Complete Guide to Middle Earth.* New York: Ballantine Books, 1978.

Hein, Rolland. *George MacDonald: Victorian Mythmaker.* Nashville: Star Song, 1993.

―――. *The Heart of George MacDonald.* Wheaton, Ill.: Shaw, 1994.

Howard, Thomas. *The Novels of Charles Williams.* New York: Oxford, 1983.

Hurnard, Hannah. *Hind's Feet on High Places.* Wheaton, Ill.: Tyndale, 1976.

Lawhead, Stephen. *Arthur.* Westchester, Ill.: Crossway, 1989.

―――. *Merlin.* Westchester, Ill.: Crossway, 1988.

―――. *Taliesin.* Westchester, Ill.: Crossway, 1987.

L'Engle, Madeleine. *A Circle of Quiet.* New York: Farrar, Straus and Giroux, 1972.

―――. *Walking on Water.* Wheaton, Ill.: Harold Shaw, 1980.

―――. *Many Waters.* New York: Dell, 1986.

―――. *A Swiftly Tilting Planet.* New York: Dell, 1978.

―――. *A Wind in the Door.* New York: Dell, 1973.

―――. *A Wrinkle in Time.* New York: Dell, 1962.

Lewis, C. S. *Allegory of Love.* New York: Oxford University Press, 1958.

————. *An Experiment in Criticism.* Cambridge; New York: Cambridge University Press, 1965.

————. *God in the Dock.* Edited by Walter Hooper. Grand Rapids, Mich.: Eerdmans, 1970.

————. *The Great Divorce.* New York: Macmillan, 1946.

————. *The Horse and His Boy.* London: Geoffrey Bles, 1954.

————. *The Last Battle: A Story for Children.* London: Geoffrey Bles, 1956.

————. *The Lion, the Witch, and the Wardrobe.* London: Geoffrey Bles, 1950.

————. *The Magician's Nephew.* London: Bodley Head, 1955.

————. *Of This and Other Worlds.* Edited by Walter Hooper. London: Collins, 1982.

————. *Out of the Silent Planet.* London: Macmillan, 1965.

————. *Perelandra.* London: Macmillan, 1965.

————. *Prince Caspian: The Return to Narnia.* London: Geoffrey Bles, 1951.

————. *The Silver Chair.* London: Geoffrey Bles, 1953.

————. *That Hideous Strength.* London: Macmillan, 1965.

————. *The Pilgrim's Regress: An Allegorical Apology for Reason, and Romanticism.* Grand Rapids, Mich.: Wm. B. Eerdmans Pub. Co., 1989.

————. *Surprised by Joy.* London: Geoffrey Bles, 1955.

————. *They Stand Together: The Letters of C. S. Lewis to Arthur Greeves 1914-1963.* Edited by Walter Hooper. London: Collins, 1979.

————. *Till We Have Faces.* San Francisco: Harcourt, Brace, Jovanovich, 1985.

————. *The Voyage of the "Dawn Treader."* London: Geoffrey Bles, 1952.

————, ed. *Essays Presented to Charles Williams.* London: Oxford, 1947.

————, ed. *George MacDonald: An Anthology.* New York: Macmillan, 1948.

Kilby, Clyde S. *The Christian World of C. S. Lewis.* Grand

Rapids, Mich.: Wm. B. Eerdmans Pub. Co., 1964.

"*Letters from Hell,*" in *Readings in European History*. Edited by J. H. Robinson. Boston: Ginn, 1906.

Lindskoog, Kathryn. *Finding the Landlord: A Guidebook to C. S. Lewis's "Pilgrim's Regress."* Chicago: Cornerstone Press Chicago, 1995.

Manlove, C. N. *C. S. Lewis: His Literary Achievement*. New York: St. Martin's, 1987.

MacDonald, George. *Adela Cathcart*. Whitethorn, Calif.: Johannesen, 1994.

————. *At the Back of the North Wind*. Whitethorn, Calif.: Johannesen, 1997.

————. *The Light Princess and Other Stories*. Whitethorn, Calif.: Johannesen, 1997.

————. *Lilith*. Whitethorn, Calif.: Johannesen, 1994.

————. *Paul Faber, Surgeon*. Whitethorn, Calif.: Johannesen, 1992.

————. *Phantastes*. Whitethorn, Calif.: Johannesen, 1998.

————. *The Portent and Other Stories*. Whitethorn, Calif.: Johannesen, 1994.

————. *The Princess and Curdie*. Whitethorn, Calif.: Johannesen, 1997.

————. *The Princess and the Goblin*. Whitethorn, Calif.: Johannesen, 1997.

————. *Sir Gibbie*. Whitethorn, Calif..: Johannesen, 1996.

————. *Thomas Wingfold, Curate*. Whitethorn, Calif.: Johannesen, 1996.

————. *Unspoken Sermons*. Whitethorn, Calif.: Johannesen, 1997.

————. *Unspoken Sermons: Second Series*. Whitethorn, Calif.: Johannesen, 1997.

————. *Unspoken Sermons: Third Series*. Whitethorn, Calif.: Johannesen, 1997.

————. *The Wise Woman*. Whitethorn, Calif.: Johannesen, 1998.

MacDonald, Greville. *George MacDonald and His Wife*. 1924.

Muir, Edwin. *An Autobiography*. St. Paul, Minn: Graywolf Press, 1990.

———. *Collected Poems*. London: Oxford, 1960.

Osborne, Charles. *W. H. Auden: The Life of a Poet*. London: Macmillan, 1982.

Reis, Richard. *George MacDonald*. Eureka, Calif.: Sunrise Books, 1989.

Sadler, Lynn Veach. *John Bunyan*. Boston: Twayne, 1979.

Sayer, George. *Jack: C. S. Lewis and His Times*. London: Macmillan, 1988.

Sharrock, Roger, ed. *Bunyan: The Pilgrim's Progress, A Casebook*. London: Macmillan, 1976.

Siegel, Robert. *The Ice at the End of the World*. San Francisco: Harper Collins, 1994.

———. *Whalesong*. Westchester, Ill.: Crossway, 1981.

———. *White Whale*. San Francisco: Harper, 1991.

Swaim, Kathleen. *Pilgrim's Progress, Puritan Progress*. Urbana and Chicago: University of Illinois, 1993.

Tolkien, J. R. R. *The Hobbit; or, There and Back Again*. London: George Allen and Unwin, 1937.

———. *The Lord of the Rings*. New York: Ballantine Books, 1965.

———. *The Tolkien Reader*. New York: Ballantine Books, 1966.

———. *Tree and Leaf*. London: George Allen and Unwin, 1964.

———. *The Silmarillion*. London: George Allen and Unwin, 1977.

Wangerin, Walter. *The Crying for a Vision*. New York: Simon & Schuster, 1994.

Williams, Charles. *All Hallows' Eve*. Grand Rapids, Mich.: Wm. B. Eerdmans Pub. Co., 1981.

———. *Charles Williams: Essential Writings in Spirituality and Theology*. Edited by Charles Hefling. Cambridge, Mass.: Cowley Publications, 1993.

———. *Descent into Hell*. Grand Rapids, Mich.: Wm. B. Eerdmans Pub. Co., 1980.

———. *Descent of the Dove.* Grand Rapids, Mich.: Wm. B. Eerdmans Pub. Co., 1979.

———. *The Figure of Beatrice: A Study in Dante.* Cambridge: D. S. Brewer, 1994.

———. *The Greater Trumps.* Grand Rapids, Mich.: Wm. B. Eerdmans Pub. Co., 1980.

———. *He Came Down from Heaven.* Grand Rapids, Mich.: Wm. B. Eerdmans Pub. Co., 1984.

———. *Many Dimensions.* Grand Rapids, Mich.: Wm. B. Eerdmans Pub. Co., 1981.

———. *Outlines of Romantic Theology.* Edited by Alice Mary Hadfield. Grand Rapids, Mich.: Wm. B. Eerdmans Pub. Co., 1990.

———. *The Place of the Lion.* Grand Rapids, Mich.: Wm. B. Eerdmans Pub. Co., 1980.

———. *Shadows of Ecstasy.* Grand Rapids, Mich.: Wm. B. Eerdmans Pub. Co., 1980.

———. *Taliessin Through Logres* and *The Region of the Summer Stars.* And *Arthurian Torso,* by Charles Williams and C. S. Lewis. Grand Rapids, Mich.: Wm. B. Eerdmans Pub. Co., 1974.

———. *War in Heaven.* Grand Rapids, Mich.: Wm. B. Eerdmans Pub. Co., 1980.

Wilson, A. N. *C. S. Lewis: A Biography.* New York: Norton, 1990.

INDEX

CHRISTIAN MYTHMAKERS

Designed by Pat Peterson
Composed in Adobe Caslon & Adobe Caslon Expert
Display lines set in Kelmscott, based on
William Morris's "Troy" typeface
Initial letters set in Morris Initials
Kelmscott and Morris Initials
available from the Scriptorium at
www.ragnarokpress.com
Printed and bound by United Graphics, Inc.
on Miami Book Natural

Books of related interest from Cornerstone Press Chicago

C. S. Lewis: Mere Christian, Fourth Edition
Kathryn Lindskoog

One of the best introductions to C. S. Lewis and his writing in print! Lindskoog draws from his fiction, poetry, essays, and radio speeches to explore Lewis's ideas on God, nature, humanity, death, heaven, hell, miracles, prayer, pain, love, ethisc, truth, the sciences, the arts, and education.

> "Lindskoog commands an encyclopedic knowledge of Lewis's life and works, and she writes with contagious passion" —*Books & Culture*

ISBN 0-940895-36-6 • 292 pages • $14.95

Finding the Landlord: A Guidebook to C. S. Lewis's Pilgrim's Regress
Kathryn Lindskoog

Finding the Landlord opens up Lewis's classic allegory, *Pilgrim's Regress*, to an audience that may not be familiar with the people and classical allusions that fill the book. Lindskoog has also shown how the journey in the book parallels C. S. Lewis's own quest to find true joy.
ISBN 0-940895-35-8 • 165 pages • $9.95

Flannery O'Connor: A Proper Scaring, Revised Edition
Jill P. Baumgaertner

Drowning in a river, the violent murder of a grandmother in the backwoods of Georgia, and the trans-genital display of a freak at a carnival show are all shocking literary devices used by Flannery O'Connor, one of American literature's best pulp-fiction writers. More than thirty-five years after her death, readers are still shocked by O'Connor's grotesque images. Dr. Jill Baumgaertner concentrates on O'Connor's use of emblems, those moments of sudden and horrid illumination when the sacred and the profane merge as sacrament. This readable volume is ideal for college students, O'Connor scholars, or those wishing to better understand Southern gothic fiction.
ISBN 0-940895-38-2 • $10.95

more books and ordering info on other side

toll-free: 1-888-40-PRESS
on-line: www.cornerstonepress.com

The Double Vision of Star Trek: Half-Humans, Evil Twins, and Science Fiction
Mike Hertenstein

Star Trek is an unavoidable presence in contemporary culture; many have tried to explain it as modern mythology, juvenile fantasy, or futuristic morality plays. What most commentators have missed is a striking aspect of *Trek's* vision: its doubleness. The vision of a brighter tomorrow is torn by internal conflicts, a double-mindedness its own creator would not admit to, of logic vs emotion, body vs soul, individual vs community, tolerance vs morality, reality vs holodeck, knowledge vs mystery, science vs fiction. Hertenstein examines the alternative and parallel universes of *Star Trek*.
ISBN 0-940895-42-0 • $14.95

The Harmony Within: The Spiritual Vision of George MacDonald
Rolland Hein

A look at the life and works of 19th century Scottish minister and fantasy writer, of whom C. S. Lewis said, "I have never concealed the fact that I regard [MacDonald] as my master; indeed, I fancy I have never written a book in which I did not quote from him."
ISBN 0-940895-43-9 • 228 pages • $11.00—You Save 15%